Teaching Global Theologies

Power and Praxis

KWOK PUI-LAN
CECILIA GONZÁLEZ-ANDRIEU
DWIGHT N. HOPKINS
Editors

BAYLOR UNIVERSITY PRESS

Cover Design by Nita Ybarra
Cover Art: "La Cruz de la Habana" 2015, Alfredo González Cardentey (detail). Acrylic on canvas, 24 inches by 24 inches, courtesy of the artist.

Library of Congress Cataloging-in-Publication Data

Teaching global theologies : power and praxis / Kwok Pui-lan, Cecilia González-Andrieu, and Dwight N. Hopkins, editors.
224 pages cm
Includes bibliographical references and index.
ISBN 978-1-4813-0285-2 (pbk. : alk. paper)
1. Theology—Methodology. 2. Theology—Study and teaching.
3. Globalization—Religious aspects—Christianity. I. Kwok, Pui-lan, joint editor.
BR118.T43 2015
230.071—dc23
2015006697

Printed in the United States of America on acid-free paper with a minimum of 30 percent post-consumer waste recycled content.

"As contemporary Christianity continues to move beyond its Eurocentric moorings to embrace a truly global and transnational World Christianity, *Teaching Global Theologies* is well positioned to become the definitive resource and yardstick for rethinking and re-visioning theological education that will prepare new leaders who are formed and equipped to lead their increasingly diverse and pluralistic communities in this new global and transnational reality."

—**Jonathan Y. Tan**, *Archbishop Paul J. Hallinan Professor of Catholic Studies, Case Western Reserve University*

"Now that Christianity has become truly global, the need to teach theology in a global and transnational context is more urgent than ever. Kwok Pui-lan and her associates, all of them veteran practitioners and teachers of theology in a variety of venues and in different countries, offer here a treasure trove of concrete suggestions distilled from their experiences. I most strongly recommend the book as required reading to all people—administrators, faculty, staff, and students—involved in theological teaching and learning."

—**Peter C. Phan**, *The Ignacio Ellacuría, S.J. Chair of Catholic Social Thought, Georgetown University*

"In a globalizing world, theology has no choice but to become global as well. The chapters of this book present helpful models for alternative ways to become truly global, addressing roadblocks, such as power differentials, and making constructive suggestions for another way forward that embraces complexity and hybridity."

—**Joerg Rieger**, *Wendand-Cook Professor of Constructive Theology, Perkins School of Theology, SMU*

Contents

PART III
PRAXIS AND RESPONSIBILITY

Acknowledgments

The idea of this book began when William A. Dyrness and Kwok Pui-lan were invited to speak at the University of Chicago Ministry Conference at the Divinity School in the spring of 2009. With Dwight N. Hopkins they discussed the critical importance of initiating conversations on teaching theology in the global context with colleagues in the field. We want to thank Matthew Richards and other students who helped organize the conference and sowed the seeds for this project.

We are grateful to the Wabash Center for a grant to support contributors in the United States while they met during the annual meeting of the American Academy of Religion (AAR) in 2011 to exchange ideas and find ways to broaden this conversation. In the fall of 2012, the group gathered again at Fuller Theological Seminary to concretize the book project. The Wabash Center, Santa Clara University, and two local churches provided the necessary financial support. Loyola Marymount University helped with local logistics, and Fuller Theological Seminary offered spaces and facilities. To these organizations, we offer our sincere gratitude.

As we worked on the book project, we had the opportunity, under the auspices of the Theological Education Committee of AAR, to organize two workshops—"Teaching Theology in a Global and Transnational World" and "Teaching Global Theologies: International Perpsectives"—at the annual meetings in 2013 and 2015. We thank John Thatamanil, Jeffrey Williams, and other members of the committee for their enthusiastic support, and we thank the panelists for their participation. The workshops generated new pedagogical insights, collegial support, and international conversation on the topic.

This book has been a collaborative project from the beginning, and we thank the contributors for their commitment to this project. Several members battled illnesses, and one had to care for a family member who was seriously ill during the writing process. Eleazar S. Fernandez flew from the Philippines to join the AAR workshop in 2013 after Typhoon Haiyan ravaged his country. Lai Pan-chiu agreed to contribute at a later stage and added a valuable international perspective.

We are very grateful to Carey C. Newman, director of Baylor University Press, for his enthusiasm for the book and for shepherding with great care the production and marketing processes. We are indebted to Taylor Hall for editing the manuscript and to the University of Chicago Divinity School for the funds supporting her work. The staff at Baylor University Press offered timely, professional help every step of the way, and we want to thank them for their meticulous work on the book.

We are grateful to Spencer Bogle for preparing the index with care. We thank the Episcopal Divinity School for support from the Theological Writing Fund. Last but not least we thank our families for their support and generosity. Their love and their care for what we do gives us the necessary space to dream new dreams for doing theology in our global age and for teaching it to the next generation.

Introduction

An important challenge for theological education today is to educate and form leaders of faith communities who are prepared to lead in a global and transnational world. The global society is formed because of increased connectivity as a result of the neoliberal economy, the Internet and mass media, technology, mass consumerist and popular culture, and migration and travel. Transnationalism refers to social, economic, cultural, and political relations and activities that transgress the boundaries of the nation-state. As the world grows closer through instant communications, technology, and easier travel, we discover new knowledge from a variety of theological scholars and religious communities. Although there has been a growing body of literature on global theology and the construction of theological doctrines from an intercultural or global perspective, theology is still largely taught in the same old way, which privileges the European and Euro-American traditions.

Theology is also often taught to the same communities that have historically had access to education, and less often to those who represent the complex world realities of the Christian church. Currently there are very few resources available on how to teach theology that specifically take into serious consideration the changing global situation and how this might affect the theological curriculum as a whole. This book aims to identify texts and resources, successful pedagogies of inclusion, and best practices in order to teach theology in a global and transnational age, and to stimulate further conversations in the wider academic community.

Some of the questions we will explore include the following: What are the possible "sources" for a global theology? How can we teach theology while bearing in mind the cultural diversity within the long tradition of Christian thought? Whose voices are missing, and how do we pay attention to the power dynamics of race, ethnicity, class, gender, and sexuality in the classroom? What are the successful pedagogies and best practices that promote students' global consciousness and prepare them as global citizens? Where today are connections being made by Christians and people of faith from multiple settings that might have potential for raising (new) theological questions? How can we approach the task of teaching theology in a global context from the perspective of comparative theology? How shall we situate global theological voices in pedagogy and across the curriculum?

The majority of the contributors to this volume are from the United States, with one from Asia and one from Europe to enrich the discussion by raising issues from other cultural contexts. A significant feature of the book is the collaboration of theologians and scholars from Catholic, mainline Protestant, and evangelical traditions. Those from the United States come from different racial and ethnic backgrounds, and each of them has sustained connections with other parts of the world. They teach in theology departments in liberal arts colleges and universities, divinity schools, and seminaries. The plurality and diversity of the contributors increase the book's relevance because, true to the vision the volume espouses, the global condition is examined from many vantage points.

All along this has been a collaborative project. The various authors based in the United States met twice and also presented panels on the book's questions and findings at annual meetings of the American Academy of Religion. Through engaging these public conversations, we were able to identify common concerns and generate ideas in shaping the text you now hold in your hand. These encounters helped sharpen the arguments of the book, avoid unnecessary overlap, and hopefully make the book more coherent and useful to our readers.

Part 1 falls under the heading "Global Theology and Why It Matters." In chapter 1, "Teaching Theology from a Global Perspective," Kwok Pui-lan discusses the challenges of globalization to the teaching of theology with attention to the expansion of capital, the relation between the global and local, and cultural and religious diversity. She analyzes the context for the globalization of theology and different approaches to the conceptualizing of "global theology." The changing Christian demographics and the shift of Christianity to the Global South require teachers of theology to be aware of Eurocentrism (i.e., presupposing Europe as the default position for theological education) and to attend to the new expressions of Christian identity and faith, coming especially from the formerly colonized peoples. The shift of geopolitics necessitates a new way of conceptualizing the teaching of theology and imagining the theological curriculum. This chapter argues that teachers of theology need increasingly to pay attention to the identity and politics in the classroom, the relation of intellectual work with community, and the promotion of global consciousness.

In chapter 2, "Listening for Fresh Voices in the History of the Church," William A. Dyrness recalls the cultural diversity within the long tradition of Christian thought, from the multifaceted patristic period with its Alexandrian, Antiochene, and Gallic accents, through the medieval centuries in its Eastern and Western forms, to the modern period of missionary and colonial expansions. The chapter examines ways the development of church authority often conspired to exclude marginal voices. This would include the manner in which Monophysite Syriac and Egyptian churches were silenced by imperial rule and in which Nestorian and Arian voices, to say nothing of women and cultural minorities, have been systematically omitted from major histories. But it also points to how denominational histories, whether in their Catholic or Protestant forms, frequently leave vast sections of the church out of account. If we take into consideration the histories that have been suppressed, we will see that the church has been post-Western for quite some time. Recovering these missing voices may help us see that global theology is not, after all, a new reality but part of the broader heritage of the Christian church.

Veli-Matti Kärkkäinen, in "Teaching Global Theology in a Comparative Mode," approaches the task of teaching theology in a global context from the perspective of comparative theology. Chapter 3 focuses on the teaching of systematic/constructive theology in a way that puts key Christian doctrines—such as the Trinity, salvation, and theological anthropology—in dialogue with other living-faith traditions. Rather than attempting a "neutral" correlation of teachings of faith traditions (as in religious studies), comparative theology usually is "confessional" in nature (in this case, from the point of view of Christian tradition) and seeks to engage particular relevant teachings of the religious Other in a hospitable, inviting, and instructive way. This chapter explores questions such as these: Are there any resources in Christian tradition to facilitate such a pedagogy? What are the specific challenges or opportunities?

What does it take for the teacher to carry on such a task? How does it shape Christian self-understanding?

The book then turns to another emphasis in part 2: identity, power, and pedagogy of teachers and learners. With "The Good of Education: Accessibility, Economy, Class, and Power," Cecilia González-Andrieu offers chapter 4 with a focus on students. While most people acknowledge education's indispensability for a thriving human community, educational systems often protect asymmetrical power dynamics and replicate exclusion rather than challenging it. In theological education, issues of power and agency take on particular urgency as students prepare to serve and lead the future church. In the work of building up a church that makes a preferential option *with* and not only *for* the poor, transgressive pedagogical strategies must be developed. This chapter discusses educational access, as well as socioeconomic factors and relationships, and their effects on theological students and the institutions that are meant to serve them. The chapter explores practical challenges and the ways in which the theological classroom may become an effective engine for the transformation of the church by building up communities of theologians trained and committed to working with the disinherited of the world and those who may even come from their own ranks.

In chapter 5, "Identity Cross-Dressing while Teaching in a Global Context," Miguel A. De La Torre investigates how the constructed identity of scholars of color, along with the power and privilege that come with cultural capital, impacts pedagogy within the global perspective. This chapter explores "honorary" white identity conferred upon U.S. scholars of color (especially those teaching abroad) and how the very act of instruction of the normalized canon, taught in the language of the colonizer, reinforces the very structures responsible for oppression. It is within the classroom—the room of class—that students are taught their class and, more importantly, their place in society. Which "class"room one is relegated to attend—or teach from—will determine the extent of one's own colonized mind. How, then, does the scholar of color engage in a liberative pedagogy, which decenters and dismantles the legitimized discourse? How do the disenfranchised resist the temptation of imitating the oppressive praxis of those from the dominant culture? By exploring these questions, this chapter elucidates the opportunities and pitfalls faced by scholars of color who engage the global context in their work.

Lai Pan-chiu then moves the conversation in chapter 6 into Chinese thought and traditions with "Teaching Global Theology with Local

Resources: A Chinese Theologian's Strategies." Teaching at the Chinese University of Hong Kong, the author presents three strategies for teaching global theology with Chinese theological sources. The first is to study the historical documents of *Jingjiao*, which was conventionally called Chinese Nestorian Christianity, and to discover its Syrian roots from the Church of the East. This church was misidentified and pejoratively labeled by its opponents as "Nestorianism" for polemical purposes. Lai exposes the Eurocentric bias prevalent in most textbooks of the history of Christianity and introduces a broadened idea of global Christianity. With a second strategy, the author analyzes several of the theological texts of premodern Chinese Catholicism, some of which were shaped by traditional Chinese culture. These Chinese concepts, he claims, may be significant transnationally or globally. The task of Chinese Christian theology should include the interpretation of the meaning of its theological traditions in a transnational or even global context, rather than restricting itself to indigenization in China. The third strategy is to use strands of contemporary Chinese Christian theological treatises to show how comparative theology can be one of the possible ways to make a contribution to the development of global theology with Chinese sources.

Dwight N. Hopkins in chapter 7, entitled "Pedagogy for Being Human in Global Comparison," asks how an educator teaches the idea of being human among different students from various nations sitting in the same classroom. The author begins by examining his experience of teaching theological anthropology for a year in Seoul, Korea. His class consisted of students representing five different countries. His pedagogical strategy presupposed the following: (1) all knowledge first arises from specific cultures, (2) the human communities in those cultures define the theological anthropology, and (3) consequently, theological anthropology lacks a universal essence or global applicability. His pedagogical techniques encouraged the students to claim their own voices by consistently and consciously using a comparative method. For instance, whatever claim a student made, he/she had to give his/her viewpoint in relation to a different culture in the class. In addition, the students each were asked to pursue this comparative method by examining their views on different levels of being human—that is, on the family level, religion/spirituality level, space and time level, and so on. At the end of the class, the students each were asked what "being human" meant in their particular country.

Part 3 makes a further turn, this time toward praxis and responsibility. With chapter 8, "Teaching to Transform: Theological Education, Global Consciousness, and the Making of Global Citizens," Teresia Hinga recognizes the urgent need for conscientization about the global ethical issues of our time. She proposes that such consciousness-raising should become a major dimension of theological education since such awakening of consciousness is a necessary stepping-stone in the making and nurturing of global citizens who would be committed to mitigating said issues. The author refers analytically to two examples: (1) the Jesuit education system (exemplified by Santa Clara University, particularly in its new emphases on global matters in its newly minted Core Curriculum), and (2) the World Council of Churches, where such experimentations with education for transformation of consciousness and the making of global citizens are taking place in the fight against HIV/AIDS. Hinga makes the case for the adjustment of theological education to facilitate transformation of consciousness and also explores what we can learn from these two cases about the rationale, best practices, and strategies to adopt when scaling up curricular and pedagogical adjustments toward teaching theology in order to transform both the students and the world.

Loida I. Martell-Otero in "*Hablando Se Entiende la Gente*: Tower of Babble or Gift of Tongues?" investigates the concerns present when the classroom is populated by communities from oppressed and/or minoritized groups, as well as by those in places of privilege. Chapter 9 specifically asks this question: Does a diverse classroom necessarily create a conscientization of global issues or of the oppression of the "Other"? How does one ensure that all students leave the institution with an awareness of global issues—and how these issues impact ministry locally, nationally, and across the world? How can our pedagogy create a space of hospitality that nurtures community amid its celebration of difference? Given these questions and concerns, the author offers an example of teaching an introductory course to illustrate collaborative dialogue amid diversity.

Eleazar S. Fernandez' chapter 10, "The Geopolitical and the Glocal: Situating Global Theological Voices in Theological Education," presents a way of understanding the global as an entry point in the discourse about transnational pedagogy in theological education. The term "glocal," which is the interweaving of the global and the local, provides such an entry point in framing transnational pedagogy. Therefore, this chapter argues that a transnational pedagogy and a theological curriculum that takes account of our globalized world must (1) promote a way of thinking/reasoning that transgresses Eurocentric assumptions, (2) be multilingual (understood in a deeper sense to be inclusive of various ways of apprehending the world through language), (3) be transcontextual-transcultural, (4) take account of the multipositionality and shifting positions of social subjects in the power-knowledge nexus, and (5) be interfaith-engaged, hermeneutically dialogical, interdisciplinary, and integrative.

We hope you will enjoy this collaborative and expansive book and conversational journey. Though an invitation to all curious seekers, the book is intended especially for people who teach or are preparing as scholar-educators in the areas of theology, ethics, and world Christianity in theology departments in colleges and universities, as well as in seminaries and divinity schools. We especially hope it will prove useful for new instructors teaching in these contexts for the first time. We also wish to serve seasoned scholars wanting to know about the challenges and opportunities of pedagogy in a changing, globalized world. Our collaborative process has sought to generate fresh ideas for navigating an increasingly diverse and transnational classroom and to prepare global citizens. Finally, we direct this work toward religious practitioners and academics who are interested in the future of theological education in general. Since the book addresses issues from Catholic, Protestant, and evangelical contexts, we hope that along with being global and transnational, it may also promote Christian relationships built on effectively learning from one another.

PART I

Global Theology and Why It Matters

✦ 1 ✦

Teaching Theology from a Global Perspective

KWOK PUI-LAN

In the fall of 2012, I taught a course on liberation theology to a class of about twenty students in Boston. The students were highly motivated and wanted to learn liberation theology from different parts of the world and various social locations. The class drew students from my own Episcopal Divinity School, which has predominantly Euro-American students, as well as from other theological schools in Boston. As it turned out, one half of the students were Euro-Americans, while the other half consisted of racial and ethnic minority students and international students from several Asian and African countries. The diversity of the students' backgrounds enriched the class discussion, making us more keenly aware of the contextual nature of doing theology.

Teaching the course raised several pedagogical questions for me: What does it mean to teach theology from a global perspective? How should one organize the course materials—geographically according to different parts of the world, doctrinally according to theological themes, or socially according to issues pertaining to class, race, gender, sexuality, colonialism, and so forth? How does the teacher help students who have relatively little knowledge of the Global South understand theology arising from these contexts? Would racial and ethnic minority students and international students have privileged knowledge of liberation theology because of their marginalization in society? How can we avoid treating students from marginalized communities as if they are "native informants," especially when there are only a few of them in the classroom? How can we help Euro-American students feel that they have something meaningful to share and not feel isolated or silenced?

As we live in an increasingly interconnected world and face a growing diversity of students in our classrooms, it is important to reflect on teaching theology from a global and transnational perspective, with its challenges and opportunities. This is important not only for a course on liberation theology but across the theological curriculum. For too long, theology has been done for the church as a reflection of faith or in the academy as a highly specialized discipline. Today, theology must be done more intentionally in the public square, to promote dialogue for the common good and to educate global citizens. Theology must address social and political issues that concern the public, engage critical thinkers of our time, and articulate the public relevance of religious faiths and beliefs.[1] In this chapter, I discuss the context of the globalization of theology, different approaches to conceptualizing global theology, and the challenges of teaching theology in a global world.

The Context of the Globalization of Theology

Globalization is often used to describe the interconnections of our world based on the neoliberal economy, the Internet and social media, mass and consumerist culture, and "complex connectivity" as a result of rapidly developing networks.[2] In a so-called global village, what happens locally is affected by events occurring far away (and vice versa) because of the intensification of global social relations.[3] In fact, sociologist Roland Robertson has suggested replacing the term "globalization" with "glocalization" and argued that globalization is in actual fact a local process and that the worldwide exchange or fusion of culture is done in local terms. For Robertson, the global and the local are not opposing forces but interdependent and mutually influence each other.[4]

But globalization is not a new phenomenon; its roots can be traced back several centuries. It began with the so-called "discovery" of the New World, when the trade routes between the Old World and the New World were connected and people from different parts of the world were forcibly brought within an orbit that had Europe as the center. The developments in industrialization, transportation and telecommunication, and large multinational corporations facilitated capitalist growth and the integration of the market. Today the Internet and social media allow real-time interconnection and affordable and fast communication across the globe, and because of this, globalization has broken down national and territorial boundaries and compressed time and space. It has brought convenience to social life and connection among people, but it has also made possible the creation of a transnational capitalist class, who are able to amass and control great wealth. Economic disparity between the rich and the poor has widened, causing social unrest, large-scale migration, and war and violence in some places. The protests across North Africa, the Middle East, and Europe in 2011 and the Occupy movement around the world pointed to the unsustainability of the world's economic system.

The growing awareness of doing theology from a global perspective must be seen against this backdrop of rapid social, economic, and political changes since the latter part of the twentieth century. In the Catholic Church, the Second Vatican Council (1962–1965) was a watershed event, for it opened the church to the modern world and encouraged the use of local languages and expressions of faith. In evangelical circles the 1974 International Congress on World Evangelization in Lausanne, Switzerland, and the resulting Lausanne movement heightened the awareness of the global connection of Christians as well as local diversity. Some scholars have urged evangelical Christians to move beyond Western theology to rethink theology in light of global realities.[5] At the same time, the World Council of Churches, the Ecumenical Association of Third World Theologians, and other ecumenical networks have provided forums for theologians from different parts of the world to dialogue with one another.

Contextual theologies began to develop in the 1960s and 1970s in Latin America, Asia, and Africa, challenging the colonial paradigms and Eurocentric domination in theology. Latin American liberation theology attracted worldwide attention with its emphases on theology as a reflection of social praxis, the preferential option for the poor, and the new understanding of people as subjects of their own history.[6] Latin American and North American theologians gathered to discuss the implications of liberation theology at the Theology in the Americas Conference in Detroit in 1975.[7] In Asia and Africa, some theologians emphasized sociopolitical liberation and shared similar concerns with Latin American liberation theology, while others focused on religio-cultural aspects, striving for inculturation or indigenization of the gospel in their own soil. Robert J. Schreiter argues that the emergence of local theologies and an increasing sensitivity to history and culture created "an important shift in perspective of Christian self-awareness and theology, both among the churches in the southern hemisphere, and among the churches of the North Atlantic communities."[8]

The proliferation of local theologies raises the question of the relationship between the universal and the particular. In the past, Western theology has been taken as the norm and the "universal," while all other theologies are relegated as "particular" or derivative. Today, we have become aware that *all* theologies are contextual, arising from a particular worldview and addressing particular social and cultural situations. Yet, while theology is contextual, our contexts are increasingly interconnected and we cannot do theology limited to our local context. Stephen B. Bevans reminds us, "Theology today needs to be done in a dialogue with one's own contextual perspective and the broad and deep tradition of the Christian church, and in a dialogue as well with the results of this interaction and the perspectives of Christians from every part of our world."[9]

The shift of Christian demographics to the Global South prompted Christians to think of doing theology in a global way. Whereas in 1900, 83 percent of the world's Christians lived in Europe and North America,[10] today the majority of Christians live in the Global South. In 1900 Africa had only 10 million Christians, about 9 percent of the population. The number has increased to 360 million, roughly 46 percent of the population. By 2025 about one-half of the Christian population will live in Latin America and Africa, and another 17 percent in Asia. At this rate, only one out of five of the world's Christians will be non-Latino whites.[11] The phenomenal growth of the church in the Global South and the demographic shift has caused some scholars to argue that Christianity is becoming a non-Western religion. Lamin Sanneh, for example, has written, "Christianity as a truly world religion [is] increasingly defined by values and idioms of non-Western cultures and languages."[12] Sanneh, Kwame Bediako, Andrew Walls, Dana Robert, and others have urged scholars to pay attention to how Christianity in the Global South is reshaping the beliefs and practices of the Christian church. Sanneh's work, in particular, has focused on the vitality and agency of men and women on the ground, new ecclesial forms and practices, the interaction of Christianity and Islam, as well as reconceiving an African Christianity free from European and imperial interests.

The study of world Christianity has made us more keenly aware of the plurality and diversity of the Christian tradition, both in the past and in the present. Instead of focusing on the history of European Christianity, scholars have shown the ways Asians, Africans, and people in what is called the Middle East today have contributed to the development of the Christian tradition. Sanneh differentiates between a "world Christianity," with its emphasis on the use of local idioms and indigenous responses and adaptations, and "global Christianity," which still places the center of gravity in Europe, as if the global church were built on replication of forms and patterns developed in Europe.[13] Although not everyone agrees with Sanneh, many have become more conscious of the shift of the center of gravity of Christianity, the interaction of global and local, and the need to go beyond European and North American frameworks in the study of Christianity.

As Christian demographics shift to the Global South, the religious landscape of Europe and North America is simultaneously becoming more and more religiously pluralistic because of immigration. New immigrants have brought religious traditions from their homelands, such as Islam, Buddhism, Hinduism, Confucianism, and so forth. They have also made Christian communities more diverse in terms of race, ethnicity, and culture. In Europe, while church membership and attendance have been in steady decline, the face of the church has changed. Walter Hollenweger notes, "In many European cities there are more black, yellow and brown Christians coming together on a Sunday morning than white Christians."[14] In the United States, Soong-Chan Rah argues that it is the immigrant, ethnic, and multiethnic churches that are flourishing, even while the white mainline churches are declining in membership. He laments, however, that American Christianity is still caught in Western cultural captivity, and he shows how individualism and materialism have influenced the megachurches and emergent churches.[15] Since there will not be a majority race in the United States by 2040, the churches will be ill-equipped to face the diverse population and the new racial and cultural reality.

Even though the religious landscape of Christianity has changed so much in the past decades, the teaching of theology in general has remained quite traditional. A review of twelve syllabi of courses in theology or systematic theology posted on the Wabash Center Website shows that (1) there is little emphasis on the global nature of theology and the growing body of literature on the subject, (2) the majority of required texts are written by European and Euro-American male theologians, (3) only one required text, and often none, is by a theologian outside North America, usually from Latin America, such as Gustavo Gutiérrez, and (4) there is not enough acknowledgment of the contribution of the work of racial and ethnic minority scholars in the United States.[16] The teaching of the theological discipline remains Eurocentric, and in terms of global sensitivity, it lags behind the teaching of other fields, such as church history, world Christianity, missiology, and even biblical studies.

I hope the publication of this volume will stimulate further discussion to remedy this and to reorient the teaching of the theological field.

Conceptualizing Global Theology

Although we have a growing body of literature on "global theology," "theology in global dialogue," or "theology in a global context," there is no consensus on the scope of the subject matter, methodology, and evaluative criteria. I would like to discuss four approaches that have been used to conceptualize "global theology" in order to push the conversation further. These four approaches are selected to illustrate the diversity of opinion; they are not exhaustive. The first approach conceives of the "globe" primarily in a geographical or territorial sense. William A. Dyrness' edited volume *Emerging Voices in Global Christian Theology*, published in 1994, includes contributions from Eastern Europe, Africa, Asia, and Latin America. Addressing a primarily evangelical readership, he stresses that theologies from non-Western settings have a lot to teach Western Christians and further argues that "any renewal that will come to western theology will come by interacting with voices from alternative traditions."[17] Dyrness notes that there is a great deal of diversity in terms of theological agenda in the non-Western context, and he takes care not to collapse the differences. The text serves the purpose of introducing readers to these newer and unfamiliar resources, but readers need help to situate these emerging voices in the larger theological field. The separation of these voices from dominant theological discourses may also inadvertently marginalize these voices, because only those who are already interested in theologies of the Global South may pick up a book like this.

Veli-Matti Kärkkäinen's volumes on global discussions on the doctrines of ecclesiology, Christology, God, and Trinity attempt to bridge the gap between the dominant and emerging voices.[18] These books are also organized according to a primarily geographical grid. Each volume begins with the classical traditions and historical development of the doctrine. The volumes on ecclesiology and Christology move on to present contemporary formulations (mostly by Western European males), followed by contextual constructions (feminist, African, Asian, Latin American, and so forth). The volumes on the doctrines of God and Trinity are more explicit in their geographical framework, with sections divided into European, North American, and non-Western perspectives. The advantage of structuring the volumes in such a way is that both Western and non-Western authors are discussed in the same volume and readers can gain a comprehensive picture of the historical, ecumenical, and contextual approaches. The disadvantage is that a temporal order is imposed onto the geographical mapping, with the non-Western section consisting of newer, emergent voices placed at the end of the book. This section is usually the shortest, as if these voices are less important.

Hans Schwarz' *Theology in a Global Context: The Last Two Hundred Years* is an ambitious project. He presents a careful analysis of the development of modern European theology in its cultural, religious, and social contexts.[19] He then elucidates North American theology and Orthodox theology in different parts of the world before turning to the "emergence of new voices" from the Global South. The Eurocentric bias of the book is evident because the section on the "new voices" consists of only 78 pages out of a volume of 600 pages. The author assumes that his readers need to know European theology and its context in minute detail but the new voices just in passing. Namsoon Kang articulates the danger of conceptualizing theology according to continents when she speaks about the Asian context. She warns against the tendency to construct theology of a particular continent in a geographically deterministic and culturally essentialist way without attending to the very broad range of experiences of Asian people.[20] In surveys of global theology, when only a small number of theological voices from Africa, Asia, or Latin America are singled out to be discussed, it is difficult to avoid overgeneralization and simplification.

The second approach to global theology does not treat non-Western sources as "emergent" or "new" voices (with Europe as the norm),[21] since Christian theology has a long history of development outside the orbit of the Western world. This approach seeks to recover the multicultural and polycentric nature of the Christian tradition. The organizing principle is not "the West and the rest," or center and margin, because there are multiple centers. As Tite Tiénou explains:

> Polycentric Christianity is Christian faith with many cultural homes. The fact that Christianity is at home in a multiplicity of cultures, without being permanently wedded to any one of them, presents for Christians everywhere a unique opportunity for examining Christian identity and Christian theology.[22]

Just as scholars of world Christianity have emphasized that Christianity has been shaped by different cultures and histories from the beginning, theologians need to develop cross-cultural competency in the study of Christian doctrines. Andrew Walls notes,

> A culture-sensitive reading of the history of Christian doctrine might reveal how the crossing of cultural frontiers develops and enlarges theology. This happens because entry into a new culture at any depth may both pose questions previously unconsidered and provide intellectual materials for pursuing those questions.[23]

Walls argues that when the early church entered the Greek world, it began a long and arduous process of attempting to think in Greek in a Christian way, asking Greek questions and using indigenous categories and conventions. The words from the Nicene Creed—"God from God, Light from Light, Very God from Very God, begotten, not made, being of one substance with the Father"—came from interaction with the Greek world of thought and questions posed by it. Similarly, when Christianity came into contact with other cultural settings, the processes of translation and transposition also brought forth new questions and dimensions of Christian thought.

Let us look at Christianity in China as an example. Christianity arrived in China in the seventh century through the activities of Syrian missionaries from what was known as the Church of the East. These missionaries had to borrow Chinese expressions from Buddhism and Daoism to translate Christian ideas. In addition, they used the Buddhist symbol of the lotus to express this new faith to the Chinese audience. As the Christian tradition came into contact with the Chinese multireligious worldview and symbolic systems, new questions were raised by the Chinese cultural context. For example, the text on the stele erected by missionaries in Xian in 681 C.E. recounted the essentials of the Christian message, covering the creation, the Trinity, the incarnation, and baptism. But there was no mention of Christ's bloody sacrifice on the cross, probably because blood sacrifice as an act of redemption was difficult for the Chinese to understand.[24]

Contacts with Western Christianity began in the thirteenth century under the Mongol rulers, but these early efforts by Catholic missionaries did not take root. When Matteo Ricci (1552–1610) and other Jesuits arrived in the sixteenth century, they wanted to appeal to the Chinese literati and dressed in the attire of the scholarly class. Ricci studied the Chinese classics and found the ideas of *tian* (heaven) and *zhu* (Lord) in the Chinese classics and combined them to translate the Christian term "God" as *Tianzhu* (Lord of heaven). He saw no problem presenting

Christianity in Chinese garb. Ricci also supported the Chinese practice of veneration of ancestors, which the Franciscans and Dominicans condemned as idolatry. The Rites Controversy, as the debate was called, led European intellectuals and theologians to learn about Confucian and other Chinese rituals. Chinese scholars also learned something about Christianity in order to defend their tradition. The controversy thus led to the comparative study of Christianity and the Confucian tradition in both China and Europe.[25]

In the early nineteenth century, when Protestant missionaries arrived from England and the United States, they worked among the lower classes and had to adapt to popular religious practices. Because *Tianzhu* was not appropriate to the context, the missionaries debated about what Chinese terms would best reflect the concept "God." The British missionaries opted to use *shangdi* (the monarch above), while the Americans chose *shen* (spirit). Even today, there is no common consensus as how to translate the term "God" in the Chinese Christian community. Christian missionaries were allowed to preach in China because of the unequal treaties China was forced to sign with European countries with superior military power. As a result, many Chinese regarded Christianity as a foreign religion and associated it with imperialism. In response, Chinese theologians such as Wu Yaozong, Wu Leichuan, and Zhao Zichen had to reconstruct Christian theology in order to show that Christianity could contribute to resisting foreign aggression.[26]

The example of China shows that when Christianity crossed new cultural frontiers, questions such as the translation of Christian terms, the interpretation of Christ's sacrifice and redemption, the use of indigenous symbols, the role of Chinese rituals and practices, and the relation between religion and politics were raised. These issues were unavoidable when Christianity encountered a multireligious context in a colonial or semicolonial setting. Doing global theology from a Chinese perspective will be very different from that in the Western perspective.[27] Becoming aware of this difference expands our horizons and enables us to see the Christian theological tradition in a polycentric and multilayered way.

The third approach also recognizes the multiple cultural homes of Christianity and seeks to understand the relationship between the global and the local when there is a central teaching office, as in the Roman Catholic tradition. In *The New Catholicity: Theology between the Global and the Local*, Robert J. Schreiter addresses the changing contexts of the Roman Catholic Church.[28] He says that globalization has made global capitalism a new reality and that the global hyperculture has created homogeneity on the one hand and provoked intensifications of the local on the other. In the face of this new reality, the church needs to develop a new catholicity, which he says

> is marked by a wholeness of inclusion and fullness of faith in a pattern of intercultural exchange and communication. To the extent that this catholicity can be realized, it may provide a paradigm for what a universal theology may look like today, able to encompass both sameness and difference, rooted in an orthopraxis, providing *teloi* for a globalized society.[29]

This "universal" theology is not prescribed by the Vatican but rather shaped by dialogue and mutual understanding through intercultural hermeneutics. Even though "local" or "contextual" theology might have emerged from a particular context, its implications and significance often far exceed its immediate context. Latin American liberation theology is an obvious example. Schreiter says that the global theological flows have been much shaped by the discourses of liberation, feminism, ecology, and human rights since the second half of the twentieth century. These theological discourses address the crises and contradictions of the global systems, and can lay claim to the new universal theologies because they are ubiquitous and are highly influential in shaping contemporary theological consciousness.[30]

Schreiter's view is grounded in the classic doctrine of the church: one, holy, catholic, and apostolic. While some scholars in the postmodern and postcolonial era might shy away from using the term "universal," Schreiter does not avoid it. But unlike in the colonial era, when dominant Western culture was "universalized" to superimpose on other cultures, Schreiter's idea of global theological flows is grounded in a global consciousness that recognizes the flows of capital, resources, labor, and ideas in our interconnected world. Theological movements and currents do not flow only from the center to the margin, but can travel in multiple directions across geographical and cultural boundaries. Published in 1997, Schreiter's book is inclusive and forward-looking, though the Vatican under Pope Benedict often harkened back to the old idea of catholicity and failed to acknowledge women's rights; the rights of lesbian, gay, bisexual, and transgender people; and the challenges of religious pluralism. It remains to be seen if under Pope Francis, the first pope elected from the Global South (Argentina) in 2013, a new chapter of the church will unfold. His statements concerning economic justice have already created controversy in the United States.

Many Catholic scholars have urged the Catholic Church to address the Christian demographic shift, as most of today's Catholics either live in the Global South or are members of racial and ethnic minority communities in the Global North. In *Idol and Grace: On Traditioning and Subversive Hope*, Orlando O. Espín argues against a Eurocentric Catholicism. He stresses that Western cultural tradition, as well as the Catholicism within it, is not monolithic but "the ambivalent mixture of the dominant and the dominated, and neither side can claim to be sole representative of this tradition."[31] In postcolonial parlance, colonized cultures have already been inscribed within the colonizers' cultures. In discussing the traditions of the church, he says, it is not sufficient to focus on the contents of tradition, authority, and related topics without paying attention to the process of reception. The contents of tradition have often been taken as propositional doctrines whose truth and authority are guaranteed by the popes and the bishops. But in fact, the contents of tradition must be interpreted and received within particular contexts for them to be passed on from generation to generation. He proposes the term "traditioning" to shift the focus to the process and context. Traditioning, as a dynamic process, would counteract the idolatrizing tendencies that take some decontextualized doctrinal propositions as a *depositum fidei*.[32]

The fourth approach offers transnational feminist perspectives to look at globalization and theology. Although the book *The Oxford Handbook of Feminist Theology* does not have the term "global" in its title, it is based on a gathering of feminist theologians from around the globe and its central theme is globalization. The editors of the volume, Mary McClintock Fulkerson and Sheila Briggs, explain that in addition to gender, race, ethnicity, class, and sexual orientation, which continue to be important in defining the contexts of feminism, globalization brings three more factors: deterritorialization, hyperdifferentiation (in that people have multiple identities and live in multiple realities), and hybridity of cultures.[33] The book opens with Serene Jones' discussion of global imagination and encourages the readers to move beyond a narrowly defined and essentialized identity politics to enter into a global conversation.

Even though deterritorialization is a defining character of globalization, the editors recognize that territorial geography still exists and devote almost half of the book to feminist theological issues by geographical regions. One of the reasons for doing so is to honor the diversity of women's experiences and their regional differences. The organization is different from that in the books I have discussed in the first approach above, in which the Global South is separated from the Global North or presented at the tail end. Here, Europe and North America are treated as one region among many and are not given any special status. In fact, priorities are given to the voices of women from the Global South and to women of racial and ethnic minority (for example, there are three chapters on African women, two chapters on Native American and indigenous women, but only one chapter on European women). Although many of the contributors are North Americans or international scholars currently teaching in the United States, the book has a wide range of voices and seeks to present an inclusive account of feminist theologies in the early twenty-first century.

Many contributors, both from former colonizing and colonized countries, are cognizant of the colonial legacy that is shaping the world and use postcolonial insights in their work. They articulate in various ways the negative impact of globalization on women in the world and the power imbalance between the Global North and Global South. For instance, Musa W. Dube from Botswana asks this critical question: In what ways does feminist theological discourse "reproduce and maintain the globalization power relations?"[34] She argues that feminist theology cannot be a "one-way traffic" from the West with responses or counternarratives from the Global South. In other examples, Ellen T. Armour and Sharon D. Welch from the United States urge readers to eradicate colonial ideologies in feminist presuppositions and misconceptions about colonized and postcolonized others.[35] Welch especially draws from postcolonial theories to interrogate the construction of "religion" and religious difference and offers helpful alternative forms of interreligious engagement.

A distinctive feature of this volume is that people from non-Christian traditions are not just talked about, as in many volumes on theology of religions and comparative theology, but invited to join the global conversation. Feminist scholars from Jewish, Hindu, Native, and Muslim traditions, as well as scholars who are knowledgeable about African indigenous religions, are all part of the dialogue. They provide critical insights about how globalization has reshaped women's religious lives, especially in the rise of fundamentalisms and gender violence, and how women's groups have critiqued capitalism and brought forth changes.

Throughout the book, there is an urgent call to combine feminist scholarship with activism, to go beyond the 1990s' preoccupation with "difference" to connect and engage, and to find new visions and imagination to address the challenges of the globalized world.

These four different approaches show that there are both advantages and disadvantages in conceptualizing global theology in geographical and territorial terms. Even as globalization has heightened our sense of a deterritorialized world, the old cartography of the world in terms of continents and geographical regions remains strong in theological discourse. Gayatri Chakravorty Spivak's notion of a "critical regionalism," which attends to the plurality and diversity of any given region, might be a helpful reminder if we continue to use continental labels.[36] What is seen as global theology is contingent upon one's social location, history, and background. The discourse on global theology in China will be quite different from that in the United States. The relation between global and contextual theologies is shaped by denominational histories, theological traditions, and institutional structures. Global theological flows are increasingly not a one-way traffic, as theology developed in one part of the world has implications for other parts. Furthermore, globalization has impacts on the configuration of gender, race, class, sexual orientation, religion, and so forth. Transnational feminist theology; transnational lesbian, gay, bisexual, and transgender theology; and renewed theological engagements with race and class that address the global situation have much to contribute to global theology.

Challenges of Teaching Theology in a Global World

Although the Association of Theological Schools in the United States and Canada has discussed globalization and theological education since the mid-1980s[37] and a growing body of literature on global theology is available, the theological curriculum in many schools is still very Eurocentric and Euro-American. There is a time lag between the field of theology and what is happening in other fields in the humanities and social sciences. For example, postcolonial theory was not introduced to the field of theology until almost twenty-five years after Edward W. Said published the foundation text *Orientalism*.[38] To many people, theology is a parochial discourse addressing only people in the church, with no significant import for the larger issues facing humanity and the planet. Even for those who are interested in theological questions, the field of theology seems quaint and outdated. In a provocative essay, Corey

D. B. Walker asks, "What is the fate of theology in a post-theological moment?"[39] By "post-theological," he does not mean we are entering an age devoid of theology. Rather, his term signifies that traditional theological discourse cannot hold the breadth and depth of what animates current intellectual discussions on theology and politics from so many disciplines and quarters. Theology is "leaking" in the sense that what was considered the central core of theology does not hold anymore. Theology pops up in categories, concepts, and languages that we may not have anticipated or recognized.

We must emphasize the public nature of doing theology in order for theology to speak to our contemporary world and reimagine the scope, contents, and pedagogy of the field. We have to engage the church, academia, and the wider public to discuss what is theological literacy and competence in the twenty-first century. We need to interrogate the curriculum, contents, courses, paradigms, staff, and pedagogies of theological departments, seminaries, and divinity schools. Musa W. Dube warns against the danger of tokenism and paying only lip service to diversity. She says we should seek to

> establish whether the contents and structures of theological programs reproduce and maintain the globalization practices of one-way traffic and tokenist paradigms that maintain Eurocentrism. In the latter paradigm, theological programs admit Two-Thirds World staff, theological perspectives, theories, and methods in the non-threatening margins and ignore the ever-changing faces, accents, and foods of its neighborhood.[40]

Dube's comments point to three significant problems in theological programs that we would do well to avoid: (1) add a few courses on theologies from the Global South, usually as elective courses, while the core courses and the general ethos of the program remain largely Eurocentric, (2) include only perspectives and theologies from the Global South that do not present radical challenges and can be domesticated or appropriated, and (3) separate theological concerns from the Global South from those raised by racial and ethnic minority scholars closer to home, because it might be easier to discuss oppression in faraway places than in our own neighborhood.

Even if a teacher wishes to include theological sources from the Global South, it is not easy to find and have access to those materials. The number of titles on theologies from the Global South published in the United States and Europe has been in decline, and some of these books easily go out of print. Only a small number of theologians from the Global South have been included in the theological curriculum, which does not do justice to the plurality of voices. Those who do not write in one of the major colonial languages will remain obscure even if they have something important to say. To add to the complexity, most of the books on "global theology" or "theology in a global context" are written or edited by European and Euro-American scholars, and filtered through their theological assumptions and epistemological frameworks. In order to overcome these challenges, the teacher and the school's librarian must be familiar with local and regional publishing programs and establish relationships with different theological networks.

The teaching of theologies from a global perspective is challenging in the United States because transnational literacy[41] is low, and many students do not possess adequate knowledge of other parts of the world. For example, students may not know the history of Peru, the influences of Marxism among intellectuals in Latin America, or the culture of Latin American churches when they read Gustavo Gutiérrez' *A Theology of Liberation*.[42] If theology grows out from lived experience and a particular context, students have a lot to catch up on to know the context before they can engage the theological material. Furthermore, students need to be aware of their own biases and presuppositions before they can enter the worldview of theologians speaking from a very different context. Rauna Kuokkanen notes that the epistemological foundations and practices of the academy are selective and exclusionary, influenced as they are by the Enlightenment, colonialism, modernity, and, in particular, liberalism. She continues:

> These traditions, discourses, and practices have very little awareness of other epistemologies and ontologies, and offer them heavily restricted space at best. Even in the academic spaces that consider themselves most open to "changing the paradigm," individuals are often unwilling to examine their own blind spots.[43]

William A. Dyrness gives an example of how this relates to the teaching of theology. He says that much of Western Christianity is indelibly shaped by the "liberal self," which gives priority to the individual and separates him or her from society. But for most people outside the West, community and relationships are seen as primary, and actual relationships take precedence over dogmatic abstractions, whether these involve the veneration of the Virgin of Guadalupe in Mexico or the presence of spirits in Africa. While the Enlightenment has determined Western people's attitude toward truth or knowledge, this does not affect many other people.[44] It is challenging, therefore, for students in the United States to understand or engage in dialogue with African notions of gods and spirits.

In a traditional and Eurocentric theology class, the experiences of international students and racial and ethnic minorities do not count much, and they are not seen as capable of producing knowledge. But in a course on theology from a global perspective, these students are often put on the spot as "authentic" representatives or spokespersons of their cultures. As "native informants," their assigned role is to educate Euro-American students about their ignorance, which has been sanctioned by the larger society. In other classes the accents or lack of linguistic skills of some of these students may be seen as a liability, but in a class on global perspective, their accent may suddenly become an asset as one of the marks of their "authenticity." The teacher should recognize there is an imbalance of knowledge among the students: international students and racial and ethnic minority students have to know the West because of Western hegemony, but the Euro-American students have not been required to know about the rest of the world. It is the Euro-American students' responsibility to educate themselves and not rely on their darker-skinned classmates to educate them. In such cases it would be helpful for the teacher to discuss some of the power dynamics shaping the classroom and offer guidelines to deal with difference at the beginning of the class.

It is also important for the teacher to be aware of the range of emotions that the class may elicit, which contributes to diverse responses. I have had Euro-American female students crying in class because they felt that they were complicit in the oppression of women in the Global South. I have also had Korean students in their twenties who found Korean *minjung* theology perplexing, because they could not relate to a time when Korea was poor and under a dictatorship. Althea Spencer Miller notes that feminist and multicultural educators have categorized responses in the classroom as "resistance," "nonengagement," and "engagement."[45] Resistance is negative engagement that dissents against the liberatory impulse and philosophy. The student is nonengaged because the process is perceived to be boring or irrelevant, or it is too alien to the student's more comfortable learning style. The student may also feel there is a lack of safe space. The desired response is engagement, when the student actively participates in the classroom and takes responsibility for his or her own learning. Such engagement, Spencer

Miller notes, "may be marked at a deeper level by self-assessing reflexivity, recognitions of connectedness, and the movement from personal experience to theorizing, a form of praxis."[46]

Although the challenges of teaching theology from a global perspective are immense, there is no turning back if we want our students to be global citizens and future leaders of faith communities in a transnational world.[47] Our students who belong to the millennial generation have grown up in a world of the Internet, instant messaging, Facebook, Twitter, Instagram, and other social media. They are the most globally connected generation the world has ever seen. They are the "digital natives" who use mobile devices to access information on the go and to connect instantly with their friends, families, and colleagues across distances.[48] The field of theology will have a bright future if we can speak to the globalized world and capture the imagination of this upcoming generation.

✦ 2 ✦

Listening for Fresh Voices in the History of the Church

WILLIAM A. DYRNESS

In this book we are seeking to highlight the rich diversity of the Christian church—a diversity that to our minds should increasingly influence the way theology, and its history, are taught in the academy. While there is a growing awareness and even appropriation of contemporary diversity, the argument of this chapter is that a Eurocentric and Western orientation of the church still dominates the reading and teaching of Christianity's history. This has had the unfortunate consequence of marginalizing not only what we call the Eastern tradition but the still-vibrant Syriac, North African, and Asian strands of the larger Christian tradition, to say nothing of the newer traditions in Africa and Latin America.[1]

This is true despite the fact that growth of the church is occurring predominately in the non-Western world, so that by 2050 only one-fifth of the world's three billion Christians will be non-Hispanic and white. In short, a post-Christian church in the West faces an increasingly non-Western church elsewhere. This calls, I argue, for a new, historical self-understanding. I will approach this possibility from three directions: issues of faith and culture show the original diversity of the emerging Christian movement; Christendom and colonialism describe the rise of imperial Christianity; and our globalized world underlines the current and future challenges of our intercultural and interfaith world.

Issues of Faith and Culture

Christianity by its very nature is a missionary religion, and missionaries necessarily take the faith across cultural boundaries. Beginning with the life and teaching of Jesus in the Middle East, Christianity spread to the Greek and European worlds, but also to Asia, North Africa, and other parts of the Middle East. At each point in its transmission, significant shifts of theology and practice had to occur to accommodate cultural and social differences. The shift, for example, from the Jewish world of Jesus to Greek and Hellenic worlds occasioned Tertullian's polemical question: What has Athens to do with Jerusalem? Quite a lot as it turned out, but not without radical changes in theology, liturgy, and lifestyle. For starters, circumcision was dropped as a precondition for Christian membership, and Christ's person and mission were reconceived in terms of the Greek idea of the Logos. As Lamin Sanneh and others have pointed out, Christianity is intrinsically a religion of translation based on Christ's own Trinitarian translation from eternal Logos to someone who assumed human form and embraced the cross in time and history.[2] Among the questions this raises are the following: What principles and criteria have guided these translations in the past? How do these criteria stand up to critical examination in the present, and how in the light of social and historical change might they be modified in the future?

As soon as the first cultural frontier was crossed, questions were raised to which the Jewish context and its theology had no answers. This related on one level to whether believers needed to be circumcised but also how they were to understand the person and work of Christ. The question had to do with both *how* they needed to act and *what* they needed to think. Christ as a Jewish messiah made no sense to Greek Christians, and so Paul suggested that Christ's status was better conveyed by a new phrase: Jesus is Lord. As Andrew Walls notes, when the apostles decided Christians did not need to become Jewish proselytes and accept circumcision, "the implications of this were huge, and no one could guess where they would lead."[3]

And the challenge was more than simply a change in vocabulary; it involved delicate cultural negotiations, for as Paul put it in his Letter to the Corinthians, "Jews demand signs and Greeks desire wisdom" (1 Cor 1:22)—the one asked what should be done; the other, what can be thought. Thus have Christian groups talked past each other ever since.

One thing is clear already in the New Testament: whatever Jewish Christians expected, Greek vocabulary and methods of thinking would now be a necessary part of Christian discourse. No one could have guessed what issues were implicit in John's daring use of the Greek "Logos" to describe Christ's person and work. But neither could anyone predict the shape of Christianity as it entered still other worlds in Syria and Egypt. Three brief case studies illustrate this transformation.

Syriac Christianity

Though often ignored in Western texts, Christianity in Syria was flourishing by the late first century C.E., influenced especially by Matthew's gospel and the *Didache*;[4] an important collection of very early Christian hymns (called "odes") survives from this period. With a probable origin in Antioch, the focus of these hymns is thanksgiving for the advent of the Messiah; their tone is Jewish rather than Greek, and their emphasis is on Christ's incarnation as both savior and model.[5] They urge believers to leave the way of error and walk in the way of truth, noting that "because I love him who is love, I will become a son" (729). In the seventh ode, Christ is praised as the one who "became like me, that I might receive him. In form he was considered like me that I might put him on" (739). With its practical and deeply emotional tone, these odes anticipate, and perhaps even defuse, theological controversy that was centuries away:

> A cup of milk was offered me
> And I drank it in the sweetness of the Lord's kindness.
> The son is the cup
> And the Father he who was milked
> And the Holy Spirit is she who milked him. (Ode 19, 752)[6]

These poet-theologians modeled a way of doing theology that would not find expression until the medieval mystics, and have not received the attention they deserve in the dominant theological histories.

Egypt

Meanwhile, a wholly different Christianity was forming in Egypt nurtured by a Greek-style academy in Alexandria. Whereas Antiochene Christianity focused on Christ's humanity and the literal interpretation of Scripture, Alexandrian Christianity under the influence of Greek philosophy favored an allegorical reading of the Old Testament and honored Christ's divinity. But Mercy Oduyoye thinks something more fundamental was at work in Egyptian Christianity. The Nile Basin was well known for its cult of Isis and Osiris. Osiris (goddess of the waters of the Nile) died yearly but was resurrected by the weeping of Isis. Thus the gospel of a man who died and was raised was naturally accepted here. But at the same time, the honor paid to Isis easily passed over to the esteem offered to Mary as the Theotokos (God-bearer). As Oduyoye notes, "As Isis brought life back to Osiris so Mary gave life to the Son of God."[7] This divine character of Christ was so important to these

Christians that they would eventually reject the Chalcedonian formulation of Christ's two natures.

In Alexandria, John's gospel and its terminology were to have fateful influence, especially on the third-century theologian Origen (185–254). Taking his cue from John, Origen identified the Son with the divine Logos, which in his thinking made him different from God and even subordinate to him. But two characteristics of the Church of Egypt, central to the controversies to come, need special emphasis for their contemporary resonance. On the one hand, the Christianity of Egypt and of North Africa more generally was known for its asceticism, and even its embrace of martyrdom. Indeed, as Oduyoye points out, the first appearance of the North African Church in the records of Christianity was to name the twelve Berber Martyrs who had refused to swear by the "Lord our Emperor."[8] This was a church that believed it was better to die as martyrs than betray their faith. This understanding of the church as de facto holy made North Africa a center for the Donatist rigorists, leading in the fifth century to an entirely separate church structure against which Augustine struggled in his later years. This focus on visible holiness, and salvation as the deliverance from corruption, found further support in the monastic movement that developed in Egypt.

But there was a second characteristic of this region that was as crucial as it was misunderstood by the dominant authorities. After Origen, the Alexandrian Church continued down its subordinationist road. Arius, an Egyptian priest, was eager to reinforce the complete transcendence of God, "who is alone unbegotten alone eternal and alone without beginning."[9] Since the Word was begotten, Arius reasoned, he must be a creature. While it is hard to piece together exactly what Arius believed since his writings were suppressed, at the heart of it, as Henry Chadwick points out, was Arius' astonishment that the one God could also be three. This bias on behalf of unity led this church, even after Arius was condemned, to focus on Christ and the Spirit proceeding directly from the Father.[10] This emphasis on the unity of God and the hankering for martyrdom resonate in this region up to the present.

This could have been one of those critical moments when the church embraced difference and sought to understand and learn from it—even to forge a vocabulary that would have helped diffuse subsequent controversies with Islam. But unfortunately that did not happen. Both the Donatists and Arius (as Origen before him) were condemned by church councils, and this history stands mostly as the story of a road not taken by the imperial church. Sadly, an opportunity was lost. Significantly, it is a Ghanaian woman theologian who points out to us what should have been obvious: that the Donatist impulse for actual purity in the church and the subordinationist focus on God's transcendence and unity both had deep indigenous roots. So strong was the continuing influence of these traditions, despite the determination of all church councils, that when the Muslim invaders swept across North Africa in the seventh century, their asceticism and monarchial focus led the church to accept this rule rather than identify with a church from which their voice had been excluded. In the year 703, Oduyoye notes, "they went over en masse to Islam, which made them more welcome than Christianity had ever done."[11]

Nestorius and the Mission to Asia

Between 325 when the Council of Nicea condemned Arius and Chalcedon in 451, a controversy raged that no council was able to quell. Indeed, for a time after Chalcedon, most major centers of Europe, and even their vandal invaders, had become Arian. A split was forming that not even the might of a diminishing empire could forestall. A central example is the case of Nestorius, priest from Antioch and eventually, for a time, archbishop of Constantinople (428–431). Consistent with the Antiochene focus, Nestorius leaned toward a literal interpretation of Scripture and emphasized the humanity of the historical Christ.[12]

Nestorius was especially troubled by the growing use of the term "Theotokos" for Mary, since it seemed to diminish Christ's humanity, and he proposed "Christ-bearer" as a better description of Mary. Modern discovery of Nestorius' writings have shown that his views were essentially orthodox. Taking his stand on the historical Christ, he accepted all the biblical teaching about Christ's divinity. As he put it, Christ was "true God by nature, true man by nature, though one person."[13] Chalcedon came to affirm the two natures, though Nestorius was condemned for separating the two natures. Meanwhile, the Egyptian church continued to affirm the single nature of Christ (thus its characterization as Monophysite), which it teaches to this day.

Again the charges and countercharges that these groups leveled against each other neglected to take account of the deep underlying reasons these views arose or why they were found so convincing. The early councils, in spite of all politics, did find broad common ground—and we might allow they were often right in what they affirmed but wrong in what they left out or simply ignored. Meanwhile, the biblical and missional focus of Nestorius led to a vital study center developing in Nisibis, from which a stream of missionaries went into Persia and China along the Silk Road. By 650 it is estimated that there may have been as many as 300 churches in China, often referred to as Nestorian. Meanwhile, the focus on Divine Kingship and ascetic practices spread from the church in Egypt into Ethiopia, where the Coptic Church prospers to this day.

But both these movements occurred outside the purview of a developing Christendom. Chalcedon may have succeeded in unifying the church in the West (though even this took almost a century to achieve), but it also, at the same time, separated the Western churches from those in Africa and Asia. Though these churches desperately needed each other, by the sixth century the alienation was complete. And the Islamic invasion only confirmed a division that had long existed. As Andrew Walls summarizes:

> A world Christian community that transcended all imperial frontiers became submerged. The world church split along linguistic and cultural lines. So bitter was the division that Syriac and Coptic Christians could welcome the Arab occupation of Syria and Egypt as liberation, and accept Islamic rule as preferable to that of oppressive fellow Christians.[14]

Some critical lessons might be learned from these case studies. First, diversity in theology has existed from the very beginning of Christianity, and we should not be surprised to find it present in the global church today—it is a major characteristic of Christianity's translatability and its global diffusion. But secondly, these differences reflected significant local differences and cultural expectations, not ignorance and unbelief. Moreover, their suppression caused divisions that were to prove harmful to the advance of the Gospel. Finally, differences, rather than promoting suspicion and violence, should provide the opportunity for mutual learning. To see why this became so difficult in the history of the church, we need to examine our second topic.

Christendom and Colonialism

When Christianity became the official religion of the Holy Roman Empire under Constantine the Great in the early fourth century C.E., it radically changed its character. What had largely been a decentralized and pluralistic faith until then became vastly more centralized and monolithic. This is not at all to aver that the dominance of Rome and its imperium were not subsequently challenged—the great schisms of the Eastern Orthodox Church and later the Protestant Reformation indicate otherwise. But it is to suggest that a certain imperial and colonialist mentality was inaugurated in world Christianity with far-reaching repercussions. Moving forward in history, it is a fact that the imperial powers of Spain, Portugal, France, Italy, Britain, the Netherlands, and more recently the United States employed Christianity as an essential cultural-political tool of their colonial enterprises. What is characteristic of this dimension of Christian history is the way political power, and even violence, has accompanied the advancement of the faith.

To understand this we turn briefly to the form of Christianity that emerged during the Middle Ages. Even a cursory review of controversies during this time lead one to conclude, as I have argued above, that differences were as often political or cultural as they were theological. Indeed, the overriding impression is that the inability to locate theological differences within their larger cultural settings made it impossible for any significant exchange to take place. In particular, even sympathetic readers of this history are troubled by the way final decisions and condemnations were enforced by imperial might. Though, from our perspective, Augustine's preaching against the Donatists appears convincing and authoritative, even though he had to appeal to the imperial court in Ravenna for a final judgment in order to put the matter to rest. And this insistence on unity and intolerance of diversity, Samuel Hugh Moffett points out, was a particularly Western characteristic.[15] Indeed, Malcolm Lambert argues that though the Byzantine (Eastern) Church struggled against competing factions, "there never was a time in the history of the Byzantine Church in which heresy is completely eliminated."[16]

We have already noted that the Christians were treated with more respect under Islam than some of them had been under a supposedly Christian emperor. This relative tolerance also characterized Islamic rule after the conquest of Spain in the eighth century. Indeed, in that century the Umayyad Caliphate reached a level of civilization that medieval Europe would not attain for another 400 years.[17]

But a single characteristic of this period calls out for attention and explanation. Students of this period have agreed that there was a remarkable tolerance toward difference during the early medieval period. Indeed, those who study what are called heresies in church history note that, while Pelagian and Arian heresies persisted up to the end of the seventh century, no new heresies appeared at the popular level until the eleventh century.[18] Of course the Eastern Church went through its struggles in the Iconoclastic movement, which was finally settled at the Second Council of Nicea in 787 C.E. But what accounts for this absence of dissent and heresy during this period? Is it due to the fact that our sources are limited primarily to the missionary outreach of the church? R. I. Moore has recently proposed a different reason: the church in the early medieval period permitted a greater variety of worship and practice because it had "not yet developed the means, or, some would say, the inclination, to demand uniformity of worship and practice across Western Christendom."[19]

What is clearly evident is that persecution faded away with the decline of the Roman Empire and did not reappear until the eleventh to the thirteenth century.[20] This fact is well established; the question is what accounts for the sudden reappearance of this determination to impose uniformity. The best guess of modern historians is that this was an extension of a longstanding impulse on the part of authorities to quell the dangerous tendency to violence of fanatical mobs.[21] Moore demurs from this standard view and argues that persecution was introduced systematically by acts of state. Rather than there being no diversity of opinions to be challenged previously, he thinks that it was only in the eleventh and twelfth centuries that "deliberate and socially sanctioned violence began to be directed, through established governmental, judicial and social institutions, against groups of people defined by general characteristics such as race, religion or way of life." This resulted from what Moore calls the formation of a persecuting society, a claim that deserves further attention here.

Medieval Heresy

In what are now three scholarly books, R. I. Moore has developed a central pair of claims. On the one hand, he notes that all the heresies that developed related in one way or another to the growing desire for spiritual purity and escape from the evils of the world, and to the equally strong and increasing sense that the church was not being true to its spiritual mission—that it had failed in fundamental ways.[22] Moore notes that the increasing wealth of society had often corrupted the church and its leadership, and the people quite naturally began to look elsewhere for religious guidance. One can even argue that it was the failure of the religious authorities that promoted heretical groups or encouraged groups in the direction of heresy.[23]

But the second claim by Moore, developed in his most recent book, is equally striking. The very process of the church to reform itself, he thinks, led to mechanisms of control that inevitably entailed violence. The process began in 1160 when five heretics were burned in Cologne, only the second execution in about seven centuries since the fall of the Roman Empire. This process culminated in the famous Fourth Lateran Council in 1215 that produced, Moore claims, a full blown "persecuting society." The canons of this council encouraged prelates to liquidate heresy in their regions, even as it required the faithful to make an annual confession. As reviewer David Collins sums up Moore's thesis, "Reform . . . encompasses intolerance for those aspects of the status quo it aims to change and not uncommonly directs violence against them in word and action as well."[24]

However one judges Moore's work,[25] the ironies that he pinpoints are compelling. The heresies that developed—or, if Moore is right, were invented—were all in the service of a piety that sought real holiness and deliverance from the trials of life on earth. But the response of the church to these movements—which can be understood, at best, as its attempt to reform itself—only increased the systematic persecution of those seen as deviant. Does this, Moore wonders, suggest an intention to destroy the ability of local populations to display the difference of understanding and acting that their indigenous traditions have given them?

One possible support of Moore's point is to point to the sorry history of the Crusades that began late in the eleventh century. These represented attempts not only to recover the Holy Land from its Muslim rulers, but they also came to be directed against residents of Europe, who for a mixture of religious, economic, or political reasons were considered pagans or heretics. Whatever wrongs were perceived in these groups, these initiatives ensured that the indigenous wisdom they represented was also left out of account—after the disastrous Fourth Crusade which virtually destroyed Constantinople, the capital of Eastern Christianity, in 1204, it would take almost 300 years to recover the riches of the Greek tradition of Christianity. Even the attacks on Islam embodied a certain hypocrisy considering all the Western Church had learned from the Muslim philosophers in Spain. Indeed, the Greek philosophical and scientific heritage passed into Europe by means of the Muslim (and Jewish) philosophers in Spain. However we understand this, it is uncontestable that it was this form of Christianity that conquistadores took with them to Latin America. As Enrique Dussel notes, such was the confidence in this Christian civilization that the Crusades against the Moors and the conquest of Latin America appeared natural. "It was," Dussel notes, "the same Latin, Hispanic Christendom which came to America."[26]

While colonialism in its many forms—economic, cultural, and political—continues, it is largely true to say that we have today entered a postcolonial era where the formerly subjugated peoples of Asia, the Middle East and Africa, and Latin America, many of whom are Christian, are trying to forge their destinies in their own cultural idiom. All of this poses a critical question: What will postcolonial Christianities look like? And more importantly, what lessons have we learned from this colonial past?

Our Globalized World

These questions lead us finally to the central characteristic of postcolonialism: a globalized world where temporal and spatial boundaries are permeable and where religions and cultures are forced to interact—for good and for ill. Even though Christianity remains the world's largest religion (followed closely by Islam), it is a fact that in a postcolonial era it cannot claim hegemony—no emperor enforces its unity—but must encounter the conditions and constraints of religious pluralism. Thanks to immigration and demographic changes, Christians are invariably brought face-to-face with people of other cultures and, often, of other faiths. This has spawned the notorious "clash of civilizations" described by Samuel Huntington but has also allowed for fruitful dialogues with Jews, Muslims, Hindus, Buddhists, and others. Some of the most valuable contributions to Christian theology and practice have emerged from such dialogues. This situation gives rise to a series of questions: What principles and criteria should guide and shape these dialogues? What about so-called religious hybridity and multiple religious belonging—are these a threat or a boon to Christian identity?

My argument to this point has made it clear why Christians have a hard time answering these questions. The habit of listening to the other and learning from difference has not been developed, or, often, even tolerated. This has become even more evident in the history of the last 500 years—evident but still surprising. For during this period the experience of movement, exchange, and difference has become inescapable. This was true almost from the beginning of the early modern period. Just as Europe was being convulsed with the Reformation, European explorers were extending the reach of knowledge and communication to America, Africa, and Asia. Indeed, the Catholic Reformation itself led to vital Jesuit and Franciscan missions to Asia and Latin America. The world was shrinking even as the reach of Christianity was expanding.

It took some time, but by the eighteenth century the Protestants had joined in this globalizing movement of Christianity, extending Christian witness into many parts of Africa and Asia. In a powerful, recent reflection on this period, Willie James Jennings describes in bitter detail the way these missionary movements, both Catholic and Protestant, encouraged a one-way traffic that imposed Western thinking and practices on these newer Christians. Jennings argues that the central dynamic of these modern movements was the way they abandoned place-centered identities in favor of a theology that displaced people from the stories of their place, even as they brought a Christian gospel abstracted from its Jewish origins. Jennings points out, moreover, that the mistake was not only missiological but theological: what the conquest brought to Latin America was theorized by the dominant missionary voices as a New Creation, a creation ex nihilo. Jennings summarized the character of this project in Latin America:

> Detached from the land, oblivious to the ongoing decimation of native ecologies, deeply suspicious of native religious practices, and, most important, enclosed within Iberian whiteness, the performance of Christian theology would produce a new, deformed, and deforming intellectual circuit.[27]

Native identities were contained, Jennings argues, indeed, imprisoned, within a new racial reality. Meanwhile, the evaluative and pedagogical character of the missionary performance, Jennings suggests, made it impossible to hear native explanations. The world had to be remade after the image of a Western Christ.

Jennings' argument oversimplifies a complex reality. There were missionaries who opposed this reading of culture—one thinks of Bartolomé de las Casas in Latin America, or the Jesuits in China. And, whatever the missionaries may have wanted, the native reception of Christianity often adopted many indigenous values and practices.[28] But in too many places missionaries were better at teaching than they were at learning, and this clearly impacted the theology that resulted.

There was a certain muddle combined with a peculiar irony in this colonial movement that I want to briefly explore. The muddle was the inability to detach the missionaries' reading of Scripture from their own Western settings. Indeed, their own reading (and the teaching that issued from this) was all they knew, and they had no framework for imagining other possible readings. This had to do with received views of race and humanity, which Jennings highlights, but it also had to do with the cultural advantages they took for granted, and that powered their enterprise.

This is where the irony appears. The technology of travel and communication that colonialists and missionaries (they were not always the same) took for granted was an inheritance fueled both by their Jewish, Christian, and even medieval Muslim heritage on the one hand, and by the resources plundered from the places they conquered on the other. Let me linger a bit on this irony. As is well known, missionaries assumed their Western culture was superior, and in some ways it clearly was. So they were not wrong to teach people to read and write, set up printing presses, and introduce the latest medical advances. Here, recent scholarship is recognizing that the modern missionary movement, sometimes in spite of itself, resulted in much that was good. The correlation between missionary presence and the rise of liberal democracies and increasing levels of development has become indisputable.[29]

But there is a dark side to this story that has to be acknowledged. The resources, both natural and human, that funded their cultural advantages were often appropriated from these very colonial lands. Moreover, recent scholars have insisted that there is even more to this side of the story than the usual acknowledgment of wealth transfer from the non-West to the West. There are also political and philosophical resources in play. Enrique Dussel has drawn a significant connection between *ego conquiro* and *ego cogito*. In other words, the Enlightenment itself was, in part, facilitated by colonial projects—no colonialism, Dussel claims, no Enlightenment.[30]

So the self-deception of the Western projects becomes clear. Despite their sense of initiating a New Creation in these places, the colonial and missionary actors were in fact playing out a story that was already globalized, and they were busy with a project that, for better or worse, would have global consequences. As the most perceptive of them were quick to acknowledge, they would soon be deeply indebted to natives they met and learned to admire—and the cultural change they initiated would impact not only this new world but sooner or later even the old world from which they came.

But for the theological establishment, the ability to learn from other voices was slow in coming. An incident played out in the Dutch setting in the mid-1800s graphically illustrates this Western inability to learn from others. In the mid-century a growing awareness of cultural and religious difference led the Dutch government to seek to discover how this difference could be explored in the universities. Could this exploration of religious difference be carried out alongside the dominant teaching of Christian theology? After a decades-long debate, it was concluded that these projects—what we call today religious studies and theology—were incompatible with each other. For religious studies seeks to place all religions on the same abstract footing, but the theologians refused to see Christianity treated in this way. As Herman Bavinck described the theologians' conclusion, "In our faith, Christianity is not one religion among many, not even the highest among many, but the only true religion, and all heathen religions are idolatry."[31] Thus the practice of religious studies is a betrayal of the Christian faith.

There is a contemporary resonance to this conclusion that it would be unwise to ignore—religious studies and theology are still too often described as opponents. But the discussion we are promoting in this book wants to challenge such dichotomies. Indeed, many in the academy want to move beyond such a simplistic reading of the alternatives. There is no need to give up one's faith commitments, or even one's convictions about what is true, in order to listen carefully to the witness of believers of other religions. This is the proposal of an important recent movement in theology called comparative theology. This project is described by Francis Clooney, a leader of this movement, as "the practice of rethinking aspects of one's own faith tradition through the study of aspects of another faith tradition."[32] This is important because it promotes the study of faith traditions not from the outside (from some supposed position of neutrality) but from within—from a position that attends to difference not as a place of tension but as a site for mutual learning.

Clearly the globalized world has added a larger challenge to the theological conversation that partly lay behind the earlier difficulty in Dutch universities. For now the differences no longer reflect intramural debates about the nature of Christ or the sacraments but reflect encounters with other faith traditions about the nature of God and salvation. Western theologians may have felt they could ignore these differences and focus on keeping their Christian house in order; Christians outside the West have never had this luxury. From the beginning of the Christian mission, Christian conversation had to include interfaith witness and translation. And increasingly, all theology in the future will have to confront and learn from religious difference.

Conclusion: Toward a Theology of Difference

The nineteenth-century debates we have cited illustrate clearly Jennings' argument that Western theology had become so tethered to the abstractions of modernism that it was incapable of listening to the other. Its discourse was so bound up with truth considered to be an abstract system that it was incapable of real encounter with difference. In another chapter of this book, Dwight Hopkins argues that all theology today is comparative. This obvious fact implies that important theological work needs to be done around the question of difference. Why are our concerns with difference focused so intently on divisiveness and conflict? Recently, A. N. Williams has made use of Leopold Senghor's notion of *négritude* to show that "encounter with the other is constitutive of what human beings are."[33] As Senghor wrote, "I feel the other; I dance the other; therefore I am."[34] The point of Senghor's focus on *négritude* was not to express pride in his identity but to see difference as a good to be valued. For Senghor such affirmation was not the product of a willful ignorance of the reality of racism and hatred—he knew these all too well. It was rather an expression of his Christian faith—a gift of God's grace, which made love of the other imaginable. This grace could even make possible an embrace of the other, what Senghor called *métissage*, an intimate exchange and mutual knowing.

Williams goes on to describe the way such exchange resonates with the long tradition of Christian reflection: the development of the notion of the "person" and the mutual influence of this on discussions of the Trinity in the medieval period, and of the similar development of Christology in the modern era. The notion of "wholeness-in-distinction," she claims, is the contribution of Christian teachings on creation and on the Trinity. She summarizes in words that speak directly to our promotion of pluralism in theological conversation:

> In all these varied theologies, the same principle holds true: that entities which are really distinct can be bound in a dynamic unity in a way that does not obliterate distinction, but in a relation which both constitutes and modulates their identity.[35]

Here at least are theological resources—in an understanding of divine creation that celebrates difference, in the Trinitarian mutual exchange among the persons, and in the mediation of Christ by the Spirit—to address the questions that have arisen to the top of the theological agenda. How do we learn not only to tolerate diversity but also to embrace it and flourish because of it? How does the multifaith environment allow greater mutual learning? What principles and criteria should guide and shape these dialogues? What about so-called religious hybridity and multiple religious belonging; are these a threat or a boon to Christian identity? And an even more important question emerges out of all these: How can the great religious traditions *together* find ways to address the deep economic and ecological challenges of our globalized world? Clearly, a critical rereading of our own Christian history is one way of beginning to answer these questions.

✦ 3 ✦

Teaching Global Theology in a Comparative Mode

VELI-MATTI KÄRKKÄINEN

The purpose of this chapter is to reflect on and resource attempts to revamp the teaching of systematic/doctrinal/constructive theology in a way comparative in nature. I am approaching the task of making theological education more globally sensitive through the lens of interfaith relevance and religious plurality. To further trim down my canvas, I am working from the perspective of my own academic field, which is systematic/doctrinal/constructive theology. Along with standard systematic theology courses, in which I engage every major doctrinal locus with some relevant insights from other religions, I also coteach a graduate-level comparative course titled "World Religions in Christian Perspective." That course consists of about two-thirds basic introduction to fundamental teachings and traditions of Islam, Buddhism, and Hinduism, and one-third engaging with Judeo-Christian teachings. The latter course naturally leans much more easily to a comparative mode. What is, however, a much wider and deeper challenge to universities, divinity schools, and seminaries (which already are offering separate courses on world religions) is the willingness to reconsider all theology courses from the perspective of religious plurality. Approaching the topic from my own discipline, I also understand that there are specific concerns and issues pertinent to biblical and historical studies as well as ministerial courses. I leave that refinement to my colleagues.

In order to locate my reflections, let me share briefly how I came to be convinced of the necessity of teaching theology in a comparative mode. Personal narratives as the way of introduction go beyond niceties and are therefore an integral part of doing theology. After finishing my theological education in Europe, focusing on ecumenics and following a typical continental model with a heavy emphasis on studying theological traditions, I moved with my family to Thailand to teach theology for Asian students. As a naive and eager fledgling theologian in a new environment, I thought it necessary to first learn the language in order to gain a deeper access to the culture. Beginning to teach theology in Thai for Thai students was quite a bit of a learning experience as well. Later, returning to Europe for a few years, I continued rethinking the challenge posed by global diversity and religious plurality. My training in ecumenics focused much on learning how to dialogue with and encounter the Other. This led to a commitment to long-term work with the World Council of Churches (WCC), both in inter-Christian and interfaith "ecumenics"; although often kept at arm's length from each other, these two have much in common and feed each other. After moving to teach in the United States more than a decade ago while continuing my post also at the University of Helsinki, I became engaged in enterprises such as the Association of Theological Schools (ATS) interfaith education project. This has helped me compare notes and learn from distinguished colleagues and sister schools. At the same time, my international doctoral students have further taught me valuable lessons about diversity.

The structure of this chapter consists of three sections. The first part seeks to reorient the task and meaning of theological education in light of religious plurality. Based on this challenge, the second part is devoted to reimagining the implications for theological education of adopting such a comparative, dialogical mode. The final part highlights a number of different types of resources I have found useful, in terms of both pedagogy and sources. Knowing that my colleagues in their chapters are presenting a number of other resources, I will focus on those with which I am most familiar, produced by the processes in which I have had an opportunity to participate over the years.

Reorienting Theological Education

A current document-in-the-making sponsored by the World Council of Churches, "Religious Plurality and Christian Self-Understanding," reminds us of the most prominent challenge the Christian church faces in the beginning of the third millennium:

> Today Christians in almost all parts of the world live in religiously plural societies. Persistent plurality and its impact on their daily lives are forcing them to seek new and adequate ways of understanding and relating to peoples of other religious traditions. . . . All religious communities are being reshaped by new encounters and relationships. . . . There is

> greater awareness of the interdependence of human life, and of the need to collaborate across religious barriers in dealing with the pressing problems of the world. All religious traditions, therefore, are challenged to contribute to the emergence of a global community that would live in mutual respect and peace.[1]

Prophetically anticipating the future that lay ahead, Paul Tillich is reported to have confessed, just a few days before his death, that if he had the opportunity to rewrite his three-volume *Systematic Theology*, he would do so engaging widely with other world religions. This was due to his brief exposure at the end of his life to some forms of Japanese Buddhism, as well as the influence of his famed Romanian religious studies colleague, Mircea Eliade.[2] One wonders what Tillich's magnum opus would have looked like had he been given a chance to rewrite it with religious plurality in mind. What's more, how different would the rest of the presentations of Christian doctrine, ethics, and philosophy have been if they had been written with the same goal in mind! The fact is that even in the beginning of the third millennium, one cannot find any full-scale presentations of Christian doctrine or ethics in which other faith traditions are an integral part of the discussion along with the best of Judeo-Christian tradition.[3]

While there is no need for finger pointing, we theological educators bear much of the responsibility for this state of affairs. Hence, the menu for training Christian theologians and ministers for the diverse global world needs to be expanded in a way that makes learning about and comparing Christianity with the religious Other an integral part of the task. This is more than merely taking elective—or even a couple of mandatory—courses in world religions, the importance of which, in itself, should not be understated. (I take it for granted that every divinity school requires at least a minimum of courses about other religions as part of the standard curriculum.)

Contributions from three interrelated academic fields of inquiry are needed to enrich, challenge, and reshape the current theological pedagogy and content—namely, comparative religion/religious studies, theology of religions, and comparative theology. Comparative religion (along with the related but distinct fields of the history of religions and other disciplines in religious studies, phenomenology of religions, and social scientific study of religions) seeks to identify, analyze, and compare "ideas, words, images and acts, historical developments—as found in two or more traditions or strands of tradition."[4] Christian theology of religions seeks to reflect critically and sympathetically on the theological meaning of religions in the economy of God.[5] "Theology of religions is that discipline of theological studies which attempts to account theologically for the meaning and value of other religions. Christian theology of religions attempts to think theologically about what it means for Christians to live with people of other faiths and about the relationship of Christianity to other religions."[6] While in principle there could be theologies of religions from the point of view of any religion (e.g., Islam), the Christian tradition has so far excelled in this enterprise.[7] Theology of religions, however, can get us only so far for reasons that are well known, such as that it tends to stay at too generic a level, and that it may fail to engage the Other from the perspective of that Other's tradition, and so forth.[8] Hence, in recent years, a complementary and more focused way of engaging in mutual dialogue among religious traditions has been attempted under the rubric of comparative theology, which, on the one hand, builds on the discipline of comparative religions that seeks to compare theologies from different religious traditions and, on the other hand, is a theological enterprise that studies two or more religious traditions by focusing on certain specific topics from the perspective of a certain confession.[9] In sum, comparative theology gleans resources not only from Christian theology and theology of religions but also from comparative religion.

Reimagining Theological Education

But is a comparative and dialogical approach feasible and useful? Does it not lead, rather, into confrontation and violence? Should not the academic preparation of religious professionals rather have the goal of negating differences among faith traditions as a way to a pluralistic society?[10]

Whereas comparative religion seeks to be "neutral" with regard to faith commitments and to look "objectively" at the features of religious traditions, North American Catholic theologian Francis X. Clooney, the leading expert in comparative theology, asserts that this field—which is "*comparative* and *theological* from beginning to end—marks acts of faith seeking understanding which are rooted in a particular faith tradition but which, from that foundation, venture into learning from one or more other faith traditions. This learning is sought for the sake of fresh theological insights that are indebted to the newly encountered tradition/s as well as the home tradition."[11] Comparative theology is robustly Christian theology and is committed to its traditions and its contemporary expressions.

There is, thus, a deep, built-in dynamic between unwavering commitment to one's own tradition and a bold openness to dialogical engagement and learning from others. "In our religiously diverse context, a vital theology has to resist too tight a binding by tradition, but also the idea that religious diversity renders strong claims about truth and value impossible."[12] Hence, comparative theology, similarly to Christian theology—as long as it is both *Christian,* rather than a "pan-religious" mixing of aspects of insights from here and there,[13] and *theological,* rather than a sociological description of church practices or merely an analysis of human interpretations of human religiosity—is both an act of faith and a spiritual practice.[14] In this way, it does not deny or compromise its status as an academic discipline that follows the strict procedures and principles of any similar academic field in the humanities.

An important part of this task is to "inscribe within the Christian theological tradition theological texts from outside it, and to (begin to) write Christian theology only out of that newly composed context."[15] Unlike the theology of religion's more generic approach, comparative theology makes every effort to undertake a detailed consideration of topics in diverse religious traditions. "It is detailed, deeply reflexive, self-corrective in the course of its own investigation, even in regard to its basic questions, methods, and vocabulary."[16]

One may hear the objection that it is only Christianity (and perhaps Judaism) that is "theological," strictly speaking. While it is true that as an academic discipline "theology" is by and large limited to the Christian sphere,[17] this is not to deny that in some qualified sense it is appropriate and useful to speak of "theologies" of different living faiths. Clooney makes the compelling case for such an opinion. He argues for "Hindu theology and Hindu comparative theology, though without arguing that 'Hindu theology' is exactly like Christian theology."[18] Hence, he states that his choice of texts from various Hindu traditions presume the possibility of making theological comparisons because "Hindu traditions such as Mimamsa[19] and Vedanta are best described as 'theological.' " Furthermore, not only is it the case that the faithful in each tradition have a "faith," but it is also true that, to a growing extent, they are aware of the growing diversity and thus the need to engage others.[20]

Scholars engaged in the enterprise of comparative theology come from two different backgrounds.[21] Some are trained as scholars of religions with the openness to learning about theology, while others are versed in theology with the desire to become acquainted with basics of other religions. An example of a theologian who has robustly taken the comparative approach is the former Oxford University divinity professor Keith Ward, who has launched the most ambitious and wide-reaching project in comparative theology ever attempted by a theologian. His four-volume work focuses on revelation, creation and God, human nature, and community, and it seeks to develop a robustly Christian account of these four key loci in intense and detailed dialogue with Judaism, Islam, Buddhism, and Hinduism. He rightly describes his project as "a systematic Christian theology, undertaken in a comparative context."[22] In other words, it is an "open orthodoxy," a faithful, open-minded, and developing construction of Christian faith.[23]

Systematicians and other theologians, of course, face the great challenge of overcoming lacunae in the detailed knowledge of religions. For example, Ward admits throughout his project that his knowledge of religions is limited in that it is based on careful reading of texts along with some important personal contacts. In my case, only Buddhism—Theravada tradition, to be more precise—is familiar at a more personal and experience-based level from the years I spent in Thailand as a teacher of Christian theology. Despite the fact that I am fluent in Thai and can thus read many Buddhist writings inaccessible to Western scholars, I still woefully remain an outsider. However, having firsthand exposure to one specific tradition should also transfer to the way one studies other traditions. As a continuing student of Hinduism, Islam, and Judaism, I read their texts differently from the way I did before my exposure living with Buddhists as a young theologian.

In order for the comparative approach to be *comparative*, and hence useful and interesting, one has to resist the modernist fallacy of the "common core" and "rough parity" of religions. Modernist ideology does not honor the Otherness of the Other and thus fails to prepare the student for our diverse and pluralistic world. A truly dialogical mode, rather than denying differences, is an essential asset in the pursuit of truth and conviction. As the German systematician Jürgen Moltmann underlines, "Dialogue has to be about the question of truth, even if no agreement about the truth can be reached. For consensus is not the goal of the dialogue. . . . If two people say the same thing, one of them is superfluous. In the interfaith dialogue which has to do with what is of vital and absolute concern to men and women—with the things in which they place the whole trust of their hearts—the way is already part of the goal."[24] Moltmann rightly says that only those people are capable of dialogue—or "merit dialogue," as he puts it—who "have arrived at a firm standpoint in their own religion, and who enter into dialogue with the resulting self-confidence."[25] Thus, Moltmann continues, "it is only if we are at home in our own religion that we shall be able to encounter the religion of someone else. The person who falls victim to the relativism of the multicultural society may be capable of dialogue, but that person does not merit dialogue."[26]

Engaging not only the cultural diversity within the vastly globalizing Christian church, but also the religious diversity, is a laborious and in many ways annoying project, as it takes theologians to the edge not only of their intellectual capacities but also of their emotional comfort zone. Clooney puts it well:

> If we are attentive to the diversity around us, near us, we must deny ourselves the easy confidences that keep the other at a distance. But, as believers, we must also be able to defend the relevance of the faith of our community, deepening our commitments even alongside other faiths that are flourishing nearby. We need to learn from other religious possibilities, without slipping into relativist generalizations. The tension between open-mindedness and faith, diversity and traditional commitment, is a defining feature of our era, and neither secular society nor religious authorities can make simple choices before us.[27]

Resourcing Theological Education

How do we go about revamping theological education with the goal of developing a dialogical, comparative mode? Regarding pedagogical moves, I have found the following ones useful. First, nothing beats the effort to provide students either with access to grassroots personal encounters with people of other faiths or, if that is not possible, at least with visits to sacred places or otherwise meaningful sites of other religions. For me, living in a cosmopolitan area such as Los Angeles, California, facilitating both efforts is not too difficult. While, of course, a more sustained face-to-face relationship with a person or group from other faith traditions is the desired form of encounter, even well-planned visits to mosques, temples, and shrines, with a presentation from the representatives of the Other and an opportunity to ask questions, is highly useful. I have found that often students are very enthusiastic about opportunities to visit the sacred sites of another religion—not infrequently for the first time in their lives. Because of this, they often go beyond the required minimum and begin to seek out contacts on their own.

Second, I make sure that the students not only read *about* another faith tradition but also read at least a minimum amount in the scriptures of other traditions themselves, whether these be their primary sources such as the Qur'an, Tipitaka, or Vedic texts, or secondary texts such as Hadith or Bhagavad Gita. Not without basis does Timothy C. Tennent, a distinguished American theological educator with intimate knowledge of the religious diversity in the subcontinent of India, observe, "In the West, it is rare to find someone who has more than a cursory knowledge of the sacred texts of other religions. In contrast, because Christians in the Majority World are often in settings dominated by other religions, it is not uncommon to meet a Christian with a Muslim, Hindu, or Buddhist background who has an intimate knowledge of another sacred text."[28] I fear that not only the theological students and professionals in the Global North but also those in the South are illiterate in the texts of other faiths: as is well known, for many, becoming a Christian means leaving behind everything in the old religion and its practice. Be that as it may, I know from experience that most students find reading the scriptures of other traditions very challenging. The reasons are many: neither the Qur'an nor Vedas have a plot; Hindu and Buddhist scriptures are so exceedingly vast that even to begin locating something is almost impossible for the beginner; terminology and forms of expression are also very different; and so forth. This means that students need quite a bit of guidance in selection and comprehension. Fortunately, access to the scriptures is easy in this Internet age.[29] Third, along with scriptures, I try to find at least some readings by representative contemporary "theologians" of other faith traditions. Fourth, as much as possible, I try to get visiting presenters from other faith traditions.

There are a slowly growing number of resources that offer guidance and inspiration as well as primary and secondary sources. Let me highlight here the two main processes and projects with which I am most intimately familiar. First, in recent years the WCC has launched significant efforts to bring together resources that the global church can use for the training of theologians and ministers in various locations. Under the rubric "Ecumenical theological education,"[30] the production of *The Handbook of Theological Education in World Christianity* (2010) was a massive enterprise.[31] Far more than just a listing of schools and institutions, the manual is an indispensable means of connecting and being informed. A promising start has also begun through an earlier project named "Teaching Christianity in Dialogue with Other Faith Traditions,"[32] which has produced some fruit so far and carries a lot of potential. Also useful is the programmatic statement "Magna Charta on Ecumenical Theological Education in the 21st Century,"[33] which includes interfaith preparedness as one of the key themes for global theological education and looks for opportunities for projects and collaboration. Another related ecumenical enterprise is the huge "Global Digital Library on Theology and Ecumenism,"[34] which currently has more than 65,000 essays and documents, reference works, journals, and special collections on ethics, theology, ecumenism, and interreligious dialogue. Indeed, that online site may well be the most resourced collection of materials for teaching theology and ethics in a pluralistic, globalizing world.

The second major set of resources has to do with the various programs organized by and related to the Association of Theological Schools (ATS) in North America. One such recent addition is the highly useful resource titled "Christian Hospitality and Pastoral Practices in a Multifaith Society."[35] It is an offshoot from a multiyear process titled "Christian Hospitality and Pastoral Practices,"[36] which initiates new courses and programs particularly with ministerial training in mind. Some of the many representative seminary-based funded initiatives that can be explored for resources, insights, and experiences include the following:

- "Taking Interfaith Off the Hill"[37]
- "Educating Parish Clergy for a Multifaith World"[38]
- "The Pastoral Practice of Christian Hospitality as Presence in Muslim-Christian Engagement"[39]
- "Christian Hospitality and Neighborliness"[40]

Other initiatives based at theological schools include Auburn Seminary's long-term labor of developing multifaceted and creative interfaith teaching and learning resources, including *Beyond World Religions: The State of Multifaith Education in American Theological Schools*.[41] I have personally benefited from looking at resources prepared by scholars from other religions who are beginning to experiment with interfaith programs. (An interesting task for a Christian theological educator, for example, is to reflect on the distinctive challenges a Jewish colleague faces when organizing interfaith programs in a Christian school!)[42]

Appeal for a Dialogical, Comparative Mode of Teaching Theology

As argued in this chapter, for theological education in the third millennium to redeem its promise requires a radical re-formation of content, approach, and resources. Other chapters in this book highlight related challenges in meeting globalization. The present chapter has focused on the dialogical and comparative aspect of the pedagogical task, with a stated focus on religious plurality.

The dialogical approach, however, is not limited to interfaith pedagogy. It is, however, the preferred mode of discussion, teaching, and learning for everything in divinity and religious studies. It calls for mature convictions and also a childlike openness to learn. It requires affirming one's own identity and willingness to be reshaped by new encounters. This theological vision is supremely captured in Moltmann's pointed statement:

> Truth is to be found in unhindered dialogue. Fellowship and freedom are the human components for knowledge of the truth, the truth of God. And the fellowship I mean here is the fellowship of mutual participation and unifying sympathy. . . . This free community of men and women, without privilege and without discrimination, may be termed the earthly body of truth. . . . It is only in free dialogue that truth can be accepted for the only right and proper reason—namely, that it illuminates and convinces *as* truth. Truth brings assent, it brings about change without exerting compulsion. In dialogue the truth frees men and women for their own conceptions and their own ideas. . . . Christian theology would wither and die if it did not continually stand in a dialogue like this, and if it were not bound up with a fellowship that seeks this dialogue, needs it and continually pursues it.[43]

PART II

Identity, Power, and Pedagogy

✦ 4 ✦

The Good of Education

Accessibility, Economy, Class, and Power

CECILIA GONZÁLEZ-ANDRIEU

The world of higher education can often resemble an echo chamber where what those inside its "hallowed halls" want to believe is reinforced by a structure designed to be a self-perpetuating system. People involved in higher education use language (such as academic rigor), build on facile and not always shared presuppositions (such as the desirability of diversity), and generally assume that the very idea of education is somehow uniformly understood and universally valued. I propose that to respond to the challenges before the communities involved in theological education, we would do well to heed the advice from biblical scholars and theologians such as Walter Brueggemann, Justo González, Sandra Schneiders, and Gustavo Gutiérrez.

I cite these four contemporary Christian theologians working in proximity to my own context in the fractious borderlands of the American continent for three reasons. First, research into issues of accessibility to education (and by inference to theological education) may be approached from multiple angles, and, indeed, major work is being done by the social sciences and philosophy of education on this question.[1] However, here I want to contribute my work as a theologian that understands the biblical law of love and care of neighbor to include educational justice. In their general conference in Aparecida, Brazil, in 2007, the bishops of Latin America and the Caribbean (CELAM) confronted the challenge presented by globalization by stressing the need to "promote a different type of globalization marked by solidarity, justice, and respect for human rights."[2] In the resulting document, CELAM insists that we must make every effort to "contemplate the faces of the suffering," counting first among these all those whose dignity is assailed because of their race, gender, or class.[3] The document makes special mention of "youth, who receive a deficient education and are unable to move forward in their studies or enter the job market."[4] The CELAM document references education multiple times, connecting diverse issues such as general education, formation toward full maturity in the home and the community, and education in the faith. The Latin American bishops claim that a quality education is a "right" that belongs to all students.[5]

Because a definition of education is necessary to argue for it, CELAM defines it in terms of what it *should* do:

> Education humanizes and personalizes a human being when it makes it possible for him or her to fully develop in thought and in freedom, allowing these to bear fruit in habits that lead to understanding and that initiate a communion with the totality of what is real. In this way, the human person humanizes the world, produces culture, transforms society and builds up history.[6]

Education is cut of one cloth, if we understand it as the process that facilitates the passing on of vital information, training in how to effectively understand such information, and, finally, training in how to use and communicate such information for the common good. Whether theological or otherwise, we can account for theological education not in discrete isolation but in the wholeness of the dynamic process of being human.[7]

Second, as the biblical tradition and its interpreters have expressed it, the fundamental option for the poor affects all areas of human endeavors and confronts the ways societies organize themselves.[8] On the shelves of the libraries that serve theological education, in the hymns of faith communities, and in their practices and ministries are stunning resources spanning centuries to help us articulate and strategize our particular role in this specific instance of doing of God's work. To paraphrase Justo González' approach to what he calls the grammar of the biblical text (a text that he insists is about neither spiritual reality nor doctrines), we should take a step back and look at our moment in time. Theological education is called to a new way of being by the very text of our globally construed life. This moment in history constitutes a new "text," and González might invite us to ask, "Who in this text is in power? Who is powerless? What is the nature of their relationship? Whose side does God take?"[9]

Third, the question of theological education from the point of view of accessibility constitutes a challenge, a judgment, an ecclesial vision, and a celebration of possibility. To take a cue from Sandra Schneiders, the challenge exists between the "is" of the good of theological education globally and transnationally imagined, and the "is not" posed by the constraints of resources and structures. The *Chronicle of Higher Education* bemoans the status of theological education in the United States (arguably the society holding the most resources), saying,

> Despite their important role in the nation's intellectual and religious life, many [theological schools] are spartan operations. The typical institution has fewer than 200 students, most of whom will go into low-paying ministry jobs. As a result, tuition is kept as low as possible so as not to saddle graduates with unmanageable debt. Few alumni become wealthy enough to give sizable donations later in life, and clergy-dominated boards do not have deep pockets. Denominational support, when available, is limited.[10]

Theological education, of its very nature, presents the requirement of embodying an option for the poor in the lives of those who are called to take up its work. Because of this, a theologically centered approach to the question of access to theological education must be done with full awareness and even in celebration of its location in this unstable periphery. Unlike most M.B.A. programs, theological education has in its very subject matter already taken a marginal position in the prevalent power structures of our contemporary society. To imagine ourselves to be speaking about "higher education" and approach theological education as just one of its many disciplines is to ignore the marginality of the theological enterprise in many of today's developed societies and to overlook the increasingly browner and poorer students called to enter its ranks.[11] Walter Brueggemann says, "Real criticism begins in the capacity to grieve because that is the most visceral announcement that things are not right."[12] I begin with what Brueggemann asserts must be the first step of the prophetic imagination. We must bring the "hurt to public expression."[13] I do so from the vantage point of those seeking education as I am privileged to accompany them here and now.

Grief as the Ground of Change

The sight of a university professor reviewing admissions applications is probably commonplace. Yet, someone who saw me at my desk late on a spring night last year might have noticed something unusual—my considerable agitation. As I sat there with bloodshot eyes, I wrote to a colleague halfway across the country, "I want to cry, I want to scream, I feel so powerless." The applications were stirring and often painful. Far from the demographic abstractions that are frequently our only sources of information about prospective students, these applications were humbling windows into the realities of our singularly complex moment in the world's developing story. My grief at reading these students' stories became compounded by four considerations I eventually uncovered. These help frame my inquiry.

First, the system. The applications on my desk were from students whose academic achievements and scores on standardized tests were "high" enough to qualify them for a university merit scholarship. Many young people had applied and some had even been accepted, but what that larger group had achieved on scoring instruments had been deemed insufficient for merit scholarships. Those students never had the opportunity to place their stories in the very small pile of applications I was given to review. There were many stories I would never read, left out by self-perpetuating systems of privilege. The applicants that had made it to this point were inordinately high achievers, and all of them had beaten a system engineered to keep them out.

Second, the funding. Of this highly unlikely group who had beaten many odds to land on my desk, many would be turned away. Our institution could fund only as many as the fingers on one of my hands. In an incoming class of over 1,500 students, only five (or 0.3 percent) would come from the most vulnerable population of young people in my corner of the globe, the aptly named "DREAMers." These accomplished students I was evaluating were more than economically disadvantaged. Lacking proper documents because they were brought to this country as young children without authorization, they live in the shadows, and for those of us who accompany them, they are reminders of the failure of global economic and political systems. As one student recounted, "The simple fact that I do not have documents turns me into a thing. I am no longer human. I live a life of fear."[14] Even if it is only five scholarships, I am profoundly grateful. These students in our midst are constant reminders among us of the indispensability of developing proactive institutional support.

Third, the resilient.[15] This 0.3 percent of the incoming class were the unlikely survivors of the convergence of economics and legislation that makes higher education one of the most unattainable of goals for many youth. The UCLA Center for Labor Research and Education reports that every year roughly "65,000 undocumented students graduate from U.S.

high schools."[16] Accordingly, the five young college applicants I eventually recommended for merit scholarships represented roughly 0.007 percent of that year's group of undocumented high school graduates.

Fourth, the discarded. Those 65,000 who graduate are the lucky ones. Focusing only on Latinos/as who have dropped out before completing high school (regardless of immigration status), a report by the Pew Hispanic Center stresses that this is "a problem that is quite grave."[17] The report reveals that about 30 percent of Latino youth never complete high school. About half of these are young "immigrants who never set foot in a U.S. school," while the other half are those who drop out after "engaging the American [*sic*] education system."[18] The applications on my desk were from the unlikely fighters who made it past both of these eventualities. The first would have left them out on the furthest peripheries of society as unschooled transnational youth, and the second would have meant they had participated in a U.S. school system that had failed them. In my ministry of teaching theology to Hispanic adults outside of the university setting, I routinely encounter those who did not make it. The figure of Latino/a high school dropouts for the year beginning the twenty-first century was a disconcerting 529,000. Thus, the five students I eventually chose represent a figure so small that it is impossible to imagine: for each one of them, there are over 100,000 Latino/a youth without a high school diploma.[19] The thought of those thousands of others should, in the words of Pope Francis, keep us up at night.[20] Accordingly, just at the level of college freshmen, the population of U.S. Latino youth is already severely decimated, and, every step along the way, the group and those whose voices they enact, evoke, and activate continues to be reduced.

From Grief to Voice

My theological method requires me to begin this chapter with the particularity of lived experience through my work with vulnerable Latino/a student populations.[21] It is because questions arise organically from the contours of such experience that insights may have some claim to authority and relevance. As theologian Stephen Bevans points out in his now-classic text on contextual theologies, "Reality is not just 'out there'; reality is mediated by meaning, a meaning we give it in the context of our culture, our historical period, interpreted from our own particular horizon and in our own particular thought forms."[22]

Cognizant that all theologies are indeed contextual, the work of theology in today's global and transnational reality ought to be done with self-consciously meaningful particularity as its starting point. It is in this way that theological work is able to apprehend and query a robust multiplicity instead of attempting a nondescript and ultimately nonexistent universality. Such a richly varied overflowing of perspectives is only activated as theologians themselves *come from* a startling variety of communities. It is here that evocative experiences become available and comprehensible to them as theological loci. As theologian and church historian Justo González argues, the goal of theology is no longer "to produce some sort of neutral—and therefore inane—interpretation of the nature of God and the universe, but rather to discover the purposes of God, to read the 'signs of the times,' and to call the church to obedience in the present situation."[23]

Access to theological education *for the excluded many* instead of *for the privileged few* is thus a requirement of doing theology; it is a necessity of the theological task that David Tracy names "conversation."[24] As responsible theologians argue, "any understanding of theology as an unchanging already finished theologi perennis is being challenged . . . in the name of relevance"; consequently, in "Asia, Africa, and Latin America, Christians are becoming increasingly convinced that traditional approaches to theology do not really make sense within their own cultural patterns and thought forms."[25] In order to create a global conversation that unites "a vision of life and a way of life,"[26] theological education must carefully inquire into who is missing from the dialogue. The very particularity of starting with one of the most educationally vulnerable populations in the United States becomes the way for me to discern problems and search for insights in the experience of exclusion. It also allows me to serve my communities of accountability. Both of these tasks need to be reproduced across experiences and communities all over our planet, because conversation, genuine conversation, requires it. Without a sufficiently diverse group in the conversation, we are just reinforcing what we already know, and thus, the efficacy of education itself is lost.

Although such carefully located theological work is never meant to stand in for a universal experience, it should however bear what theologian Alex García-Rivera says are the marks of "insight." These marks are breadth and coherence joined to that which is personal and moves our heart.[27] I propose that theological insights are severely limited as long as voices are missing that could help mediate expansive, coherent, and personally moving insights. Access to higher education that has the capacity to undermine the history of power and exclusion built into educational systems is thus inextricably joined to the very task of doing theology responsibly in this twenty-first century. In truth, if theological education remains a privilege, theology itself suffers.

I would need to do some very creative covering of the sun with my thumb to claim that theological education does not suffer from an acute problem of exclusion. This is because, even as it strives for inclusivity, theological education is only the top rung of a long climb that begins early in a student's life. The statistics surrounding Latino/a students in the United States are by no means the most dire or disturbing in the world—not even close—but they are those I know intimately.[28] Although I was not undocumented, I was brought to the United States as a "refugee" child before completing the sixth grade in my native country. The inability to understand the English language and complex North American customs and history, the poverty of my family, and the vulnerability of being a Latina surrounded by the multiple cultures of Los Angeles that toxically encouraged hedonism, sexism, and survival of the fittest all conspired to make me one more discarded youth among the many. Like many of my current students, I am certain that without the formative faith experiences of early childhood that convinced me of my identity as a beloved child of God, and without the active intervention of teachers, financial aid counselors, scholarship donors, and a veritable web of extended support, my seat in many classrooms would have remained empty. My work with what sociologists call "low-status youth"[29] like myself is made necessary by the insights that my firsthand experience facilitates. What is more, as a Christian theologian I understand there to be a nonnegotiable requirement presented by biblical faith—the imperative to embody the true universality of God's love. To paraphrase theologian Roberto Goizueta, we cannot speak of theological education as in some way having a real connection to the search for God without speaking of such education as available to all. Anything else is a contradiction.[30]

Undoing Systems of Privilege

Returning to my late night review of applications, the demographics make it clear that the students who make it as far as their first year of college are a grain of sand in a vast desert. It is among this small group of survivors that I came upon this letter from a young man I will call Ignacio.[31]

> Last spring, I told my younger brother that I was accepted . . . but was unable to attend because of my legal status. He said, "The great ones failed multiple times before being successful." . . . I was denied [admission while in] high school but since then, I have been accepted to the school four consecutive times.
>
> Since high school, I wanted to become a counselor and help students get to college especially in low-income communities. Several people have told me to quit . . . but I want to be [a] mentor [to students] and give them every opportunity to succeed. . . . If my economic situation does not change in the next couple of months, I will probably not be able to attend college in the fall. I have failed to attend [this institution] five times but the great ones failed more than that. I will not be content until I attend . . . and if I fail a sixth time, I will apply until I am successful.[32]

As I sat at my desk, surrounded by the many privileges of elite education, I was humbled by this young man's determination. I was also reminded of my story and the obstacles I faced decades before. We could say that both our stories had a happy (if highly unlikely) outcome—Ignacio joined us that fall—but admission into an exclusive club when you represent one in 100,000 is far from easy. Although some theological schools attempt to broaden entrance requirements by not mandating minimum scores from GPAs and standardized tests, the truth is that in order to "demonstrate . . . academic preparation to engage in graduate-level theological study,"[33] a student with low scores in the aforementioned tests would be at a great disadvantage. How does someone demonstrate academic preparation without having access to academic preparation? Can such a circle of impossibility be subverted?

Higher education broadly, and theological education more precisely, has to come to terms with the fact that there are multiple obstacles to gaining admission into our classrooms. Recruiting the most talented survivors of unjust systems cannot be the answer to the requirements posed by both the radical inclusivity of God's love and the particularly embodied task of doing theology in the globalized reality of the twenty-first century. As Archbishop Desmond Tutu makes abundantly clear, the search for ways to provide wider access to theological education stems from "the biblical foundation that all God's people are called to ministry and mission and the concern to enable all to gain relevant skills for their mission."[34]

As has been widely studied, there is considerable evidence that Ignacio's determined survival is the outstanding exception, not the norm. As studies of what researchers term "shadow education" show, a hard-to-quantify educational advantage in gaining admission and then thriving in any educational environment is created by access to "educational activities outside of formal schooling [which tend] to confer advantages on already privileged students."[35] These activities are many and can begin in prekindergarten, but some of the most obvious examples are private tutoring, extra classes, enrichment experiences, specialized test preparation, and admissions counseling. These happen before any student "dares" to knock on the doors of theological education and are in many ways quite at odds with our efforts at equity. For instance, the costs for preparing for the Graduate Record Examination (GRE) can range from $4,599 for one-on-one personal tutoring to $499 for online prepackaged video instruction.[36] In Japan, an equivalent service called "Kawaijuku" provides extra ongoing academic support for high school students and costs $450 per subject for just three sessions in a term.[37] In many parts of the world, and clearly only accessible to a particular clientele, for-profit centers of shadow education sell the dream of gaining a competitive advantage in the admission process as they advertise,

> Wouldn't it be great to get feedback from the admissions committees *before* you submit your applications? Kaplan Admissions Consulting is the next best thing. Get expert advice from our team of admissions experts on choosing the right program, writing application essays, and positioning yourself in the most compelling way.[38]

This preadmission service costs $2,500. I know Ignacio is struggling to pay even the most basic health insurance, which costs slightly less than this admissions preparation package. If we want to take seriously the scandalous absence of certain types of students from the theology classroom, we must first realize that they have been absent for a long time, that the lack of advantages began decades before. Beyond straight academic subjects, these "low-status" students have been missing from multiple settings that contribute to what the gatekeeping mechanisms of academic culture identify as the marks of an educated person. We can argue that keeping these marks for the few and away from the many is what makes them desirable.[39]

Sitting in the Lobby

In a perceptive essay in the *New York Times*, writer Anand Giridharadas recounts how one black teenager ducks into the Brooklyn Museum day after day to escape the stifling summer heat. She sits in the vestibule "because she could not afford the $8 suggested student admission—one that she, like so many others, understood to be required." On this particular day Giridharadas spots the girl "on her usual bench, where she perched because of her belief that it cost money to roam further." When Giridharadas explains that the donation is "suggested" and accompanies young Chanel Baldwin and her cousin to the turnstile, he empowers the youngsters to enter a world that just moments before was forbidden to them. As Chanel attentively examines every piece of art encountered, Giridharadas ponders, "Watching her, I realized how the inadvertent exclusion from these rooms must have trained her eyes." It is precisely as she drinks in all the beauty unjustly kept from her that Chanel's critical sense grows and she becomes "irritated with the museum" for never explaining that the entrance was "somewhat free." Giridharadas comments, perhaps rethinking his own assessment that the exclusion was inadvertent, "New York is run on the kinds of understandings that kept the cousins in the lobby, with so many places formally open to anyone but protected in their exclusivity by invisible psychic gates."[40] I would add, not just New York, but most of the world is run this way.

Viewed through the lens of educational access, Chanel Baldwin's story as she patiently waits in the lobby of the museum is paradigmatic. Systems of privilege survive owing to practices that guarantee that only a select few will gain access to the markers of such privilege. As in many cases where lip service is given to the ideal of "diversity," the museum's anemic attempt at inclusivity through inserting the word "suggested" (which on the website appears only as a footnote)[41] is only part of a sophisticated system through which our society can continue to differentiate the "haves" from the "have nots." The aesthetics of geographic location, architectural styles, the types of people visibly in charge and present, and other more or less subtle clues contribute to the forbidding exclusivity of many cultural institutions. Both the church and the academy participate in this system of exclusivity. Ross Kinsler's collection of case studies dedicated to documenting the progress made "in the urgent task of opening access to and equipping God's people for ministry and mission" since the 1960s identifies multiple barriers, some of them psychic, many more of them also practical. His team of researchers concludes that access to theological education is constrained by issues that may be geographic, economic, cultural, ecclesiastical, and also based on gender, race, class, pedagogical styles, or spirituality.[42] The campuses of theological schools often brim with just these types of barriers. Predominantly male and white in their leadership, and identifying themselves as cultural institutions that are historic, venerated, and selective, they speak the same forbidding language of the museums. Without the translation and accompaniment provided by people like Giridharadas (himself a man of color), access is denied implicitly if not explicitly.

What Chanel Baldwin's story also makes clear is an experience many educators may recognize as we teach students from historically excluded communities: the desire to learn, to work, to be simply awake to what is new is heightened in those who have been "kept in the lobby." As I sometimes teach Hispanic adults in nondegree-granting theology programs, it is their desire for the bounty of education that makes them stay behind after class, give up their few leisure hours in order to learn, and ask about alternatives for continuing their education after these short-lived programs end.

Intervening for Access

By the time a student seeks a program in theological studies, the lack of access to the privileges provided by "shadow education" will affect that student's ability to "demonstrate academic preparation" in the competitive marketplace of higher education.[43] Because of this, the turnstile will remain closed. How do theological educators and their institutions address this problem?

To subvert a self-perpetuating system of power, the way the system works must be exposed.[44] The prevalent and significant global spread of the "shadow education" phenomenon is profoundly worrying. As UNESCO cautions, this privatized system available only to those who are already economically advantaged "could negatively influence formal educational systems in terms of both equity and quality" and "can magnify inequality and confound a nation's ability to provide equitable and high-quality education to the general population."[45] Before we address those who never apply to our programs, we theological educators can look for ways to undo systems of privilege for the ones already waiting in our lobbies. We can do this through a heightened awareness of the social location and educational background of applicants. This will: (1) provide mindfulness of the multiple biases at work in admissions policies (ours and those that may have preceded us), (2) provide effective clues about which genuine gaps need to be actively addressed once underrepresented students are admitted (language/writing and critical thinking, etc.), and (3) consciously highlight valuable assets brought by these students but routinely discounted (speaking multiple languages, cultural competencies, and grassroots activism).

However, this is not enough. We are also called to differentiate between our *desired* students and those who are actually applying. We may routinely receive applications from an applicant pool that is homogenous and replicates the systems of privilege outside our doors. Even as we continue to serve these students, we need to devote resources to finding the Chanel Baldwins of the world and helping her get past the turnstile. Identifying our desired students (and that student, that global "other," will be not on the far side of the world but very often right at our door) will suggest the kinds of outreach and intervention a school or its sponsoring denomination should undertake to actively provide alternative "shadow education" to those desired populations. All of this calls for careful examination of the institution itself and how it may be "inadvertently" perpetuating exclusionary systems.

In order to create the possibility of such clear vision, institutions do well to make central to their operations a version of the principle of subsidiarity that Pope Pius XI first articulated.

> It is an injustice and at the same time a grave evil and disturbance of right order to assign to a greater and higher association what lesser and subordinate organizations can do. For every social activity ought of its very nature to furnish help to the members of the body social, and never destroy and absorb them.[46]

An application of this principle in an admissions and financial aid setting insists that decisions be made as close as possible to the student whose life will be affected by the decision. In such a setting, the lack of "academic preparation" that may be apparent in a particular student's application can be creatively and proactively addressed. Is there a language deficiency? An admissions office actively engaged with the problem at its source would understand that such difficulties are often the result of living with non-English-speaking parents in culturally segregated neighborhoods. What is more, such a consistent finding among a pool of desired applicants would argue for the creation of "bridge" programs that could include intensive English writing classes and consistent tutoring. Beyond this, such findings could suggest the inclusion of courses in languages other than English to allow students to grow their ability to lead and minister within their communities. The application of subsidiarity here would also make evident that students like Ignacio are best served by actively helping them to meet high academic standards, as these are necessary to thrive in the difficult work that follows graduation. A "watering down" of standards for particular populations—or the setting up of two separate tracks, one degree granting and another only providing certificates—perpetuates exclusionary systems.[47] Although in theological programs some students will be preparing for ministry, others for teaching, others for research, and so on, the "currency" that grants authority within ecclesial communities and wider social structures and ensures at least a modicum of economic survival is an actual degree. Every effort must be made to structure theological programs that can make academic degrees available to those who are not represented in the halls of power but quite overrepresented in the pews.

A concrete example is provided by the present state of the Catholic Church and two intersecting problems. First, as it does with many other global resources, the United States is voraciously consuming the priests of other nations. As journalist John Allen points out, in the United States "one out of every six priests is now foreign-born, and we add 300 international priests [to U.S. parishes] every year."[48] Contrary to the feel-good idea that these priests are reaching U.S. shores out of evangelizing zeal and a surplus in their home countries, bringing these priests north from the Global South robs those regions of their urgently needed clergy. "In the United States and Europe, the priest-to-baptized Catholic ratio today is 1 in 1,300; in Africa, it's almost 1 in 5,000; in Southeast Asia, it's 1 in 5,300; and in Latin America, it's a staggering 1 in 7,000."[49]

This practice has profoundly problematic implications, and Archbishop John Onaiyekan of Nigeria sounds a caution against continuing a situation

> where a European priest feels overwhelmed having to say three Masses on Sunday, and so he wants a black man to say them. Surely this is not where the church wants to go, getting poor people to do jobs that the rich don't want to do, as today happens in other walks of life.[50]

Like Ignacio's parents as they made their way to the United States for economic survival, African priests serving in the United States also send part of their salaries home to Africa. By working in U.S. dioceses, they are also able to forge relationships and make appeals for aid for their impoverished communities from affluent U.S. congregations.[51] These priests are migrant workers, helping communities at home survive.

As this situation makes abundantly clear, the U.S. Catholic Church cannot continue to drain away the clergy of poorer nations. Rather, it must increase its reliance on lay ecclesial ministers to carry out its pastoral work, while also moving needed resources to the Global South. However, in a denomination obsessively centered on its ordained clergy, trusting the laity with ecclesial responsibilities is no easy proposition. As the U.S. bishops express it in the document "Co-workers in the Vineyard of the Lord,"

> Inadequate and faulty formation harms rather than helps the mission of the Church. *Usually, a master's degree, or at least a bachelor's degree,* in an appropriate field of study is preferable. Degree work provides a systematic knowledge base and methodology in a given discipline. If the degree is pursued at a reliable Catholic school and if it includes theology and related disciplines, it can provide a foundation in Catholic teaching and lay the groundwork for a well-informed pastoral practice.[52]

The document elaborates in a footnote, citing that "in 2005, 48.1 percent of lay ecclesial ministers hold a master's degree or better,"[53] while admitting that only half of those master's degrees are in fields related to theology or pastoral ministry. The reality is, then, that less than one quarter of those already fulfilling the duties of lay ecclesial ministers have the desired degrees to do so. The other reality, not mentioned, is that those holding master's degrees are not representative of the congregations where they serve but predominantly white.[54] We have already seen the shocking numbers of Latino/a high school completion and the immigration laws and economic systems that encourage "brain-drain" from needy countries rather than investing in educating those who hunger for education but who have been kept outside of the education system. Theological education that provides "certificates" does not address the need for a college degree for Latinos/as that will satisfy the requirements for lay ministry leadership set by the bishops. The urgency is even more pronounced because as of 2013, the majority of U.S. Catholics under thirty are Hispanic (54 percent), and of almost seventy-eight million Catholics in the United States, over thirty million are Latinos/as.[55] Access for young Latinos/as to higher education broadly, and theological education particularly, would go a long way to addressing the shortages now filled by creating a brain-drain on the rest of the world.

So, are the seats in theological schools filled with these young Latinas/os ready to serve the church? Today, Hispanics represent less than 6 percent of students in programs accredited by the Association of Theological Schools, and of those 6 percent only a very small fraction are Roman Catholics.[56] Thus we return to Ignacio's story. The likelihood that he will graduate in four years and, even more, that he will be able to continue on to a graduate degree is tragically small. Ignacio was awarded enough financial assistance to make it possible for him to attend a university, but funding is just the proverbial tip of the iceberg. Several weeks ago, now beginning his senior year, Ignacio sat in my office visibly distressed. As a result of the rigor of his junior year of college, he acknowledged tearfully that the community colleges he had attended had not provided him with the necessary preparation to succeed academically. Beyond this, he felt overwhelmed by the structures, power dynamics, and barriers that seem to govern the physics of the complex system of higher education in the United States. What is even more distressing is that an ad hoc team endeavors to mentor Ignacio but is stymied by many existing structures. What is higher education like for the other Ignacios and Ignacias at institutions of higher learning lacking even our makeshift resources?

Ignacio's seat at our table of privilege, our table of higher education, had been empty for years as he cobbled together what funds he could find and attended a sequence of different low-cost public institutions in his quest for higher education. His story, before he finally took his place among us as a transfer student, was tragic and complex, but admission alone could not change the accretion of obstacles, self-doubts, internalized racism, class-based insecurities, and the lack of social capital that had been part of his entire life.[57] Ignacio's journey, a difficult one, was just beginning when he walked through our doors.

I also know that Ignacio's plight in this privileged land of the United States pales in comparison to that of millions around the world who lack access to education. This landscape of inordinate inequality and disenfranchisement becomes even more complex when approached theologically and when applied to people on the margins, young and old alike, seeking the particular good of a theological education, an education that does good, around the globe.

As a Christian theologian I thoroughly identify with Gustavo Gutiérrez' description of what it means to "do theology," which is the goal of a theological education. He states,

> To do theology is to write a love letter to that God I believe in, to that community I belong to, and to that Church of which I am a part. A love that is no stranger to what is perplexing and even to what is bitter, but [a love] that is more than anything a source of profound joy.[58]

Following the stark reality of Ignacio's story and the statistics he has defied, Gutiérrez' densely packed affirmation helps set the parameters for the questions I want to pose here. First, theological education deals with a complex constellation of concerns that have as a starting point a knowing awareness of God's abiding and loving presence. This God that Gutiérrez "believes in" is a God of love, unfailingly deserving of the love letter Gutiérrez is writing. This God of love, as the theologian also asserts, is not encountered in isolation, only to be an object of our private devotion, but, precisely *because* God is love, God calls us out of ourselves and into God's beloved community. This community, Gutiérrez tells us, is also the glad recipient of our love letter, each name appearing, as in Jesus' great commandment, alongside God's.[59] Consequently, in such a theological context, a commitment to the good of the close or distant Other, a commitment to Ignacio's education and that of the many like him, is not predicated on a civil right or even on demands for equality (laudable as those are), but it appears as a nonnegotiable requirement of authentic Christian faith.

Second, this love letter that is the work of theology is also directed at the church. Because of this assertion, we know that Gutiérrez does not equate "the community" he so dearly loves with the church, and there is no claim for the task of theology to be directed only to other Christians: the love letter is universal and to be universally proclaimed. However, as he adds the "Church" to the recipients of the work of theology, he does so acknowledging himself a part of that church. The church, this living body of Christ to which he and I both belong, needs love letters, complex and exacting ones, precisely from those who are part of its body, and who know its pain. The one society shuns, the one who has battled the obstacles, the one whose only strength has been God, *that one* needs to be given the tools to speak; we must not be content to speak only *for* her.[60] As Gutiérrez asserts, the love communicated in theological work "is no stranger to what is perplexing and even to what is bitter" but is, above all, "a source of profound joy." Our perplexity, even our bitterness, should not pull us away from love, because even when painful, honesty is constitutive of love's requirements. Thus, the very particular situations surrounding our present global and transnational reality call for the fecundity of the work of justice, the work of love, that can result from seriously engaging with our perplexity and bitterness.[61]

As a Latina Roman Catholic theologian in the United States, I live in the midst of the pain associated with my community's scandalous educational marginality in all sectors of society, and theological education is not only not an exception but perhaps one of its most urgent features. As Gutiérrez takes us back to "profound joy," he reminds us of the work of the theologian as the love letter writer and that, without theologians, perhaps such love letters will not get written. To love the universal Other in the human community requires the facilitation of a constant stream of lovers of God in each place, time, language, and voice—people willing to also write letters to the church. This is the urgency: to ask difficult questions about educational access to theological education is to be involved in what educational theorists call "changing the world."[62] What could be more Christian than that?

✦ 5 ✦

Identity Cross-Dressing while Teaching in a Global Context

MIGUEL A. DE LA TORRE

I am an international cross-dresser; that is, I am a "cross-dresser" between different constructions of identity, and the power and privilege that comes with the identity I happen to be wearing due to geographical location. Within the United States, I am constructed as brown and Other, relegated to marginalized spaces. But race is not solely socially constructed depending on skin pigmentation. Language spoken, accent in speech pattern, and/or geographic location can determine the race to which one is relegated. For example, as a Cuban refugee who has lived within the United States since the age of one, the Latino/a Miami community where I was raised during my formative years reinforced the notion that I was "white." Thus, when I gazed into the mirror, I saw the constructed reflection of a white Hispanic man.

Upon leaving my Miami neighborhood for Louisville, Kentucky, I took a job teaching Spanish to seminary professors at the institution I was attending. One day, I decided to test my students on their ability to pronounce colors in Spanish by pointing at an item in the room and asking the students, "¿Qué color es esto?" ("What color is this?"). After pointing to several items throughout the room and soliciting numerous responses, I realized I had yet to ask a question where the answer would be *blanco*, white. Not finding anything white in the room, and seeing myself as white, I pointed to my skin and asked in Spanish, "What color is this?" To my surprise, the class in unison responded, *moreno*, brown. At that moment, an epistemological break occurred concerning how I see myself, for I realized for the first time that the dominant culture saw me as brown, even though I saw myself as white. Regardless of my skin pigmentation, or how my particular culture defines race, the dominant

Eurocentric culture classified me as nonwhite, thus making me their Other.

Being Latino, even though I have light skin pigmentation, makes me brown in the eyes of those with the power to gaze and construct my identity. To be gazed upon, to be seen, defines the Object's existential self. To gaze implies a position of authority, a privileged point of view for the one seeing. To gaze is not an innocent metaphysical phenomenon concerning the transmittal of light waves, for it encompasses a mode of thought that radically transforms the Object being gazed at into an object for the possession of the one doing the gazing.

Those from the dominant U.S. culture who look into a mirror to see themselves construct an identity superior to the Latina/o Object of their gaze through the distancing process of negative self-definition. Specifically, "I am what I am not." The subject "I" is defined by contrasting it with the Objects residing on their margins. In the formation of the "I" out of the difference from the "them," there exist established power relations that give meaning to those differences.[1] Hispanics are lazy. When I look in the mirror, I don't see a Hispanic; therefore I am industrious. Latinas/os are barbaric. When I look in the mirror, I don't see a Latino/a; therefore I am civilized. By projecting the "I" upon the marginalized, those of the dominant culture are able to define themselves as worthier of the benefits society has to offer, because they either are more industrious (the Protestant work ethic) or are simply occupying a higher evolutionary stage.

Those who become the Object of the subject's gaze fall into the trap of learning to perceive reality through the eyes of those doing the gazing. The dominant culture possesses the power to make its subjective interpretation of reality the objective worldview for everyone else. Hence, those who are relegated to their underside, regardless of any aggressive rebuff employed against the colonization of their minds, remain nonetheless subjugated to how reality has been constructed by those who, in the act of seeing, create that which legitimizes and justifies their position, vis-à-vis the colonized and disenfranchised. The colonized also perceive reality through the eyes of the dominant culture, even seeing and defining themselves as they are seen and defined.

Since childhood, those residing on the underside of history have been taught to see and interpret reality through the eyes of the dominant culture, specifically white, heterosexual, middle-upper-class, patriarchal eyes. The triumph of the colonizing process is best demonstrated when people of color, including scholars of color, define themselves and their disenfranchised communities through academic paradigms that consciously or unconsciously continue to contribute to their marginalization. Academic rigor is measured by how well the marginalized parrot and incorporate scholarly paradigms that more often than not are incapable of liberating oppressed communities. Consequently, the particularity of scholarship emanating from non-Eurocentric communities poses the risk and danger in the minds of those privileged by the dominant culture of negatively impacting the prevailing so-called academic rigor.[2]

For the dominant culture to gaze upon the materiality of my particular Latino body imprisons said body. The Hispanic body is not simply confined to any prison; rather, it finds itself in panopticon's perfect paragon. The panopticon—as originated by eighteenth-century philosopher Jeremy Bentham and later resignified by the twentieth-century philosopher Michel Foucault—becomes the model prison designed to keep inmates under constant surveillance and scrutiny without their being aware of their observers. In effect, they are consistently being gazed upon.

Theoretically, constant gazing, coupled with an inability to know when one is being watched, reduces the inmates' so-called bad behaviors, since they are always fearful of being caught. The gaze of the guard confers power on the observer while serving as a trap to those being observed, even when the surveillance is neither constant nor available. The mere possibility of being watched forces the object of the gaze to internalize the power relationship. The prisoners who are being subjected to a field of visibility assume responsibility for policing themselves. The prisoner assumes the power relationship in which he or she plays the roles of both disciplinarian and disciplined, becoming the principal enforcer of his or her own subjugation. Prisoners learn to see themselves through the eyes of their guards.[3]

In a chapter titled "Colonial War and Mental Disorder," Frantz Fanon writes, "That imperialism which today is fighting against a true liberation of [humanity] leaves in its wake here and there tinctures of decay which we must search out and mercilessly expel from our lands and our spirits."[4] I would argue that these volatile "tinctures of decay" include how the colonized is constructed through the gaze of the colonizer. And yet, this call for action to move beyond the mental disorder of colonialized minds is more complex and problematic than simply taking an aggressive stance over and against the never-blinking dominant gaze. To move beyond what Edward Said terms "the rhetoric of blame" encompasses more than simply denigrating the colonizer for being white and Eurocentric.[5]

Neither power nor oppression flows hierarchically, with blame always residing with those whom the culture privileges. It would be naive to understand power as centralized, residing in the hands of some elite group. Power is everywhere, forming and passing through a multitude of institutions. It is formed in relationships, which in turn sustain, advance, and maintain power. Power is most effective when coercion appears neutral and natural. Those scholars of color who submit to societal norms and adopt the dominant culture's worldview are rewarded with inclusion in the privileges the culture has to offer. But for those who challenge the prevailing mores, punishment occurs in the form of marginalization and exclusion.[6]

The complexity of shifting identity depending on geographical location (teaching within the United States or teaching abroad) leads me to conclude that I am indeed a "cross-dresser." The fluidity of identity allows for different significations of power depending on geographical location—thus allowing me, as a teacher of theology and ethics, to cross-dress and wear identity based on where my particular classroom is located. In the U.S. classroom, even though I occupy a space of power as professor, I remain the Object of the dominant gaze; yet, when my classroom is located abroad, my Latinoness is submerged as my overseas students see me as white and Euro-American—along with all the powers and privileges that come by materially occupying that particular space. Because of the fluidity of identity worn by the U.S. scholar of color, different—and at times conflicting—challenges, pitfalls, and dangers are manifested when attempting to engage theological education within a global context. Identity cross-dressing, I would argue, complicates the ability for scholars of color and the students occupying classrooms abroad to effectively participate in production of theological knowledge. Specifically, through the use of actual autobiographical case studies,[7] we will explore some of the challenges faced, concentrating on (1) when color folk become white, (2) gazing through the eyes of the colonizer, (3) teaching through risk-taking praxis, and (4) considering when the oppressed become oppressors.

When Color Folk Become White

Those from the United States, regardless of race or ethnicity, who go abroad to teach theology soon discover that in certain cases they cease being racially categorized. To some degree, regardless of actual skin pigmentation or ethnic origins, they all become navy blue—the color of the cover of U.S. passports. The navy blue passport signifies the global imperial might of the most privileged Empire ever known in human history. The cultural influences of the Greek Empire, the imperial might of the Roman Empire, the religious supremacy of the Holy Roman Empire, and the global reach of the British Empire all pale in comparison with the cultural dominance, the military might, the capitalist zeal, and the global influence of the U.S. Empire.[8] Indeed, the sun never sets on the dominating influence of the United States. At no other time in human history has one nation enjoyed such economic, political, and cultural supremacy. While empires of old relied on brute force, the U.S. Empire relies mainly on economic force (not to disregard the fact that it also has the greatest fighting force known to humanity). Through its economic might, the United States dictates terms of trade with other nations, guaranteeing that benefits flow to the U.S. center and the elite of countries that approve the trade agreements.

All who carry this navy blue document not only fall under the protection of Empire but also become the global signifiers of Empire, even if they find themselves marginalized within the confines of Empire. Those defined as nonwhite due to the domestic dominant gaze become honorary whites when traveling abroad to teach. This became obvious during an immersion trip I led for a group of U.S. students to Mexico. One of the participants was an African American male. He expressed surprise as to how well he was being received. He intimated that when he went out for the evening, many young women wanted to get to know him and develop a romantic relationship, regardless of his race.

What he failed to realize is that the color of his passport cover trumped the color of his skin. If he would have been *un negro latinoamericano*, a Latin American black, with no access to what navy blue signifies, these same nonblack Latin Americans would probably not have bothered to give him the time of day. Racism is as much an oppressive phenomenon south of the border as it is to the north. But by crossing borders southward, he ceased to be black and became American, along with all the privileges that identity confers. I witnessed a similar phenomenon while a Fulbright scholar in Indonesia. During my time there, I quickly became familiar with *bule* hunters. *Bule* is a nonderogative Indonesian term that simply means white people. My Javanese students, along with friends I made, warned me of not falling prey to *bule* hunters. These were women and men (mainly women) who stalked hotels, restaurants, and lounges that catered to white tourists. Well-educated *bule* hunters sporting Western fashions were not attracted to this particular middle-age body that I occupy; rather, they were attracted to the navy blue documentation that I held and all the privileges it possessed. Ironically, while the colonizer's gaze always defined me as their Hispanic Other, I had to travel halfway across the world to be defined (only through the gaze of the colonized) as a white American.

In the eyes of many of my students abroad, I am not perceived as belonging to a marginalized group; rather, I am seen as a full-fledged member of the Empire. When teaching in Indonesia, many of my students there had difficulty seeing or accepting that I could understand what it meant to be marginalized. They simply saw me as white, with all the benefits that globally come to those who possess the navy blue signifier of identity. There was a refusal to accept that within Empire, spaces exist where the descendants of the Global South face and experience similar disenfranchisement to those still residing in their countries of origins. Part of my responsibility in teaching theology on a global level became making simplistic hierarchical understanding of how race and ethnicity are constructed more complex.

I have spent my entire life being defined through a hyphenated existence: either Cuban-American or Hispanic-American. Ironically, the term Cuban-American is an artificial designation amalgamating "who we are" with "where we live." This is the name given to us by the dominant culture, not a name we chose. When we talk among ourselves, we seldom use the word "Cuban-American" to refer to our being. The act of uttering a word that names us simultaneously subordinates us to the power of the one doing the naming. The word "Cuban-American" constructs us as an object for the dominant culture to possess, and it shrouds us in the very act of appropriation. This phenomenon is described by what Pierre Bourdieu calls objectivism. According to Bourdieu, "Objectivism constitutes the social world as a spectacle presented to an observer who takes up a 'point of view' on the action, who stands back so as to observe it, and, transferring into the object the principle of his relation to the object, conceives of it as a totality intended for cognition alone, in which all interactions are reduced to symbolic exchanges. This point of view is the one afforded by high positions in the social structure."[9]

Thus the term Cuban-American creates a hyphenated identity, attempting to reconcile two distinct and separate cultures into one being. This locution erects within our very being a schizophrenic (Latin for "split mind") existence. This phenomenon was manifested during my first trip back to Cuba, my homeland, some forty years after I left. While walking through the streets of La Habana, I was approached by one of the city's *jineteros* (street hustlers) who asked me where I was from (no doubt to determine what types of services or vices he could attempt to procure for me). With pride I stated I was from here, from this very city; to which he replied, "You may be from Cuba, but you're obviously no Cuban." The imperial capital I possess due to my navy blue passport, and cultural capital I obtained through my U.S. college education, impressed upon me a very different way of being. The way I dress, the way I carry myself, the way I conduct myself, the words I use in speech all betray that I no longer belong to the group from which I came. I can no longer claim my own identity; identity is chosen for me. I realize that I will always be too Cuban ever to be fully accepted within the United States and too Americanized ever to be accepted by my native compatriots. In effect, I occupy utopia (Greek for "no place"—*ou topos*), for literally there is no place on earth to which I and other U.S. scholars of color can belong. Hence, how do those of us who come from no place teach theology on the global context of place?

Gazing through the Eyes of the Colonizer

My students and I were sitting in a dirt-floor hut in a squatter village on the outskirts of Cuernavaca, Mexico. Bugs crawled along the walls of the shack constructed of discarded wood, cardboard, and plasterboard. Empty plastic bags and trash littered the flimsy structure, hugging the hut as if they were adornments. Joining me were mostly white, economically privileged students who sought to learn about God from the wretched of the earth. The "owner" of the house, an indigenous woman who had been aged prematurely by the ravages of poverty, patiently engaged us in conversation (with me serving as translator).

Routinely, I bring my students to Mexico on "missionary" trips. Usually, the purpose of missionary trips is to evangelize "nonbelievers," to convince them to accept the doctrines of the missionary, worshiping and believing like North Americans. My missionary trips, however, are somewhat different from the normative colonizing venture. We go to be evangelized by the poor, to learn from the disenfranchised and dispossessed who is God. In a real sense, we are the ones who go to "get saved."

Our host welcomed us into her home and offered hospitality. She prepared a snack of jam on stale saltine crackers, giving what she could barely afford to give. As in past encounters, I encouraged my primarily Protestant Euro-American students to ask this poor, illiterate, Catholic indigenous woman about her faith. My students began asking, "Who is God? Who is Jesus? Who is the Virgin Mary? What is the church?" Like a sage teacher instructing the young, she began to provide us with her understanding of faith, doctrine, and church teachings.

It soon became obvious that her responses to our queries were a mixture of local indigenous teachings, medieval Roman Catholicism, and a sprinkling of self-help New Ageism. She obviously lacked orthodoxy—correct doctrine. This was more than my trained theological mind could handle. In spite of my fluency with postcolonial theories, I easily reverted in seeing, and thus constructing, her as theologically unsophisticated. I fought the urge to correct her, to reveal the incongruities in her beliefs. Through my gaze, I, the one who is usually gazed upon—either unconsciously, or maybe consciously—relegated her to my theological Other as I slipped into the traditional missionary role of becoming her savior and righting her theological wrongs. Although I continued faithfully to translate her words, I began to contemplate how I could gracefully challenge her with theological "truth."

Just then her dirty, undernourished, barefooted boy (about eleven years old) shyly entered the one-room hut and meekly interrupted his mother. He handed over about fifteen pesos that he collected—during school hours—selling Chiclets to tourists. As she collected the money, she placed one peso aside. I asked her what that was for. She replied that it was for the poor. At that moment, the orthopraxis, the correct actions, of this poor woman taught my students (and me) more about divinity than all of the academic theological books we had read. Seeing the giving of the "widow's mite" was more effective than any lecture I could have possibly delivered.[10]

When those who have so little *do* their faith by providing for those who have even less, then those of us from so-called First World nations, privileged by class and theological sophistication, should be profoundly humbled. It is the privileged who see the oppressed and do nothing that are the ones that neither understand theology nor know God. I may have had the educational training to tease apart the inconsistencies in this woman's beliefs, but she knew far more about theology than I did. This is not to romanticize the poor, for surely there is nothing romantic about poverty. Rather, it is a truth concerning teaching in a global context that I learned directly from this poor woman's actions. In a sense, orthodoxy—correct doctrine—is not that important (I say as a working theologian!).

Teaching through Risk-Taking Praxis

Regularly I take students to a foreign country while technically remaining within the United States. While we may not necessarily cross borders, we do cross Border Patrol checkpoints. We go to the borderlands that separate poverty from privilege, Eurocentrism from Latinoness, the United States from Mexico. We straddle an imaginary line reinforced by walls and guns to protect the wealth accumulated on one side from those stuck on the other side, on whose backs a major portion of that wealth was created. This space we call the borderlands is undergirded by racial and ethnic suppositions that fuel capital-building assumptions geared to justify the transfer of wealth from those forced to live south of this line to those who live to the north. The colonized, who live along and on both sides of our southern border, are defined, due to decades of gazing, as uncivilized, diseased, animals. The borderland where my students accompany me is a geographical space dividing Subjects from Other, a space that must be defended with walls, guns, and personnel, lest Objects slip through demarcated perimeters. My students witness the display (symbolically and at times materially) of violent power. We define ourselves, through the negation of our Others, as a beacon of human rights for the world; yet it is not an exaggeration to say that the borderlands are the epicenter of what is probably the greatest human rights crisis presently occurring within the United States' borders.

My students and I spend our time learning about the consequences of neoliberalism by placing food, water, and clothes on the trails taken by those crossing, without proper documentation, into the United States. We walk on trails covered with footprints and littered with empty water bottles, plastic jugs, clothing, and other personal effects. Along the way we pass religious shrines, a reminder that there are symbols of the divine and celestial promise of life on these trails of death and terror. Not long ago the organization with which we work, No More Deaths, found the body of a teenage girl. We say we are the land of plenty, but thousands die in this region because they lack water or food. Every so often we come across lost migrants. We give them food and water and point them northward. We have witnessed some of these migrants picked up by the

Border Patrol and placed in what appeared to be a covered dog cage in the back of a pickup truck during unbearably hot desert days, where certainly no air-conditioning exists. We say we do not torture prisoners, yet the organization with which I work has documented the sadistic treatment of incarcerated undocumented immigrants.[11]

At times, my students and I have been detained by the Border Patrol. On other occasions, we have been detained by local police. Our crimes: feeding the hungry, giving water to the thirsty, clothing the naked, welcoming the alien within our midst. Today a Good Samaritan can receive up to twenty years in prison for providing transportation to the closest hospital for a dying immigrant, making us one of the only countries where providing humanitarian aid is a crime.[12]

Scholars are usually trained and taught to be objective, not to become involved with the objects of their research. We analyze and develop theories from the safety and security of campuses and research centers. Yet I continue to discover that unless scholarship is rooted in the real life experience of people, specifically the world's dispossessed, such scholarship has little relevance. For me, to be a scholar teaching theology and ethics in the global context means being an activist, using scholarship to bring about change, to improve the quality of human lives, and to mitigate injustices.

Teaching theology in a global context, even in the Global South spaces found within the center of Empire, is conducted mainly as a scholar-activist participating in solidarity with the marginalized. The praxis of dealing with oppressive structures within dispossessed communities is more crucial and more educational than books published by the "experts." Employing a scholar-activist methodology, unapologetically grounded within the social context of the disenfranchised, attempts to perceive divinity from within the social location of marginalized people. Such a process analyzes their reality, a reality tied to perspectives that demand a sociopolitical response to oppression. A relationship develops between the disenfranchised and intellectuals aware of the structural crises the disenfranchised and dispossessed face.

To be a scholar-activist means standing against Empire. At times, this may require loss—loss of livelihood, loss of freedom, maybe even loss of life—for to share in the lives of the marginalized means sharing in their fate. Loss is not sought for, but at times it may become the consequence of teaching theology in a global context. All too often, Euro-Americans enjoy the privilege of driving to a march. To get arrested for some movement earns them a liberal badge of honor. But for disenfranchised communities, arrest is a frequent risk of living in marginality. Scholar-activists who do their scholarship in solidarity with the disenfranchised by definition place their bodies in similar risks.

Normatively, those from the Empire teaching theology in a global context find that the theology on which they elucidate is more often than not linked to the colonizer's worldview and the political structures designed to protect the interests of the privileged few, thus reinforcing the colonizing venture on native minds. By contrast, scholar-activists (especially those from the liberationist or liberative perspectives) focus on human needs rather than ecclesiastical dogma. They believe scholarship can never be neutral in the face of injustices. When the scholars stand in solidarity with the marginalized, then theology begins to move beyond simply being an extension of the Empire. This understanding separates scholar-activists from most academicians, mainly because they work as "organic intellectuals" à la Antonio Gramsci, connecting the intellectual enterprise, which is informed by the grassroots, with popular movements where they participate in contributing to its consciousness-raising. These scholar-activists theorize and theologize for the express purpose of changing oppressive social structures, as opposed to simply better understanding said structures for the sole sake of scholarship.

There exists a presupposition that providing effective teaching entails a response to injustice and oppression. By forcing students with economic and social privilege to occupy the uncomfortable space of the marginalized (i.e., walking migrant trails), from which to approach religious studies, they are provided with a unique outlook on the normative discourse, a view that enhances traditional curricula. Because individuals enter the educational system with a lifetime of experiences and knowledge, courses must bring their suppositions into conversation with those who many may consider have nothing to offer the intellectual dialogue (i.e., the poor woman of Cuernavaca). Only by being organic intellectuals can my students and I contribute toward the struggle against oppression that has become normalized, legitimized, and institutionalized.

The major failing of teaching theology in a global setting today by scholars of color is that some fail to problematize the praxis of cross-dressing, putting on the clothing of power and privilege. We adopt the Eurocentric understanding that theology is a way of thinking rather than a way of living. Many respond in words to the inhumane conditions forced upon the dispossessed when it is much more important to respond in deeds, in actions, in praxis. Theology, as well as ethics, is action—action that leads to salvation and liberation for both the oppressed and their oppressors. For this reason, I constructed a "roadmap" that assists in reaching the goal of action, based on the Catholic social-teaching model of *seeing—judging—acting*.[13] I use this five-step hermeneutical circle when teaching in a global context: (1) observation—to understand why the present moral dilemma exists, (2) reflection—to understand how social structures contribute to and maintain the moral dilemma, (3) prayer—to understand what our responsibility as men and women of faith should be, (4) action—to respond to what we claim to believe, and (5) reassessment—to ensure faithfulness to the gospel message of liberation.[14] Maybe then are we able to live out what Francis of Assisi called us to do when he supposedly quipped, "Preach the Gospel at all times and when necessary use words."

When the Oppressed Become Oppressors

The oppressed can easily detect the oppressive structures perpetrated against them and yet remain oblivious of their own complicity with oppression. Even within colonized communities, structures of intraoppression flourish; while the oppressive structures of the dominant culture should never be minimized, it is also important to be aware of and active in dismantling the ways the marginalized emulate the dominant culture in oppressing segments within their own communities. The danger of any decolonization process is the creation of new oppressive structures where the faces and/or ethnicity of the new oppressors are the same of those who remain disenfranchised.

All too often, those more likely to be privileged by internal oppressive structures are the very students who have experienced colonization but now occupy our classrooms. This phenomena became obvious during a class I taught in Yogyakarta, Indonesia. Within the Indonesian system, citizens are required to carry identification cards that, among other things, indicate religious affiliation. All citizens must indicate to which of the six official religions they adhere (Islam, Protestantism, Catholicism, Hinduism, Buddhism, and Confucianism).[15] The classroom where I taught was mainly composed of Muslims, who represent close to 90 percent of the country's population. When I asked why a faithful follower of indigenous traditions could not indicate their faith preference, I was told that it was best for society if primitive religions based on superstition were eliminated in the country's continuous march toward reason and civilization. To that end, the government has routinely passed legislation that attempts to restrict indigenous expressions of faith. My students' consciousness was raised when I reminded them that the previous Dutch colonizers also referred to their ancestors as primitive and superstitious. In effect, I accused them of being the new colonizers, the new oppressors, imitating those who once subjugated them.

We cannot ignore the power structures existing within marginalized communities that cause injustice and require exposure and dismantling. It is crucial to recognize that oppressive structures also exist within and between marginalized communities and that they also demand attention. Domination exists within domination-creating margins within the margins. Many marginalized communities can be as sexist, homophobic, classist, and racist (based on who is closer to the white ideal) as the dominant, global, Eurocentric culture.

The marginalized often shape themselves in the image of the dominant culture, learning to mimic the attitudes, beliefs, behaviors, and actions that they have been taught to see as superior. Colonized minds reinforce the marginalized lack of self-worth that often leads to self-loathing. Some marginalized persons seem to attempt becoming "whiter" than the dominant culture. At times they exhibit greater disdain and less patience or compassion than their white counterparts for those within their own communities who fall short of the white ideal. If salvation requires assimilation—at least in terms of the dominant culture—then proof of worthiness lies in being accepted by the dominant culture, even if this leads to actions that are contrary or damning to one's own indigenous community.

The lure of becoming new oppressors at the expense of other marginalized groups is a reality that finds expression in various forms of oppression within marginalized communities, such as internal racism, sexism, heterosexism, and classism, where proximity to the white heterosexual male ideal remains the standard for measuring superiority. The closer one is to the white ideal (either in physical attributes or in geographical proximity), the more privilege—although still limited within the overall dominant culture—exists.

Educator Paulo Freire noted that everyone in some part of their being seeks to be a "subject" who is able to act and transform her or his environment. Thus, members of marginalized communities who are objects acted upon rather than subjects who do the acting have an escape route. While habitually alienated and acted upon, they desire acceptance and want to become subjects in their own right. The safe route is to imitate the dominant society whose acceptance they crave. In a very real sense, their consciousness becomes submerged; they become unable, or unwilling, to see how the operating interests and values of the dominant culture are internalized.[16]

For this reason, the (class)room is appropriately named, for it is indeed a room of class—a room where students learn the class they belong to or aspire to join, along with all the power and privilege (or lack thereof) that comes with that class.[17] The fact that some students are able to pay sufficient money to attend particular rooms of class located on prestigious campuses throughout the world indicates that they will have certain opportunities that are denied to those of lower economic class, those who are more often than not residing on the margins of society.

The pedagogy I employed in Yogyakarta (as well as here in the United States) in my constructed room of class seeks to uncover social ethics through the rich diversity found among those who are usually excluded. Succinctly stated, what occurs in my room of class is the construction of a collaborative theology and ethics and the study of its impact upon the reflection of marginalized people who struggle in understanding their faith and vocation as it is contextualized in their lives and circumstances.

Far from being an objective neutral educational system, students who attend (class)rooms can be conditioned for either domestication by or liberation from the existing social structures. All too often, educational systems serve to normalize power structures as legitimate. My task as an educator in a global context, specifically as one who calls himself a liberationist, is to cultivate the student's ability to find his or her own voice by creating an environment in which individual and collective consciousness-raising can occur. Teaching from the margins of society must be done if I, as a teacher, hope to participate in the consciousness-raising venture.

As a scholar-activist, unapologetically grounded in the social context of the colonized and the disenfranchised, I attempt to create an environment within the "room of class" that attempts to perceive divinity from within the social context of marginalized people—that is, those who are usually unable to participate in the (class)room where I teach. Such a process analyzes their reality, a reality tied to perspectives that demand a sociopolitical response to oppression. A relationship develops between the marginalized and intellectuals aware of the structural crises people face.

Conclusion

The act of decolonization, specifically decolonizing the mind, is a dangerous process and at times a violent process. Identity cross-dressing experienced by scholars of color, nestled in the Empire, who traverse borders to teach in a global context is in danger of replicating the colonizers' pedagogical methodology, making the colonized abroad—through the gaze emanating from the center—new Objects. The theological contempt the former colonizers held for the colonized can easily be duplicated through obscure theological and theoretical Eurocentric abstract paradigms that simply reinforce the supposed universality of Eurocentrism. The task of the scholar of color teaching in a global context is the raising of consciousness that can lead the oppressed toward a more just reality based on their own cultural symbols and worldview. The scholar teaching abroad ceases to be the expert and instead participates in the task of also having her or his consciousness raised. The call is not for mastering the theological canon of the West but to explore divinity through the eyes of the marginalized who have resided for centuries on the underside of the colonizers. This journey of solidarity becomes a liberative pedagogy, which can be implemented (not just by scholars of color) within a global context.

✦ 6 ✦

Teaching Global Theology with Local Resources

A Chinese Theologian's Strategies

LAI PAN-CHIU

Teaching Christian theology in Chinese is a very tricky task, especially in a global and transnational context. In addition to the challenges constituted by the language barrier between Chinese and other languages, the most challenging problem remains how to overcome the psychological or theological barriers that privilege the European and Euro-American theological traditions and hinder the participation and contribution of Chinese Christian theology in a global and transnational context.

At the moment, the majority of the theological publications in Chinese are either translations of books originally written in Western languages or introductions to individual Western theologians and/or schools of theological thought, even though there have been many proposals concerning how to indigenize or contextualize Christian theology into China. The European and/or Euro-American theological tradition is still taken as the normative or more advanced model of theology, with some sort of demarcation between Chinese theology and Western theology. This Western tradition often overlooks the fact that there are many other theological traditions as well as cultures or civilizations in this world. As the Christian population in contemporary China is dominated by Catholics and Protestants, other forms of Christianity—such as the Orthodox Christianity flourishing in Russia, eastern Europe, and the Middle East (or West Asia)—are often neglected in the ordinary Chinese Christian's perception of Christianity. This neglect further reinforces not only the impression of Christianity as a Western religion introduced into China by foreign missionaries associated with Western colonial powers but also the tendency of assuming the superiority or normative status of the Western theological tradition in contemporary Chinese Christian discourses. From time to time, the task of Chinese Christian theology is understood mainly, if not exclusively, in terms of indigenization or contextualization of Christian theology (or even Western Christian theology) in China. The question of how Chinese Christian theology may contribute to the global developments of Christian theology, including those in the Western world, is often not considered.[1]

In order to help students to take seriously the cultural and theological resources in Chinese, to widen their ecclesiastical and theological horizons, and to overcome their theological "inferiority complex," I adopt the pedagogical strategy of teaching global theology with Chinese resources, instead of relying lamely on the books available in Western languages concerning global Christianity or global theology. Many of these books are very useful and can make the students aware of the global context of Christian theology. However, they need to be supplemented by concrete examples from Chinese Christian theology, which may be more effective in helping students to rethink and retrieve their own theological heritage in a global context. In this chapter, I would like to share my ideas, observations, and experiences as well as the strategies and resources I employ in my attempts to teach Christian theology in a global and transnational context.

Resources and Strategies Based on the Legacy of *Jingjiao*

In an undergraduate course on the study of Christianity, I attempt to introduce the idea of global Christianity to the students and to correct the misconception of Christianity as a Western religion. In the lecture concerning the diversity of Christianity, I include a section on *Jingjiao,* which means literally "luminous religion."

To start, I draw students' attention to the emblem of Chung Chi College, one of the nine colleges of the Chinese University of Hong Kong, which houses a divinity school under its auspices. Featured at the center of the emblem is a cross placed on a lotus and surrounded by some fortune-clouds, symbolizing the vision for the unity between the Christian faith and Asian or Chinese culture. After raising the question about the origins of this symbol of the cross, I remind the students that the same symbol can be found in a picture hanging in the lounge of the library of Chung Chi College and that the picture is a true-to-scale inked paper copy of a monument unearthed and kept in Xi'an, China. According to the Chinese characters inscribed on the monument, it is quite clear that it is from a religion named *Jingjiao*, which flourished in China during the Tang dynasty (618–907 C.E.). The follow-up question put to the students is where this *Jingjiao* came from and which denomination of Christianity it belonged to.

I then tell the students the story concerning the discovery of the monument and the seven ancient Chinese texts associated with *Jingjiao*, and how, based on the Syrian names on the monument and some other evidences, most scholars identify a Syrian origin of *Jingjiao*, and many of them associate it with Nestorianism.[2] Upon reading some of the extracts from the monument and the texts, which include many Chinese expressions used by Buddhism and/or Daoism, I challenge the students to see if any one of them can prove from the monument and/or the ancient Chinese texts left by *Jingjiao* that it committed the heresy of Nestorianism. I then raise the question of whether "Nestorianism" is an accurate label for *Jingjiao* at all.[3]

At this juncture, I refer to the christological controversies in early Christianity. Similar to some other works in this field, my analysis of the controversies highlights that the disputes and the related "ecumenical" councils, including particularly the Chalcedon Council, involved not only theological tensions among divergent traditions but also power struggles within and outside the church circle.[4] I further propose that no matter whether Nestorius' own theology is Nestorian or not, it is problematic to label *Jingjiao* as "Nestorian." This is because, historically speaking, *Jingjiao* was established by the missionaries sent by a Syriac-speaking church known as "the Church of the East." As Syria was quite different and independent from the Roman Empire culturally, linguistically, and politically, this Church of the East also differed from the theological traditions in Rome and Alexandria, which were quite influential in the Roman Empire at that time. Regarding the relationship between this Church of the East and Nestorius (d. 451), it is important to note that Nestorius had served as the patriarch of Constantinople, but he was not the founder of this Church of the East, nor had he ever served formally as the leader of this church. In terms of theology, the theological tradition of the Church of the East was pioneered by Diodore of Tarsus (d. 390) and Theodore of Mopsuestia (350–427), while Nestorius was merely a follower rather than the founder or champion of this theological tradition. Even though there might have been some followers of Nestorius who joined the Church of the East after the disgrace and condemnation of Nestorius, and though the Church of the East refused to accept the councils of Ephesus and Chalcedon, it remains misleading to impose the label "Nestorianism" on the Church of the East, which had been established long before Nestorius.[5]

More importantly, this church, which is nowadays officially called the "Holy Apostolic Catholic Assyrian Church of the East" or "Assyrian Church of the East," has begun to reconcile with the Roman Catholic Church and some other churches, and it is recognized as one of the member churches of the World Council of Churches. Thus the question is, if it is no longer condemned or rejected as heresy anymore, why should the label "Nestorianism" be applied to the Church of the East or the *Jingjiao* established by it? In short, no matter whether Nestorius' own theology is Nestorianism or not, it is inaccurate and inappropriate to call the Church of the East or *Jingjiao* Nestorian. The popularity of the practice of imposing the label "Nestorian" on the Church of the East as well as on *Jingjiao* in most of the prevalent textbooks of the history of Christianity exposes the hidden and yet deep-seated Western or Eurocentric bias in Christian theology, especially that emanating in the West. The students are thus alerted to the power relationship in this kind of pejorative labeling.

I then take the history of the Church of the East as an example to alert the students that there might be some other branches of Christianity being neglected in most of the existing textbooks on the history of Christianity. These branches of Christianity were overlooked because they might have flourished outside the Roman Empire, ceased to exist, and/or might be considered heretical by some other Christians.[6] However, they did play important roles in the history of Christianity and should not be forgotten, for their stories remind us how Christianity was a global rather than a European or Western religion in the entirety of its history.

The lesson to be drawn from the resources left by *Jingjiao* is that as a global religion with rich cross-cultural experience, Christianity has divergent theological and ecclesiastical traditions, and the Western theological tradition is merely one of them. A theology that was rejected or condemned as heresy by the Western churches is not necessarily wrong or false. This is because this kind of condemnation might be based on misunderstanding or miscommunication, and might have been influenced by church politics, political ideology, and/or even racial biases. It is thus problematic to privilege the Western theological tradition against other theological traditions in a globalized world. Furthermore, although the Antiochene theological tradition associated with the Church of the East—including Theodore of Mopsuestia, Nestorius, and so forth—was not "universalized" or "globalized" by being adopted to the exclusion of other christological traditions, it became one of the most important contributors, alongside the christological traditions from Alexandria and Rome, to the influential christological definition articulated at the Council of Chalcedon. In a similar vein, with its rich cultural resources and sociopolitical experience, the Chinese theological tradition can also make its contribution to the global development of Christian theology, in dialogue and collaboration with other theological traditions.

After the Chinese government introduced liberalization policies in the late 1970s, many Chinese intellectuals were attracted to Christianity without formally becoming church members. Some of them studied and published rather extensively on Christianity and were identified as "cultural Christians." A cultural qua theological movement called "Sino-Christian Theology" emerged.[7] In the last decade or so, the theological publications by Chinese scholars have significantly improved in terms of both quality and quantity, and the scope of study has become more comprehensive as well. It is probably due to economic development and the dramatic increase of research funding in China that similar uprising trends took place in many other academic disciplines. On top of the funding support, in comparison with the Chinese scholars of Christianity active during the 1980s and 1990s, many of the younger researchers of Christianity are better trained in theological studies and have more overseas experience and connections. They may have better chances and greater potential to further enhance the international visibility of Chinese theological scholarship.

Resources and Strategies Based on Chinese Catholic Writings

After establishing the possibility and legitimacy of overturning the dominance of the Western theological tradition and making a contribution to global theology with Chinese resources, the next question may be what are the "homemade" Chinese resources or materials to be explored and retrieved for this purpose.

The second strategy I employ is to analyze some of the theological texts left by the Chinese Catholics during the Ming dynasty (1368–1644). Many of these Chinese Catholics, especially the intellectuals, studied Confucian classics as part of their education and had certain knowledge about Buddhism. After their conversion to Catholicism, many of them employed traditional Chinese concepts and made references to the Chinese classics, especially those from Confucianism, to explain Catholic faith and practices to their fellow Chinese.[8] My aim is to show how some Chinese Catholics integrated some traditional Chinese concepts with Christian theology, and some of these Chinese concepts may be meaningful in the contemporary context.[9] Among the numerous documents available, I particularly focus on those related to the concept of *da-fu-mu*, which literally means "the Great-Father-Mother" or simply "Great Parent,"[10] and the concept of "forming one body with the myriad things of Heaven and Earth" (*yu tiandi wanwu cheng wei yi ti*) or simply "the ten thousand things of one body" (*wanwu yi ti*). These concepts are adopted from Chinese intellectuals, especially the Confucians at that time. Unlike Matteo Ricci (1552–1610), who accepted *da-fu-mu* while rejecting "the ten thousand things of one body" in order to uphold the distinction among different kinds of creatures,[11] many Chinese Catholics accepted both concepts. For instance, in his "Treatise to Supplant Doubts" (Dai yi pian), Yang Tingyun (1562–1627) interpreted these ideas with the Confucian metaphysical concept of one principle with diverse manifestations (*li yi fen shu*),[12] which, according to Neo-Confucianism, is the metaphysical basis for the Confucian ethics of love with distinctions. In his "Sequel to 'Treatise to Supplant Doubts' " (Dai yi xupian), Yang expounded this discussion of the ethics of love with distinctions in terms of one's love toward God, self-love, familial love, love of other human beings, and benevolence toward all creatures.[13] The ethical implications derived include not only one's love toward God, oneself, and family members but also one's moral obligation toward all creatures, without denying that some sort of prioritization has to be made, because one's love may have different kinds of expression and different degrees due to the diverse relationships involved. In other words, the Confucian affirmation of the unity of all things does not neglect the distinctions or differences of all things in ethical and metaphysical terms. In fact, this idea of love with distinctions is not only comparable to the concept of the order of love (*ordo caritatis*) in Augustine and Thomas Aquinas but also relevant to contemporary discussions on ecological ethics and the interdisciplinary studies of altruism, especially the dialogue between Christianity and Confucianism on these issues. These lines of theological discussion have been picked up recently by some Chinese scholars, including Wang Tao, one of my former doctoral students.[14]

A similar example can be found in Han Lin (1601–1644), whose *Book of the Bell* (*Duo Shu*, c. 1640) was used as one of the major sourcebooks for a postgraduate class on "Selected Original Texts for Chinese Christianity" offered at Peking University in 2004, and resulted in an annotated commentary published in 2008.[15] As Sun Shangyang, the teacher of the course and editor of the volume, mentions in the preface to the book, Han converted to Catholicism together with other family members around 1620 and then wrote many books defending the Catholic faith. Though Han was successful at the provincial level of the state examination, and thus qualified for appointment as a government officer, he never served as a government official and even participated later in the rebellion against the government. This book was written under the invitation of the local government officials to lecture at a bimonthly meeting organized for the education of the local people. Han was asked to write and lecture on the six moral instructions of an edict issued by the first emperor of the Ming dynasty.[16] Han took this opportunity to use the seemingly Confucian concept of Great-Father-Mother to integrate the Catholic and Confucian ethical traditions. Based on this concept, Han affirmed not only the fear as well as the love of God but also filial piety (*xiao*), which is one of the cardinal virtues in Confucianism. This was quite different from many of the Catholic missionaries, who might emphasize fear or respect for God or God's love toward human beings but not a spirituality that integrated and equally emphasized both the human love and the fear of God. When expounding the meaning of the commandment "love thy neighbor as oneself," Han further elaborated the ethical implications of the concept of Great-Father-Mother to affirm a universal and egalitarian love among fellow human beings as brothers and sisters or children of the same Great-Father-Mother.[17] In order to explain and implement this commandment, Han employed the concept of "one body of the ten thousand things" to affirm a compassionate, altruistic, or benevolent attitude toward all human beings—especially the poor, who might be neither our relatives nor our friends or neighbors—without neglecting the differences in terms of one's emotional attachment and moral responsibility toward those who are nearer as different from those afar.[18]

Because Sun and his students studied the book against the context of the historical interaction between the Catholic and Confucian traditions and focused on the exegetical details of the text, the significance of the book and its relevant ideas have not been properly explored against the contemporary global context. However, as I would like to suggest, other than the possible implication of the Great-Father-Mother as a nonsexist title for God for feminist theology, the concepts of Great-Father-Mother and "one body of ten thousand things" are quite relevant to contemporary discussions on ecological theology, especially if one understands that as the Great-Father-Mother, God is the parent or creator of both human and nonhuman beings. These concepts, especially the latter, play important roles in one of the recent attempts to develop ecological theology in dialogue with Confucianism.[19] This approach to ecological theology attempts to advocate for a passionate rather than a rationalistic or even managerial attitude toward nature, and to develop a middle path between the extremes of anthropocentrism and eco-centrism.[20] This attempt has attracted the attention of scholars not only from the Chinese-speaking world[21] but also those from Germany.[22]

These are merely a few examples to demonstrate to the students that Chinese cultural resources may include useful materials for the articulation of Christian theology, which may be meaningful not only to Chinese Christian theology but also to Christian theology in another cultural context. Even those ideas or resources rejected by prominent Western missionaries in the past can be meaningful or useful, and deserve to be further explored and retrieved in the contemporary global context. This may imply that the theological judgments made by Western missionaries or theologians are not necessarily better than those made by the Chinese Christians, whose attempts to integrate Chinese culture with Christian theology demonstrate vividly that Christian theology can be done in a Chinese, instead of Western, style. As their attempts may be meaningful transnationally and contribute to the globalization of Christian theology, their contributions can be understood also in terms of globalization or, better, glocalization, instead of merely in terms of indigenization, contextualization, or localization. It is thus misleading to posit a sharp demarcation between the local and the global, or identify Western with global or superior, and Chinese with local or inferior.

At the moment, though there are not so many students exploring particularly the theological significance of the concept of Great-Father-Mother, there are many postgraduate students studying Chinese Catholic writings. Some of these studies focus on the interaction between Chinese culture and Christianity, as well as the formation of the Chinese Christian identity. They appreciate how Chinese Christians made use of their cultural heritage to enrich the Christian tradition by offering their

Chinese interpretations of the Bible, Christian doctrines, and Christian ethics rather than querying whether these Chinese interpretations were heretical or not.[23] It is rather obvious that the strategy of studying these Chinese Christian texts can be very effective in helping Chinese students to cultivate their Chinese Christian identity and to enhance their awareness of the cross-cultural, transnational, or global character of Christianity.

Resources and Strategies Based on Contemporary Christian Publications

After pointing out possible resources or materials, the next issue to be addressed is the method. The third group of teaching resources I employ consists of mainly contemporary publications in Chinese. The intent is to introduce and demonstrate the approach of comparative theology, which is one of the possible ways of doing theology in a global context, and to overcome the dominance of Western theology and the bias of privileging Western theological tradition. My strategy is to refer to the relevant pioneering works published in Chinese and to demonstrate this method through conducting experiments in comparative theology by contemporary Chinese theologians, including myself.

In order to introduce the basic ideas or methods of comparative theology to the Chinese-speaking world, I edited a special issue for a theological journal published in Chinese.[24] In that special issue, I advocated that comparative theology as an approach to doing Christian theology is particularly suitable for Chinese Christian theology for at least two major reasons. First, in comparison with the confessional or denominational theological approach prevalent in Western theology, this comparative approach is more suitable for teaching theology in the universities in Mainland China. This is because in Mainland China, theology is identified as a practical training for Christian ministers. It is allowed to be taught at the theological seminaries run by the official church in China but not at the universities that are under the Communist government's control. The universities are allowed to teach religious studies as an "objective" or "critical" (in the sense of antireligious rather than self-critical) academic discipline, but not any "confessional" theology presupposing or advocating the validity of Christianity. Though theology cannot be formally offered at a university setting, certain "theological" elements can creep into the courses with certain philosophical, historical, and/or cultural outlooks, such as philosophy of religion, history of

Christian thought, and Christianity and Western culture. Since the religious and philosophical traditions in China are intertwined, the comparative studies of, say, Christian and Buddhist ideas can be taught in the name of, say, comparative philosophy (of religion) or comparative ethics, and not necessarily comparative religion. Second, the comparative approach can make use of the Chinese cultural or religious resources and help Chinese theologians to make contributions to the global development of Christian theology.[25]

In line with the Confucian educational principle "teaching through one's own body (example) is more important than teaching through one's own words (precepts)," I conducted several thought experiments in comparative theology and published them as a book.[26] The book attempts to rethink and articulate some basic theological issues through comparison with Mahayana Buddhism. The issues discussed include Christology, the doctrine of the Trinity, the doctrines of sin and humanity, soteriology, eschatology, revelation, theological language, and the theological diversity among the scriptures.[27] Instead of constructing a coherent theological system, the book aims to demonstrate concretely how the approach of comparative theology can be practiced in the Chinese context and how Mahayana Buddhism can provide useful resources for the articulation of Sino-Christian theology or Christian theology with Chinese characteristics.

The book mentions that though there are advocates of Mahayana Christian theology in the English-speaking world, it is by no means new to Chinese Christian theology, for there have been some advocates of Mahayana Christian theology in China.[28] For example, Zhang Chunyi (1871–1955), who had been trained as a scholar of Chinese classics, attempted to explain and defend the Christian doctrines in Buddhist terms after his conversion to Christianity. He continued to interpret Christian theology with a Mahayana Buddhist framework, but in a much more critical way after his later conversion to Buddhism and change, in a sense, from a Buddhist-Christian to a Christian-Buddhist. Even when Zhang remained primarily a Christian, he was very critical of the kind of Christianity preached by Western missionaries. He argued that this was not the true Christianity Jesus Christ attempted to promulgate. Since most of Jesus' first disciples failed to understand this true Christianity, not all the books in the Bible are of equal value. Zhang thus pioneered the practice of applying the Chinese Buddhist method of doctrinal classification (*pan jiao*)[29] to the study of the Bible. Following this method, he evaluated and ranked different books in the Bible according to their different levels of theological or spiritual maturity. Similar practices can be found in the Christian tradition,[30] but the criteria employed by Zhang were Buddhist rather than Christian. He took particularly the Mahayana doctrine of Buddha-nature as the most important criterion. He ranked various books of the Bible according to whether and how far they can express this doctrine, which affirms that the Buddha-nature is the divine nature innate to human beings and also identical with the human nature shared by all human beings.[31] A corollary of this is Zhang's pneumatology that the Holy Spirit abides always in human beings and is basically identical with the human spirit. It is thus inaccurate or even wrong to talk about the "comes and goes" of the Holy Spirit.[32]

It is noteworthy that Chinese and Western scholars may approach Mahayana Christian theology in different ways. In fact, there have been debates in the Chinese- and English-speaking worlds concerning Mahayana Christology, and the foci of the debates are significantly different.[33] This might be partially due to the fact that scholars in the English-speaking world may make more references to the Indian and/or Tibetan schools of Mahayana Buddhism in their discussion concerning Mahayana Christology, whereas the Chinese scholars prefer to interpret Christology with the framework provided by some Chinese schools of Mahayana Buddhism. Whereas the former may focus more on how the Mahayana Buddhist framework may enrich the Western theological tradition, the Chinese scholars may pay more attention to its relevance to the Chinese context. This seems to suggest that the same theological idea, originating in a particular local context, can be meaningful in a transnational context, though the reception may be different in different cultural contexts. Anyway, suffice it to show that comparative theology can be a method through which Chinese Christian theology can make its contribution to the global developments of Christian theology.[34]

In fact, a similar comparative approach can be adopted in some other areas of theological studies. For example, in an article I criticize the Western-centric bias in many of the textbooks in philosophy of religion in the English-speaking world. Although most of them are titled "philosophy of religion," in terms of actual content they are merely philosophy of the Christian or Western religion. This is because the philosophical issues addressed in these books are almost exclusively derived from Christianity or monotheism, while issues particular to other religious traditions are neglected. As there is a rising trend of development in philosophy of religion attempting to adopt a "global," "cross-cultural," or "comparative" approach, Chinese scholars, with their bilingual and bicultural backgrounds, may be better equipped for this approach to philosophy of religion and should take this opportunity to make more significant contributions to this field.[35] In order to highlight that this approach is by no means new to Chinese academia, I mention the pioneering work of Xie Fuya (1892–1991), whose *Philosophy of Religion* (*Zongjiao zhexue*), published in Chinese in 1939, already adopted a global or cross-cultural approach, long before many of the philosophers of religion in the English-speaking world began practicing it.[36]

Xie's book consists of five chapters. It starts with an introduction to philosophy of religion, covering the issues concerning the definition and task of philosophy of religion, the history of philosophy of religion as an academic discipline, and methodology, which highlights the "empirical" approach and the important roles of history of religions and psychology of religion. In line with these emphases, the second chapter deals with the origins and evolutions of religions in three parts. The first part introduces the theories concerning the origins of religion and outlines the basic features of primitive religions. The second part presents Buddhism, Confucianism, and Christianity as examples of what Xie calls "rational religions" (*lixing zongjiao*), and the third part spells out the principles of the developments of religions illustrated by the historical developments of these three religions, including how these three rational religions evolved from primitive religions; how they take human affairs instead of nature as the starting point, shifting their emphases from collectivity to individuality; and so on. The third chapter turns to psychology of religion and focuses on the religious consciousness and related issues such as prayer and religious experience, especially mysticism. It addresses the traditional issues of philosophy of religion (e.g., concept of God, problem of evil, human destiny, etc.) in the fourth chapter on religion and metaphysical questions. In the concluding chapter, Xie attempts to respond to the criticisms of religion in general and Christianity in particular. The book aims to clarify the misunderstanding of religion presupposed by these criticisms through rectifying the mistranslation of the term "religion" and aims to affirm the positive value and meaning of religion. It is rather obvious that the book was occasioned by the anti-Christian and antireligious movements in China during the 1920s. In this sense, it was very local and belonged to the past. However,

Xie's comparative approach to philosophy of religion with particular emphasis on interdisciplinary study finds its echo in the vision for the future of philosophy of religion articulated by some of the philosophers in the twenty-first century.[37]

Similar to the strategy employed in teaching students the method of comparative theology, I also show the students my own experiments in cross-cultural philosophy of religion, which were actually based on my term papers for an undergraduate course taken in the mid-1980s.[38] Likewise, the comparative approach can be used in the study of scriptures. Given the long Chinese tradition of exegesis or the study of scriptures, the prominent role scriptures played in the encounter between Christianity and Chinese culture, and the recent attempts in cross-textual interpretation by some Chinese scholars such as Archie C. C. Lee,[39] comparative scripture will be a promising field of study for Chinese academics.

Other than the comparative studies between biblical and Chinese classical texts,[40] there are also studies concerning how Chinese Christians in the past interpreted the Bible in comparison with, say, Confucian classics. For example, scholars have studied how the Lord's Prayer and the Decalogue were interpreted or appropriated by Chinese Christians with Confucian cultural background.[41] It is noteworthy that a new journal titled *Journal of Comparative Scripture* has been jointly launched by the Institute of Comparative Scripture and Inter-religious Dialogue, Minzu University of China (Beijing), and the Institute of Sino-Christian Studies (Hong Kong), with "Comparative Scripture and Late-Ming China" as the main theme for its inaugural issue in 2013. The bilingualism of the journal—together with its broad scope, which crosses the boundaries between Western and Eastern (particularly Chinese) religious and/or cultural traditions, rather than being restricted to the comparison of the scriptures among the three Abrahamic or monotheistic religions—may signify that comparative scripture can become an important area in which Chinese scholars may make significant contributions globally. Admittedly, biblical studies in China remains relatively underdeveloped. However, the potential for making distinctive contributions globally should not be ignored or underestimated.[42]

It is rather obvious that the method of comparative theology requires solid training in the religious traditions to be compared. It is thus more appropriate to doctoral-level work than undergraduate studies, though many doctoral students may be specializing in a particular religious tradition and may not be equally knowledgeable of another religion. However, most of the students are capable of reading classical Chinese, though the levels of proficiency may be quite different. Some might have certain basic understandings of Chinese religious and/or philosophical traditions—either studying them at undergraduate level and/or being part of their cultural or educational background. So, it is not too difficult for them to pick up this comparative method or approach to theology. Even if they do not or cannot conduct comparative studies individually, based on their specializations, they can contribute to the group discussion when research projects related to comparative theology are presented in the classroom, such as at graduate seminars for doctoral students specializing in various subareas of religious studies or theology.

Concluding Remarks

Through these local resources and the related strategies, I attempt to help students to become aware of the subtle yet influential Western bias that they might have inherited knowingly or unknowingly, and to encourage or even empower them to take active participation in the global development of Christian theology through demonstrating possible methods to them as well as showing them the resources at their disposal.

Of course, the aforementioned resources and methods are by no means exhaustive. In fact, there are some recent impressive attempts at exploring Chinese Christian theology in the global context.[43] There may be many other methods and/or resources in Chinese or other contexts deserving to be further explored and disseminated.

✦ 7 ✦

Pedagogy for Being Human in Global Comparison

DWIGHT N. HOPKINS

For one year I taught theology to graduate and undergraduate students in Seoul, Korea. In addition to my "Black Theology: 1st Generation," "Black Theology: 2nd Generation," and "Theology and Cultural Studies" classes, perhaps the most globally comparative pedagogical challenge evolved in my "Being Human" course. The students hailed from Korea, Ghana, Thailand, Pakistan, China, and the United States. After a long semester of my lectures and classroom conversations, I posed to the students a simple question: In your home context, what does it mean to be human? The Korean students mentioned food; the Thai students indicated knowing which of the three hand positions one uses when greeting another person; the Chinese student pointed to family; the Ghanaian student embraced "the ancestors"; the Pakistani student asserted "no daily violence"; and the two students from the United States (both black Americans) affirmed "individual rights." During this same period, I was one of the initiators and an international coordinator of a fourteen-country network (defined by South Africa, Botswana, Zimbabwe, Ghana, Hawaii, Fiji, Japan, Australia, India, England, Cuba, Brazil, Jamaica, and the United States). The network identified the creation of new knowledge by way of transnational pedagogy as one of its stated goals.[1]

Presuppositions to Pedagogy

These two effervescent undertakings of intellectual engagement raise this query: How does an educator teach the idea of being human among different nations situated in the same classroom?[2] My pedagogical fluidity presupposes that (1) all knowledge first arises from specific cultures, (2) human communities in those cultures define the theological anthropology, and (3) consequently, theological anthropology (being human) lacks a universal essence or global applicability from the top down.[3] Such a valuing of particularity, respect for local cultures, and accenting of the human role in theological anthropology nurtures a universal spirituality of invitation, graciousness, humility, and listening in the classroom setting. When it comes to global experiences of the transcendent and human relationships found among students in the classroom, all stand on equal ground. So the professor engenders a double encouragement. Each student recognizes the facticity and truth of his/her own being human or theological anthropology from his/her home country, and each student recognizes the surface validity of other foreign students' claims to authentic human being. It is a pedagogy of self in conversational engagement with many foreign neighbors bringing to the market of idea exchanges the fruit of their own cultures.

Culture

Indeed, culture cultivates resurfacing and enactment of memory. Such a capacious definition can teach the educator how to peel back the layers in the dynamic of collective culture.[4] Memory circumscribes collective recollection—for example, family, neighborhood, region, country, and/or hemisphere—of all that human being has produced and reproduced. One obvious memory is the theological, which entails the dialectic or harmony and balance among multiple experiences between the penultimate and the ultimate, respectively the next to last and last telos established by human being. In the effort to go beyond the boundaries of penultimate and ultimate in the human past of production and reproduction, human being confronts an inability to decipher all things outside of itself. Consequently, the reasoning about or intuition of lack in self-storied history can open being human to a possibility of a larger narrative in being human's resurfacing of and enactment of memory. In other words, human existence contains an impulse to supersede its own past recollections. In the impulse, one can discern an overflow out of bygone eras. Yes, that which human being can touch, see, feel, taste, and smell points to culture. But, concomitantly, a larger, overarching, and invisible energy (i.e., opened up by the inability and the lack) agitating the life of the cosmos, ecology, plants, animals, and the laws of nature breathes vigor into the material sensory operations evident in all of creation. This energy is synonymous with the larger narrative.

Moreover, remembering of human production and reproduction of all that being human entails differentiates among student legacies sitting in the classroom setting. A variety of international students originate from intergenerational, interconnected resurfacing. For instance, some students from around the world can literally trace blood ties for one thousand years. More specifically, one can find this manifestation in written family records passed down to subsequent offspring.[5] On a more limited-time microlevel, an individual can resurface the direct memory of his/her personal experiences from family and broader communal relations. In a classroom of global students, one can surmise personal historical memory beginning roughly between ages five and eight. However, if bad or good trauma impacts a child at a much younger age, that polyvalent trauma, due to the severity of its indelible consequences, has the potential to brand the spirituality and physicality of the adult human in such a way that he/she can resurface memory from age two. To resurface culture points to the conscious (i.e., specific goal-setting turn) and unconscious (i.e., inevitable force of habit reflex) dynamic of historical regurgitation of the intentional and unexpected dimensions of being human.

But culture is more than resurfacing. It is enactment as well. Thus it is the agential spontaneity and pioneering subjectivity of future production and reproduction derived from human being's visioning. In this sense, therefore, culture brings together the fuel of resurfacing the past with enacting the already done into the present for realizing the new of the future. To a large degree, parts of culture as human resurfacing and enactment flow out of the flexible impact of nature, time, and space. Such three-dimensional realities delimit and unbound the human being's culture. Culture resurfaces how being human crawls out of longitudinal exigencies. And culture is pregnant with the possibilities of human being's enactments.

Theological Anthropology

Regarding theological anthropology, my pedagogical approach leans toward the following explication. "Theological" carries with it a connotation of some transcendence beyond one individual human being. "Theological" by definition lives an international resonance. It entails Greek words at its root—*theos* and *logos*—evidencing Greek origins. Then Jewish Christians (Paul being part of this meaning expansion) adopted and thought together the Greek and the Jewish traditions of concepts and belief about Gods. "Theological" migrated from Northeast Africa and West Asia to Europe,[6] where "theological" (a Greek and Jewish fashioning) became absorbed in disparate European tribal and city wisdoms. Now "theological" drifted into various streams of local humanistic and spiritual currents. As European missionaries spread an already multinational, layered definition of "theological" to parts of the globe, "theological" recruited and mobilized and was recruited and mobilized by local primordial transcendent orientations toward the world. "Theological" is traditionally and historically multinational (and multicultural) and it forged further multinationality when it went out to recruit others, into its own meaning-making, transcendence argumentation.

The anthropology aspect of theological anthropology connects *anthropos* with *logos* and, likewise, embodies multinationality along a similar traditional and historical trajectory. Furthermore, if "theological" points to the transcendence beyond one individual human being, then anthropology delimits the fact of human beings creating stories about transcendence beyond the individual self. Stories of intergenerational family journeys, specifically how a people collectively came to terms with maintaining the relation between wealth (i.e., earth, air, and water) and family structures (i.e., the intraduties of production and reproduction of the family),[7] make up the basis for narrative traditions about spiritualities, self-cultivation practices, and religions through times and spaces.

Comparative Method

Moreover, a pedagogical technique of "cultures-specificity-human agency" encourages students to identify their own realities by consistently and consciously utilizing a comparative method. For instance, whatever particular claim a student makes, he/she has to give his/her viewpoint in relation to a different culture represented in the class. And each student is asked to pursue this comparative method by examining the comparisons on different levels of being human—that is, on the family level, spirituality or religion level, indigenous tradition (space and time) level, and economic level. At the end of the class, each student is asked what "being human" means in his/her particular country in the present dynamics.

Such a comparative approach applies directly to my own pedagogical definition of theological anthropology. In the classroom, I begin the conversational journey deploying theological anthropology and being human as synonymous instructional realities. Students from different nations are invited to challenge this stance from their own literate textual references and common sense wisdom experiences. As professor, I maintain my position of corresponding relationally between theological anthropology and being human. Students have to struggle for and defend their own denotations and connotations (that is to say, whether they agree with my pedagogy equating the two or not). To study being human in a multinational classroom calls on the professor and students to act out the definition of being human in the actual pedagogy. Restated, students and professor embody a fundamental trajectory in theological anthropology—to debate and defend one's view of theological anthropology with compelling evidence in a public arena saturated with the instructive excess of multicultures.

Pedagogy's Content

Within the comparative transnational classroom, pedagogy consists of conversation,[8] questioning,[9] and opening up traditions to new perspectives.[10]

Lectures and assigned texts initiate and are the bases of the conversation. Through these two media, professors assume certain traditions are important for the conversation. These legacies—history of ideas, transcendent transferred human experiences—serve as launching pad and loose framework for the ensuing conversations. Thus, on the one hand, conversation is not circumscribed by the dogmatic display of the professor's ego. On the other, neither is it simply students telling their personal stories. It is, again, the conscious and meticulous assertion of certain crucial traditions relative to the class subject matter. In this regard, conversation hovers around and breathes in traditions as intellectual legacies yielding provocative insight for today. The lectures and assigned texts speak to this.

In global pedagogy, the professor's lectures need to be comparative. A deep grasp of his/her cultural foundation and some appreciation of other cultural contours enable the lectures to be imbued with a sense of comparative legacy engagement. To have a life-giving, enriched, and truly enjoyable international conversation within the pedagogical moment and process mandates the professor be cognizant of and an authority on his/her own cultural gifts to the present. International pedagogy, by definition, does not presuppose, at the beginning, that students grasp or nuance cultured conversations different from their family of origins. At the end of the class conversational journey, we can expect this way of being in the world. The professor, to produce effective lectures welcoming the challenges from global conversation partners (which, indeed, signify the roles of students from different countries), must surface openly the historical instantiations of the cultural proclivities he/she brings to the table. Only with self-cultural legacy awareness can the lectures provide a basis for comparative conversation. Thus, the professor's lectures act as one plumb line to engender critical discovery and crucial disagreement. This models for the students how to offer their own family of origin insights. It is a gracious invitation for us to talk. In addition to self-asserted culture, the professor's presentations need to include comparative dialogue. For example, it enhances the lectures if the professor can compare his/her own culture with the cultural tradition of another people. One need not be an absolute authority on another culture to facilitate the give-and-take of classroom energy. However, it does help immensely to comprehend dimensions of one or two diverse cultural legacies as comparative paradigms.

In addition to the lectures, assigned books serve as a second plumb line, nurturing and nudging the global comparative conversation in the class. If we announce the necessity of worldwide discourse connection, the assigned bibliography can motor us toward succeeding in that proclamation. In actuality, mandatory readings serve as one easy way of honoring the pedagogy of comparative transnational exigencies. Specifically, as the larger subject matter unfolds within its constituent parts, each subset of the syllabus indicates perspectives from books emerging from different regions of the world (specifically, Africa, Asia, the Caribbean, Europe [inclusive of all cultures in Europe], Latin America, North America [inclusive of all North American cultures], and the Pacific Islands). The comparative bibliography, if properly handled, can avoid the missionary pedagogue; that is to say, the West (i.e., the United States and Western Europe) designates other world peoples on the syllabus in order to, ultimately, sublimate them into a Western European way of being and thinking—the dominant episteme of the U.S. academy loving and embodying this (conscious or unconscious) subterranean missionary pedagogy.[11]

Assigned and recommended books, if truly regionally representative, moreover, can avoid the proclivity and the pressure for the (in particular, North American and Western European) professor to self-proclaim authority over and authenticity about the Rest—the non-West. If patiently done well, the syllabus bibliography can serve as preparation, as tools, as living testimony to collaborative pedagogy framed within the overall syllabus, inclusive of assigned readings, and energized by the professor's lectures. In addition, the assigned and recommended readings on the syllabus need to facilitate comparative and interdisciplinary approaches to pedagogy. Because teaching being human globally, by definition, denotes multinational investigation of the subject matter, the syllabus, then, has to reveal texts from different countries. But just as important is an interdisciplinary representation of texts in the syllabus. Theologically Christian doctrines of being human will be present. However, one must be intentional in one's definition of being human. A global pedagogy, even if biased toward Christianity, needs to realize that Christians are not the majority of the 7.2 billion people of the world population. Thus being human in the world presents multiple ways of being human, inclusive of Christian dogma as discipline as well as a variety of human theories as disciplines. We realize therefore in teaching method that human being denotes world diversity across spiritualities, self-cultivation practices, and religions.

We recognize, moreover, in teaching method (that is to say, in lectures and syllabi), human being fluctuates and differentiates even among self-professing Christian adherents, as Christianity is believed and practiced in different nations represented in the classroom. For most Western professors, the idea that there is one Christianity in the world underscores, at least, two possible myopias. Either that American or Western European professor has never had classes packed with students from the majority of the world or he, as a purported academic seeking new knowledge, has never travelled around the world. In short, the notion of a pedagogy of the one Christian thought, belief, or practice regarding being human is a phantasm.

And so, one realizes, in pedagogical conversations, that Christian expressions of being human globally include syncretistic expressions of indigeneity and missionized Christianity.[12] This should not be a startling fact. Indeed, even within the United States, the different Christianities manifest a syncretism between missionized Christianity, originally from Western Europe, and the indigenous spiritualities and cultures of those who were missionized in the United States. Similarly, as Christianity spread from the early church to different parts of Europe, this missionary Christianity itself took on and incorporated local indigenous European cultures into the Christian missionary arrivals.[13]

The New Testament Paul serves as Exhibit A. The Christianity that Paul mixes together is his creation of at least two ingredients. The first part juxtaposes his interpretation of Jesus' stories with Greek culture, which is the second aspect. The result of this two-dimensional recipe is Paul's faith in and experience of Christianity. In particular, witness the prologue of John (1:1): "In the beginning was the word [Christian culture]" who is the logos [Greek culture]. Similar to John, for Paul the word is Jesus, the highest principle of the reality in the world he knew around the Mediterranean Sea. In order to convert or recruit part of the Greek world, he had to find the Greek idea for the highest principle in Greek culture. For the Greeks, the highest principle was "logos": reason. So Paul equated—intentionally syncretized—Jesus, a Jew, with reason from Greek culture. Paul's Christianity is the ultimate syncretism for people who call themselves Christian. Paul is syncretistic in his interpretation of Jesus' narratives and compromising in his inclusion of non-Christian sources. We have to remember that Paul never met Jesus.

In other words, even before Europe sent missionaries to other parts of the world to recruit other people, European Christianities were themselves paradigmatic expressions of syncretism termed orthodoxy. Hence, when teaching being human, with a heavy or implied Christian intent or affect, internationally, the teaching effectiveness increases when the professor foregrounds the reality of disparate (religious, spiritual, and self-cultivation) means of being human. In a word, the professor should state up front that Christianity, itself, is a syncretistic way of being in the world; and in the world there are many, many ways of being human. This theoretical analysis, at the beginning of the class, can free up the recesses of critical thinking deep within the students' brains. The students can, if facilitated properly, claim the polyvalent voices of their local religious, spiritual, and self-cultivation stories (derived from their own familial and communal traditions) without pausing to self-edit themselves in class for fear of being positively orthodox or negatively syncretic on the being human question.

Questioning

Indeed, in addition to a complex dimensional *conversation*, global classroom pedagogy entails perpetual and unencumbered *questioning* relative to lectures, assigned texts, and scholarly concepts broached during discussion periods. Though one has to be sensitive to avoid personal ad hominem attacks (especially with students from around the world where language nuance, body rhythm, and ritual themselves can define what it means to be human), good pedagogy fosters, at times, very intense pointed questioning. Fundamentally, questioning realizes at least three purposes: (1) to teach students (i.e., give them permission) not to accept anything as given, (2) to challenge students to defend the fundamentals and presuppositions of their arguments, and (3) to remind both questioner/challenger and responder/defender to always make clear the local cultural context of the challenge and the defense. Questioning surfaces from and situates itself in the local cultural realities of students debating their argumentative claims among the whole class as the professor makes sure to broaden the open-ended process of queries.

Fostering a sense of the communal value of not accepting anything "as is" requires patience on the part of the professor due to the transnational makeup of the classroom. Naturally and understandably so, students from diverse nations assume that each pedagogical participant acts as a unique authority and lives his/her own knowledge and location of wisdom as an expert. As a corollary, it might, at first, appear rude to not embrace the opinions of classroom colleagues from another international region. However, the professor encourages probing beyond the given as profound compassion for the ideas of different global students. The professor constructs a pedagogical and theological atmosphere where students can deconstruct their own initial shields of false politeness. Students eventually learn to love the wisdom, theories, and thought systems of others to such a degree that they are willing to take them so seriously and listen so carefully that they will not automatically agree with all initial arguments. All nations are made of the same brilliant and fallible human beings. And seeing the human being in each classroom neighbor suggests a visual perspective, valuing recognition of the weight of another human being's verbal contribution to dialogue and debate. Therefore perspectival recognition is a multicultural philosophy, a groomed-daily habit of existing open to challenges from and deploying challenges toward foreigners seated next to each other.

Such compassion and worldview couple with the notion of interrogating presuppositions and fundamentals. To show sympathy for and recognition of the other human's individual creativity to think aloud as a way to vivify communal processing demands a teaching atmosphere of dissecting fundamentals and presuppositions all the way around. What are the assumed common sense wisdoms and taken-for-granted reflexes breathed like natural air in the home countries of the students?

Each student has to learn that epistemologies emerge from materialities embedded deep within each nation's personality. Fruitful scholarly class adventures begin when student speakers confront one another's fundamentals (that is to say, the tangible substructure of ideas). For instance, a student speaker might assume an immense amount of human diversity and opposite thinking and practice when he/she is arguing among other citizens at home in his/her own country. However, in a transnational classroom, other international students can see how what might appear as opposite views of citizens in one country are, in fact, a manifestation of what truly defines the national common character of all the citizens in that same country.

Citizens of the United States, as an example, pride themselves for fighting over racial uniqueness and asymmetrical power relations domestically. But in a class of nations, even black American students can be very, very *American*, especially in the revelation of that religious-like American presupposition of the fundamental American God of individual rights. It can be a sacred preoccupation, particularly when U.S. citizens become insensitive to host countries granting these Americans, of all colors, the kind privilege of a visa for entrance. At home, many Americans dispute race and variegated power positioning; yet, all Americans have a tendency to fight for their individual rights even though a host country has done them a favor by granting them a visa, which calls for Americans to abide by the local laws and customs of the host country. Hence, in this classroom of multinational comparison, American students can discover the basic value of what it means to be a human being from the United States when probed by other foreign students' foundational insights. In particular, other global classroom neighbors can aid the clarification of an American being human by assisting the students from the United States in distinguishing between a deleterious mode of thought and life defined as individual rights from another American gift designated as individuality—the inherent sacredness of individuality serving the collective.

In a word, querying presuppositions inevitably shines the pedagogical spotlight on the cultural contexts of both the student challenger and the student defender of arguments. Students in divergent nations might relish a certain type of claim about wealth, structure, time, body space, or family duties. Culture determines decisively these notions. Take Christianity. In a multinational classroom, pedagogy, even pedagogy about purported universal Christian dogmatics and ritual, hinges on the culture surrounding dogma and doing. If students could learn about each other's supposedly universal Christian talk and walk by visiting each other's nations, they would, for the most part, witness unique human productions and reproductions from long cultural traditions determining the acceptance and practice of Christian orthodoxy and ortho-practice. Human culture, therefore, vivifies thought, duty, and feeling. It classifies and colors the Christian deity. And it manages and filters being human.

Traditions

Both *conversation* and *questioning* inspire the multinational classroom to a pedagogy of opening up *traditions* to new perspectives.[14] New knowledge for the world's common good can burst forth from interrogating, in a global comparative sense, legacies handed down through centuries and millennia. It is this comparative inter-nation dialogue that facilitates a student who is foreign to another student's reality to see something new in an ancient memory. On the one hand, a student upholds a sense of insight in his/her own tradition. On the other hand, the student foreign to this intergenerational path can bring fresh eyes to bear. Hopefully, mutual queries about divergent histories will lead each student to appreciate more profoundly traditional aspects making sense out of times gone by, the instructions of the moment, and the potential of journeying into the future. It can, likewise, instruct each student to walk some critical distance away from less meaningful moments in the genealogy of ideas of his/her tradition.

For instance, various countries accent the family structure and familial duties as premier to being a civilized human gathering. In contrast, other nations accentuate each family member's highest allegiance to his/her own individual voice to pursue his/her own individual preconceptions of being human. In a similar fashion, different nations concoct notions of wealth ownership; some privilege private accumulation; others prioritize collective participation. Both perspectives flow from and are implicated in enduring subterranean forces of habit where human cultures craft the contours of human being. Adherents of both perspectives think something good lives within his/her own country's tradition. Classroom pedagogy then teaches these students to be gracious enough to accept the warm invitation from other foreign students to compare and contrast, thereby deriving new interpretations out of the past. Basically, opening up ancient periods from teaching students to speak about and hear each other's traditions emerges into new, collective, life-enhancing ways of being in the world.

Moreover, opening up traditions can foster the potential of world peace and material and spiritual collaboration. As foreign students unravel on a conscious level the long histories of divergent traditions, understanding can ensue as an ultimate pedagogical revelation. In my classroom experiment referenced at the start of this chapter, a recurring query pressed for clarity about why so much of the West clings to Christianity. Actually, Christianity served at points, and especially during the Middle Ages, as glue and transmission of Western civilization when forms of state power and attendant structures weakened. Likewise, Western Christian thinkers have been one medium of preserving Western culture.[15] In addition, many people of color in the United States reappropriated certain styles of imperialistic introductions of Christianity in their communities to create their own syncretized Christianity, so that these communities of color then could make meaning out of materiality and self-apply their new-forged Christianity as a balm for psychological wholeness.[16] Thus, the passed-down stories of Christianity in the West (among the so-called normative narrative line in the dominant's eyes and among many people of color, too often the underside collateral damage of these "mainstream" narratives) enabled various sectors of the West to maintain civilization and life in the face of death.

Likewise, the students' comparative pedagogy of digging into the taken-for-granted inheritance in other global regions sitting in the classroom can compare and contrast their historical journeys that lead directly to who they are and their family structures and manipulations of wealth, three components, among others, of being human in the micro one-to-one dimension and in the macro political-economy dimension. The increased understanding of where neighbors come from hopefully can engender peace and prosperity for all countries. This pedagogy has a profound spiritual valence. Legacy denotes the transcendent transference of things greater than the individual self; thus it is spiritual because it lives on intergenerationally for years into the future. Perhaps this long view of history relative to family and wealth constitutes a major potential for mutual comprehension among the multination classroom of foreign neighbors. I would argue family-wealth perspectives undergird divergent local spiritualities, self-cultivation practices, and religions.

For example, even in the Christian narrative, a disproportionate number of Jesus' stories (in the memory of Matthew, Mark, Luke, and

John) refer to wealth and, one could add, to the notion of the family's relation or lack of relation to wealth.[17] Relatedly, from the Christian appropriation of the Hebrew legacy, the Hebrew Bible unfolds as Yahweh promises, molds, and struggles with family relations of the ancient Hebrew people (from Abraham to the thirteen tribes) while they deliberate over wealth accumulation. Yahweh promises Abraham an abundant family offspring gifted with prosperity. Later Yahweh removes the ancient Jewish families as material wealth from Egyptian material slavery. Then, in the book of Numbers, Yahweh promises the accumulated remnant of families posed at the edge of the wilderness a land of wealth, flowing with material milk and honey. By unwrapping this memory of human imaginations, one can better appreciate why today's adherents of these past creative narratives do what they do now.

So too, by divulging each foreign student's passed-down written and oral talk intergenerationally, other students have the possibility of grasping why students (representative of their diverse countries) and their respective nations think, believe, and do "as they are"—that is to say, the intertwined necessity of legacy and being human. Opening up traditions to new perspectives can circulate exchanges of knowledge toward understanding, toward friendship, toward peace.

Music and Language in Pedagogy of Being Human

In addition to the formal lectures, syllabi, and crucial debate among students, discussions about music and language among foreign neighbors in the classroom present an invigorating challenge of eventual mutual trust and understanding. Furthermore, oftentimes music and language concerns are linked to ultimate-meaning matters such as spiritualities, self-cultivation practices, and religions.

Teaching the community-building effects of music offers several approaches. A professor can decide on or solicit one song known across the world and have the students construe the substance and impact of the chosen piece in their local context. Here too music differentiates between explicit religious lyrics and "so-called" secular tunes, though in the porous and malleable walls of division there hardly stands an impenetrable partition. In either case, a common tune provides the basis for exploring being human. With the shared song, each country's representative can disclose what the lyrics mean in his/her interpretive perspective. Specifically, each elaborates on the implications for being human. On the one hand, everyone is familiar with and knows the words to one global song. Hence, the class has a provision for collective knowledge. On the other, the sparkles and fusion of new knowledge emerge in the mix of multiple, oftentimes competing, claims to significance from particularity. Even with a given transnational song, each country nuances its implications for being human differently. At the same time, each context brands the global song with each local cultural personality when local artists sing the song with their own cultural presuppositions. The being human of the local morphs the globalness of the song into a hybrid local-global humanity. What import for human being is found in the transnational and the particularity when a Korean student from a Confucian background enjoys black American soul or gangster rap music? How do the Negro spirituals facilitate the new understanding of being human when embraced and sung by citizens of the former Communist Union of Soviet Socialist Republics?[18]

Additional collaborative pedagogical awareness appears when students present songs from their native nations. The sheer novelty and strangeness of each song to other classroom neighbors can yield a rewarding result. The student describing his/her artistic piece usually resorts to the human or family or spiritual heritage undergirding the song. The student often describes the ritual setting in which the song is sung or even performed. This varies from the mundane (i.e., song for walking) to the intimacies of nurturing (i.e., song for a mother to her baby) to the more micro-regularized event (i.e., song for family singing traditions) to the obligatory (i.e., song for the dead ancestors) to the more advanced complexity (i.e., song for national festivals). To share with depth, each student will respond further to this question: What is at stake in the theological anthropology of the song in the present? How has the orthodoxy and orthopraxis of the song mutated, and how has the mutation (comprised both of things held on to and of things newly introduced) impacted previous and emerging constructions of being human? At some point the student attends to both the material tangible and the spiritual transcendent. The very unfamiliarity of the tune allows for other foreign students to raise questions for clarification that the student describing his/her song had never thought to think about due to the force of habit brought on by the routine of the familiar. The growing collective energy in the room snakes throughout the class. Some students try to situate the song within their own local musicology. Others try to map and thus control the song by framing it within superficial stereotypes of the nation from which the song hailed. Whatever the case, students can begin to ask questions such as what type of people would produce such a song; what existential and theoretical purpose does it serve; how does it relate to building communities; what spiritual endurance does it portend? And what does all of this collective cacophony and communal consensus say about my own limited notion of being human or theological anthropology in a world of foreign neighbors?

Like music, language can open up new vistas for teaching being human in a multicultural and transnational classroom situation. The professor can commence the process by choosing one word, in this case, a word in English, since foreign students have often assimilated English in order to operate at a worldwide academic level.[19] Students are challenged by the professor to contemplate both the meaning of the word for them and their particular accented way of pronouncing the English word. For instance, in U.S. English, most give a hard accent on the last letter or syllable in a word. In Putonghua (i.e., Chinese Mandarin), one can pronounce lightly the ending of a phrase or a word.[20] One could speculate that two distinct students articulate the same English word differently because the diverse method of pronouncing the common term signifies two unique ways of being human on the spiritual, intergenerational, transcendent plane. Putonghua is linked to a long Confucian and Daoist legacy of what constitutes a good person. The Confucian person is modest and learned. The Daoist master might appear as a beggar or homeless individual. A distinction divides and unites appearance and essence, surface and depth. A crouching tiger and hidden dragon warns us that behind the outward ordinary shines the hidden heroic. In usual contrast, the American human being can at first seem pushy, loud, aggressive, and demanding in a global conversation. Both law and faith undergird this apparent individualism. The very first amendment to the U.S. Constitution grants the right to shout out each person's personal voice. And the second amendment gives each citizen the right to kill someone who infringes on this individual speech. One might add to the U.S. personality a proclivity for Christianity, a major U.S. religion inextricably woven into the politics and economics of the U.S. society. Linked to the law, one, in addition, feels one has to boldly proclaim the Christian word and then aggressively travel the world recruiting people based on this word.[21]

Akin to the pedagogical exercise of music, the professor can move from articulating and interpreting a commonly known English word to positing an idea and having each foreign student speak the term in his/her own native tongue. For example, what does the word "greetings" denote for being human in disparate global classroom tongues? In U.S. English, one usually states, "How are you?" or "Good to meet you." Yet, in certain African countries, citizens recognize one another in a communal fashion. Instead of "How are you?" they embrace each other with the sayings "I see your family" or "Health to your family." The usual U.S. greeting speaks to the spiritual definition of being human. An individual, especially the Christian American person, stands before his/her maker alone, without one's father or mother. And each singular individual is accountable to this deity based on the individual's faith and witness. Certain African paradigms postulate a spirituality of collectivity with a family recognition inclusive of the unborn, dead family ancestors, and living family kin. To be human is to embody and recognize family ancestors and living family relations in each person. Or rather, one sees the individual not as an individual acting on his/her own. The communal family lives in that one individual. In actuality, a person is not one individual but someone part of a collective chain, a collective, family, spiritual personality.

Here we selected music and language. For pedagogical purposes, the professor could choose food, smells, architecture, the purpose of furniture, or a broad array of the quotidian and the extraordinary. For indeed, the being human from all countries hold this in common: all people are people who soar high and low in living out their transcendent and intergenerational connections to meaning-making in communities.

Conclusion

We began this investigation with a plumb line marker: How does an educator teach the idea of being human among different nations situated in the same classroom? Theoretical curiosity can, rightfully so, prompt such a fundamental direction. Yet, such a theoretical study, indeed any such study, will be immensely elevated when grounded in the realities of the twenty-first-century practical implications of technological, microwave-like instantaneity. Specifically, contemporary invisible communication media allow a human being to never sleep and to be present in any place in the world without physically being there. Today is what many fantasized about with Dick Tracy and his "magical" wrist watch, which was a combination of television and telephone and beyond.[22] In a sense now the world is Dick Tracy. My class of students from China, Korea, Pakistan, Thailand, Ghana, and the United States, cited at the top of this chapter, could have participated in my global pedagogy simultaneously on Skype or ooVoo. With coordination of time differentials among the various global regions present, we would all have been present in the "same" classroom at the same time without being present together physically at the same time. This is a form of transcendence of time and space. The materiality of accumulated human scientific risk taking, thinking differently, and replication of experimentation in information technology results in the nature of human being transcending the physicality of one's own individual self, transcending the exact limitations of the tangible and touchable place of the one individual. Some might cross-pollinate philosophies of being human or theological anthropology in relation to Christianity and the prohibitions of religions. Others might express a taste for the more freewheeling open-endedness of spiritualities. Still others might embrace the self-cultivation practices from thousands of years. Whatever the gardening process, we might all agree that the pedagogy of being human will probably sprout the most rewarding intellectual and existential buds of hope in a global and transnational horticulture of cultural plurality. And that ripe pedagogy could be one healthy fruit for world peace and friendship.

PART III

Praxis and Responsibility

✦ 8 ✦

Teaching to Transform

Theological Education, Global Consciousness, and the Making of Global Citizens

TERESIA HINGA

In recent years, the global community has witnessed a heightened awareness of the reality and impacts of globalization. At one level, globalization refers to an unprecedented hypermobility of people, ideas, and capital around the world, a mobility facilitated largely by tremendous technological breakthroughs in the past few decades. At another level, globalization also refers to the consequences of that mobility and the emerging acute awareness that we are not only living in "One World"[1] as Peter Singer points out but also living in it with a heightened intimacy that is reminiscent of living in a "village," albeit a global one. This sense of living in "one world" is magnified by the fact that humanity is under the sway of global capitalism, which reaches its tentacles throughout the world, especially since the collapse of communism in 1989. The robust success of global capitalism itself is linked to the tremendous technological breakthroughs that allow the mobility of goods, labor, and capital across borders with a speed and magnitude that is largely unprecedented. Such breakthroughs, according to Thomas Friedman, have flattened the world.[2]

While much that is positive has been said regarding this phenomenon, globalization has also led to many problems and issues. The global capitalist economy, for example, has simultaneously yielded, on the one hand, extreme riches and wealth, concentrated in the Global North, and, on the other, extreme poverty, concentrated in the Global South, where one-sixth of the world's population lives in utter indigence. The unprecedented technological and scientific breakthroughs have been celebrated by all for the many opportunities they offer in raising the material welfare of humans. At the same time, such breakthroughs have, in substantive ways, exacerbated human anxiety over the impact of new technologies and their potential—and often real—threat to human and other forms of life.[3] Moreover, globalization of the economy, coupled with technological breakthroughs, has also demanded and enabled people to move around the world in greater numbers and more rapidly. As a result, the scale and magnitude of transnational migration has grown to totally unprecedented levels. In turn, this has triggered in many cases nationalistic immigration policies and practices designed to control the perceived destabilizing effects of such immigration on host countries. Some of these nationalistic policies have been considered by many to be morally ambiguous at best and often morally outrageous.[4] Such complex intersecting ethical challenges of our time have made it urgent to raise awareness of these issues in order to find morally viable ways of addressing them. In particular, the various ways in which globalization has subverted rather than enhanced human and other forms of flourishing call for urgent interventions based on a critical understanding of the phenomenon of globalization, its positives, and its "discontents."

This chapter recognizes this urgent need for conscientization about the global ethical challenges of our time. It argues that such consciousness-raising should become a major dimension of education, including theological and religious education. Such awakening of consciousness is a necessary stepping-stone in the making and nurturing of global citizens who would be committed to mitigating said issues. I will refer to two pertinent cases. The first is the Jesuit education system, exemplified by Santa Clara University, particularly in its new emphases on civic engagement, multiculturalism, and attention to global matters in its Core Curriculum launched in 2009. The second is the World Council of Churches, where such experimentation with education for transformation of consciousness and the making of global citizens is already going on.

Based on insights from these two examples, I will argue for adjustment of theological and religious education so that it facilitates transformation of consciousness and the nurturing of global citizenship. I will also explore what we can learn from these two cases about the rationale, best practices, and strategies that can be adopted and scaled up to enhance the teaching of theology/religious studies so that it transforms both the students and the world.

Teaching to Transform: Some Pertinent Precedents

In making the case for "teaching to transform," I am inspired particularly by insights from the works of four scholars, including Martha C. Nussbaum in *Cultivating Humanity: A Classical Defense of Reform in Liberal Education*, and Paulo Freire, who makes the link between education and freedom in his classic *Pedagogy of the Oppressed*.[5] In addition, Sambuli Mosha argues for a reappropriation of African indigenous education systems as a stepping-stone toward diffusing the multiple crises that Africa faces.[6] bell hooks makes the case for what she calls "teaching to transgress" and calls for a pedagogy that enables educators and students to think "out of the box" in order to enhance freedom.[7]

For Nussbaum, the goal of liberal education is to "cultivate humanity" both in the students and in the world. According to Nussbaum, education promotes cultivation of humanity by nurturing three capacities in students. The first is the capacity for a critical examination of oneself and one's tradition—that is, the capacity to live what Socrates calls "an examined life."[8] This implies the ability to question all beliefs and test them for "consistency of reasoning, correctness of fact, and accuracy of judgment."[9] The nurturing of this capacity leads to the emergence of "citizens who can think for themselves rather than simply deferring to authority, who can reason together about their choices rather than just trading claims and counterclaims."[10]

The second is the capacity for cosmopolitanism, world citizenship, or global citizenship. In Nussbaum's words, those who cultivate their humanity need also the ability to see themselves, "not simply as citizens of some local region or group but also and above all, as human beings bound to all other human beings by ties of recognition and concern."[11] Education enhances cosmopolitanism by raising awareness about how humanity's "common needs and aims are differently realized in different circumstances."[12]

The third is the capacity for empathy, or what Nussbaum calls "narrative imagination." This is the capacity "to think what it might be like to be in the shoes of a person different from oneself"[13] and is not to be confused with uncritical acceptance of the views of the "other" regardless of consistency with reason or morality. She insists that this capacity is an essential first step if we are to make responsible judgments about others. As she puts it, "We do not know what we are judging until we see the meaning of an action as the person intends it."[14] For Nussbaum, then, education equips and nurtures in the students the above three capacities, which cumulatively are essential to the emergence of and sustaining of authentic humanity in the world today.

The second theorist, Paulo Freire, challenges "the banking concept of education" and proposes what he calls "pedagogy of the oppressed" as a practice of freedom through conscientization. He, too, makes the case for educational reform so that it serves to facilitate transformation of consciousness (i.e., conscientization) and to equip citizens to work for positive social change. Freire argues that traditional pedagogies are problematic because they assume students to be empty receptacles into which the teacher "deposits" knowledge that he or she thinks needs to be transferred to the students.[15] In this banking concept of education, the role of the student is minimal, since the student is reduced to "receiving, filing and storing the deposited 'knowledge.'"[16] In Freire's view, this banking approach diminishes the humanity of students, who end up being "filed away for lack of creativity, transformation and knowledge."[17] He concludes that "apart from inquiry, apart from praxis, individuals cannot be truly human."[18]

Furthermore, the banking concept is not morally neutral because it serves and supports oppressive regimes. Freire writes,

> The more students work at storing the deposits entrusted to them, the less they develop the critical consciousness which would result from their intervention in the world as transformers of that world. The more they completely accept the passive role imposed on them, the more they tend simply to adapt to the world. . . .
>
> The capability of banking education to minimize or annul students' creative power . . . serves the interest of the oppressors, who care neither to have the world revealed nor to see it transformed.[19]

Like Nussbaum, Freire proposes an alternative education that builds rather than subverts the humanity of the students. He refers to this as "education as the practice of freedom," which contrasts with education as the practice of domination. For Freire, education as the practice of freedom empowers people to perceive critically "*the way they exist* in the world *with which* and *in which* they find themselves."[20] Education as the practice of freedom allows students to "see the world not as a static reality but as a reality in process, in transformation."[21] Moreover, education as the practice of freedom "affirms men and women as beings in process of *becoming*—as unfinished, uncompleted beings in and with a likewise unfinished reality."[22] For Freire, the "unfinished character of human beings and the changing character of reality necessitate that education be an ongoing activity."[23]

In defining men and women as beings in process of becoming in an unfolding world, Freire echoes the definition of human in the context of indigenous Africa. The third theorist, Sambuli Mosha, sets out to discover how the indigenous African education systems participate in the formation of *Ubuntu*—that is, "becoming human" for Africans. Mosha, who belongs to the Chagga people of northern Tanzania, attempts to find out how the Chagga humanize themselves and their society through *ipvunda* (i.e., education).[24] He would agree with both Nussbaum and Freire on the goal of education as nurturing the humanity of the students and, by extension, humanizing the world we inhabit so that life—both human and nonhuman—can flourish.

Furthermore, Mosha points out that the content and goals of *ipvunda* flow from four aspects of the African worldview: (1) a firm belief in and profound reverence for God, the eternal Divine Mystery; (2) the awareness that from birth to death, a person must go through a rigorous process of spiritual and moral formation, reformation, and transformation, as well as the awareness that the forming and reforming of a person's moral core is fundamental in the emergence of genuine humanity and essential for harmonious living with all that is; (3) the awareness that there is an intrinsic unity between the individual and the community;[25] and (4) the awareness of a living, interconnected, and interdependent universe in which each component of the universe is intimately connected with all others. Besides facilitating awareness of this worldview, *ipvunda* also nurtures the virtues that mark one as authentically human. He writes,

> One of the important fruits of the indigenous education systems . . . is that individuals and the society in general develop an awareness and understanding of certain modes of behavior that are viewed as crucial in the formation of a sane and civil society. Indigenous society expects everyone to have these positive dispositions or tendencies that help strengthen the society's worldview and realize its goals, such as building strong and caring families and communities, nurturing responsible citizens, and strengthening the harmony already in the universe. In short, indigenous society views these virtues or positive tendencies as the *heartbeat* that keeps society healthy and vibrant . . . without this healthy heartbeat . . . society disintegrates and chaos reigns.[26]

Like Nussbaum, Mosha reinforces the view that a key goal of education is the making of good, responsible citizens motivated and sustained by a life of virtue. He identifies six such cardinal virtues, including reverence, self-control, silence or thoughtfulness, courage, diligence in work, and communality.[27] Mosha notes that communality is the central virtue:

> Communality brings forth community and continues to sustain it. If the virtue of communality is eroded in a significant number of people, a community's survival is seriously threatened. Such a community bounces back on its feet when many of its people begin to feel deep in themselves that they belong together.[28]

Through *ipvunda* the student's humanity, or *Ubuntu*, deepens and broadens as he or she grows in the positive dispositions or virtues education facilitates and nurtures. *Ipvunda* reminds one that he or she is a participant in "an ongoing dance that is kept alive by the creative and sustaining power of the Divine Mystery, the caring and protective presence of human beings, and by the inherent active participation of everything that is."[29] Like Freire, Mosha suggests that human beings are in the process of becoming. It is the goal of education to help shape and direct the student's process of becoming *Ubuntu*, authentically human. Such a process of human blossoming is lifelong and enduring.[30]

The fourth theorist whose insights are relevant here is bell hooks, who builds on Freire's thought and articulates a feminist perspective on education as "practice of freedom" and, one might add, practice of justice—particularly gender justice. In *Teaching to Transgress*, she reflects on her own autobiography both as an educator and as a student. She resonates with Freire's views that education ought to spell out freedom and should facilitate the self-actualization both of the educator and of the student. She writes,

> When education is the practice of freedom, students are not the only ones who are asked to share, to confess. Engaged pedagogy does not seek simply to empower students. Any classroom that employs a holistic mode of learning will also be a place where teachers grow, and are empowered by the process.[31]

For hooks, teaching to transgress implies the transformation of both the educator and the student so that they are each better equipped to transform the world. As she puts it, education as practice of freedom provides them "with ways of knowing that enhance their capacity to live fully and deeply."[32] In other words, engaged pedagogy enhances their capacity to flourish as human beings.

In her proposals regarding education as the practice of freedom, bell hooks is clearly inspired by Paulo Freire, a fact she acknowledges in *Teaching to Transgress*.[33] At the same time, she sees great resonance and convergence between Freire's thought and feminist educational theory and practice. Rather than seeing Freire and feminism as competing or antagonistic, hooks celebrates the overlap and mutual enrichment. Drawing from both, she weaves what she calls a pedagogical "tapestry"[34] by taking threads from Freire's work and weaving them into feminist pedagogy.

One of the major threads she picks from Freire is that education is a shared enterprise that helps both the educators and the students learn from and with each other for a more enhanced sense of freedom. Quoting Freire, she speaks of "authentic help" as the kind of help in which

> all who are involved help each other mutually, growing together in the common effort to understand the reality which they seek to transform. Only through such praxis—in which those who help and those who are being helped help each other simultaneously—can the act of helping become free from the distortion in which the helper dominates the helped.[35]

All these authors would agree that the central role of education is the enhancement of authentic humanity in the educator and the student and, by extension, the world. In light of the rampant subversion of humanity for many in the wake of globalization,[36] the rediscovering and implementation of the role of education as a way of challenging dehumanizing forces as well as cultivating, nurturing, and repairing desecrated humanity—or better still, as a means of creating prophylactic strategies to preempt the dehumanizing aspects of globalization—becomes a noble goal worth pursuing as a matter of urgency.

All these authors also agree that true education ought to equip for citizenship, even global citizenship. Nussbaum makes a strong case for education as a means of nurturing multiculturalism, for she argues, "We [in the West] need to learn more about non-Western cultures . . . for . . . reasons of good citizenship and deliberation in an interlocking world."[37] Similarly, bell hooks devotes a chapter to reflection on the challenges and opportunities of "Teaching in a Multicultural World."[38] For her, the reality of teaching in a multicultural world demands pedagogical paradigm shifts. Any efforts to transform institutions so that they reflect a multicultural standpoint must take into consideration the fears that teachers have when they are asked to shift their paradigms. She concludes, therefore, "There must be training sites where teachers have the opportunity to express those concerns while also learning to create ways to approach the multicultural classroom and curriculum."[39]

For hooks, teachers themselves need to be equipped so that they can teach to transform, as she writes,

> Multiculturalism compels educators to recognize the narrow boundaries that have shaped the way knowledge is shared in the classroom. It forces us all to recognize our complicity in accepting or perpetuating biases of any kind. Students are eager to break through barriers to knowing. They are willing to surrender to the wonder of re-learning and learning ways of knowing that go against the grain. When we, as educators, allow our pedagogy to be radically changed by our recognition of the multicultural world, we can give students the education they desire and deserve. We can teach in ways that transform consciousness, creating a climate of free expression that is the essence of a truly liberatory liberal arts education.[40]

Jesuit Education and Teaching to Transform: Santa Clara University

One major site where efforts have intentionally been made to teach in ways that transform consciousness and create a climate of free expression that is truly liberatory is in Jesuit education. This intentionality is rooted in the history of Jesuit tradition, which for the last 400 years or so has embraced education as a key dimension of their Jesuit apostolate or charism. In a speech given during the 150th anniversary of Santa Clara University in 2000, Peter-Hans Kolvenbach, S.J., former superior general of the Society of Jesus, stressed that education is a means of achieving the mission and goals of Jesuit charism. Citing insights from the Jesuits' 32nd General Congregation in 1975, he reaffirmed the view that Jesuit mission and calling is "the service of faith and promotion of justice."[41]

While efforts to implement the ideals of the Jesuit mission through education are found in all of the Jesuit educational institutions, I will use as an example Santa Clara University (hereafter SCU), one of the twenty-eight Jesuit institutions of higher learning in the United States. Particularly in recent years, SCU has been explicit and deliberate in embracing education as a means for social transformation. Laura Nichols, director of the Undergraduate Core Curriculum at Santa Clara, sums up this intentionality and organic link between Jesuit mission and Jesuit education at Santa Clara. She celebrates the fact that

> integrating the values of our 450-year-old tradition of Jesuit education with the skills and knowledge needed in the 21st century, our core brings together global understanding, critical judgment, reasoning, clear communication, ethical decision making, and concern for others.[42]

Several factors related to education at SCU reveal that education is intentionally meant to facilitate the holistic formation of the student, not only at the intellectual academic level, but also at the ethical and affective levels. This approach resonates significantly with the views of the theorists we have discussed so far. Martha Nussbaum, for example, would applaud the fact that Jesuit education at Santa Clara is a means of cultivating humanity in several ways.

SCU states up front that the educational goal is the intentional formation of students, facilitating their becoming persons of "competence, compassion and conscience." This process of formation starts with the very recognition that before, during, and after his or her education in a Jesuit university, the student is a human person, and not just a statistic or a number in the enrollment rosters. This recognition is explicitly stated in the view that the student is entitled to be cared for as a whole person, or, in Jesuit parlance, *cura personalis*. This notion calls for a deep respect for the students as people and for their potential to grow and blossom as human beings.

More specifically, cultivation of humanity through education at Santa Clara entails the nurturing of the humanizing capacities that Nussbaum speaks about: (1) the capacity to question and critique the world around them, (2) the capacity for global citizenship, and (3) the capacity for empathy, compassion, and consequent advocacy for justice. Santa Clara education is meant to form students who are intellectually competent but also who, motivated by empathy and compassion for others, are inclined to advocate for those who suffer various injustices.

The intentionality and determination to cultivate the humanity of students and through them to change the world is palpable in the recently introduced Core Curriculum. Both in its contents and pedagogical method, the new curriculum resonates with Nussbaum's call for education that is informative, formative, and transformative. For example, in efforts to engender the first capacity that Nussbaum identifies—namely, nurturing a Socratic questioning and analytical mind in the students—the SCU curriculum mandates two courses in critical thinking and writing. The stated goals for these critical thinking and writing courses are to nurture students' capacities to read and write with a critical point of view that displays "depth of thought" and capacity to make "well supported arguable theses that demonstrate personal engagement."[43] As indicated in the Core guidelines, these critical thinking and writing courses are foundational, and all students are enrolled in them even before they arrive on campus for orientation.

The curriculum also deliberately attends to the making of global citizens, Nussbaum's second goal of education. To this end, students have to take "Cultures and Ideas" as a three-course sequence. These courses are designed to foster an analytical understanding of global cultures. One of the goals of these courses is to facilitate students' capacity to "reflect on and examine both shared and diverse human experiences so that they recognize the similarities and differences across cultures as well as historical periods; comprehend the relevance of the past to their understanding of the present while coming to understand the perspective of their own cultural assumptions and values."[44]

It is in this intentional context of simultaneously nurturing critical thinking and global citizenship that SCU expects students to complete courses in religion, theology, and culture in a three-course sequence (i.e., RTC1, 2, and 3). The foundational courses in RTC1 introduce students to the study of religion as a phenomenon and as a lived reality. One of the goals of courses listed under RTC1 is to enable students to "describe and compare the central religious ideas and practices from several traditions or within one, and from at least two globally distinct regions."[45]

One of the popular RTC1 courses is entitled "Ways of Understanding Religion" and is designed to facilitate students' awareness and appreciation of the diversity of expression and interpretation of religious ideas and practices around the world. In this study of religion across cultures, students are expected to "use critical approaches to reflect on their own beliefs and the religious dimensions of human existence."[46] In other words, they are expected to apply critical thinking skills even as they seek to understand, appreciate, and engage their own beliefs and those of others with whom we share the world. Other courses that fulfill the requirements of RTC1 include those with intriguing and thought-provoking titles, such as "Texting God" (with a play on the term "text") and "Magicians, Athletes and God." The course "Franciscans and Jesuits: An Introduction to Catholic Spiritualities" is also included in RTC1.

The Core also explicitly addresses Nussbaum's third capacity of cultivation of empathy and compassion. As she explains, students may know many facts about other peoples' lives and still not be equipped for world citizenship. Citing Marcus Aurelius, she says that to become world citizens, "we must not simply amass knowledge. We must also cultivate in ourselves the capacity for sympathetic imagination that will enable us to understand the motives and choices of people different from ourselves, seeing them not as forbiddingly alien and other."[47]

To cultivate this capacity among Santa Clara students, the Core Curriculum includes courses that are designed to enhance their capacity for civic engagement. The curriculum has a segment entitled "Civic Engagement." Courses under this rubric nurture students' capacity to "critically evaluate and express reasoned opinions about the role of public organizations (governmental, nongovernmental, multilateral, or international) in civic life." They also nurture their capacity "to analyze and evaluate civic issues by engaging in active and collaborative learning with peers and others."[48]

It is noteworthy also that civic engagement, global citizenship, empathy, and compassion as a springboard for socially transformative action is not only nurtured through the rich and vibrant curricular content. It is complemented by a deliberate adoption of pedagogies that enhance human encounter locally and globally. In ways reminiscent of Freire's and bell hooks' calls for pedagogies of engagement, Santa Clara's Core Curriculum nurtures experiential learning and, specifically, experiential learning for social justice through specific and deliberately structured courses. Courses that include experiential learning involve a required placement in real-life contexts, where social justice is actively being sought, so that students can learn through experience rather than just from textbooks. In short, teaching civic engagement through experiential learning is meant to transform students' consciousness as a way of equipping them to transform the world.

In concluding this analysis of the SCU educational experiment as an example of teaching to transform, it is noteworthy that the structure of the curriculum palpably resonates with the Jesuit mission and imperative to nurture humanity by transforming consciousness. The very structure and sequencing of the curriculum is built on the underlying assumption that the world we live in is in process and not complete. As Freire and Mosha point out, the world is in the process of unfolding. This incompleteness and unfolding-ness allows the possibility of the world to be transformed. Therefore, there is room for all to participate in the making and the becoming of the world so that it can be more just, humane, and livable.

Similarly, both Freire and Mosha point out that a defining feature of being human is that we, too, are incomplete and in the process of becoming. This means that humans by definition are not reducible to some predetermined defining features. Instead, our lives, too, are unfolding. It is the goal of education to shape the direction of this becoming, so that students blossom and grow in the direction of authentic humanity.

Presupposing students' potential to grow and blossom, the SCU curriculum is deliberately designed around three phases or themes: foundations, explorations, and integrations. These very terms suggest movement and dynamism as the students, building on certain "foundations," continue to grow through "explorations" and ongoing "integrations" of insights garnered through their participation in the various dimensions of the curriculum. In this process, the content and even the methods embedded in the curriculum become a means to this goal of shaping and directing students' growth and blossoming. In this journey, the banking concept of education, which presupposes a static world and essentializes learners and teachers in ways that inhibit their mutual blossoming and flourishing, is indeed problematic. It is noteworthy in this context that SCU education eschews banking and invests in a program of education that nurtures the becoming of the students into well-informed, compassionate, yet analytical citizens of the world. This is a trajectory that Kolvenbach would endorse and support, as he says,

> Our students are involved in every sort of social action, tutoring drop outs, demonstrating in Seattle, serving in soup kitchens and we are proud of them. But the measure of Jesuit universities is not what the students do, but who they become and the adult responsibility they will exercise in future towards neighbor and the world.[49]

Nussbaum, Freire, Mosha, and hooks would agree that the role of education is the shaping and molding of these responsible citizens and the nurturing of students toward their fullest blossoming as human beings. Such molding is not exhausted by four years of formal schooling. Rather, it becomes a lifelong process.

World Council of Churches and a Global Syndemic: Implications for Teaching to Transform

HIV/AIDS is one of the most enduring crises that the world has faced in the last thirty or so years. While the crisis is global, Africa has been hardest hit. The crisis has been exacerbated by a variety of issues, including a stigma against people living with HIV/AIDS and the African continent, gender injustices based on sexist and patriarchal responses to the crisis, and poverty. These exacerbating factors make it possible to describe HIV/AIDS not just as a *pandemic* but as a *syndemic*. That is to say, it thrives in symbiotic relationships with other diseases and comorbidities, such as tuberculosis. It also thrives in the contexts of "metaphorical viruses," including the viruses of stigma, denial, structural injustices, and other situations affected by what Paul Farmer calls "pathologies of power."[50]

During the earlier days in the history of HIV/AIDS, faith-based responses to HIV/AIDS contributed to the exacerbation of the disease. This was because many embraced an interpretation that suggested that those infected were reaping the fruits of their "sin," particularly sexual sin. Many thought that AIDS was the disease of the sexually promiscuous and a just punishment for the sexually incontinent. The impact of this interpretation of diseases as a consequence of sin betrayed a distorted theodicy or theology of suffering.[51]

This simplistic and distorted theological response to the HIV/AIDS crisis was most costly. Not only did it contribute to the condemnation and stigmatization of many infected and affected by the disease; it also distracted from a timely development of responses more conducive to the interruption of and containment of the rampage of the disease.

Fortunately, due to the determined intervention of many resilient activists and HIV/AIDS advocates, the syndemic nature of the disease has come to be better recognized over the years. The exacerbating impact of the metaphoric "viruses" of stigma, structural sin, and violence (including racism, sexism, and colonialism) are better recognized as contributive to the escalation and magnitude of the HIV/AIDS crisis in Africa. Recognizing the syndemic nature of the disease, churches and faith communities have begun to address not only the medical and epidemiological dimensions of the disease; but also the root causes, particularly where those root causes are embedded in structures and pathologies of power. The World Council of Churches through its Ecumenical HIV and AIDS Initiative in Africa (hereafter EHAIA) has made concerted efforts to address the root causes of HIV/AIDS.[52]

Launched in 2002, this initiative of the World Council of Churches was intended to enable churches in Africa to deal with the problem of HIV/AIDS in their communities by helping them access pertinent information and by connecting them with other communities and churches, particularly in the Global North. To date, the initiative has grown to be a powerful, strategic, and successful platform through which churches in Africa have been enabled to become what Susan Parry has called "HIV/AIDS competent."[53]

While time and space will not allow a detailed account of the program as a whole, I explore here how this program has fostered teaching to transform as a necessary tool in the struggle against HIV/AIDS. I will explore sample strategies, which stand out in this context.[54] This includes what has been called in literature "mainstreaming HIV and AIDS into theological education."[55] At the helm of these strategies is the work of several socially engaged African theologians, who have worked closely with EHAIA to transform consciousness by transforming the theological thinking and ethical responses to the crisis. Such theologians include Nyambura Njoroge, who heads the EHAIA project in Geneva. Other key theologians are Musa Dube, who was appointed a theological consultant by EHAIA in 2002, and Ezra Chitando, who succeeded her in this role.

Regarding the main strategy (mainstreaming HIV/AIDS into the theological curriculum), the mandate for Musa Dube, a theologian and biblical scholar from Botswana, was to invite and facilitate curriculum change in theological institutions—a task she embraced with passion and even "missionary" zeal. Chitando describes her as a "missionary" against HIV/AIDS, zealous and determined "to take her gospel to theological institutions across Africa calling for the conversion of students and lecturers."[56]

Dube's own "conversion" to such a "missionary" mode arose out of the fact that, like many in Africa, she had witnessed firsthand the devastating impact of the disease on families and communities. In her "missionary" work, Dube "sought the resurrection of individuals and communities from the death and paralysis wrought by stigma and discrimination."[57] She was convinced that theological colleges were strategically positioned to transform the churches' thinking on HIV, and consequently she sought to ensure that graduates of African theological schools and departments of religious studies were adequately equipped for the task.[58]

Dube used a multipronged strategy in this project of mainstreaming HIV/AIDS into Africa's theological and ethical imagination and thus transforming the church. First, working with EHAIA's regional coordinators, Dube organized "training of trainers" (TOT) workshops across the continent. This TOT strategy focused on a variety of themes designed to address the various dimensions of church thinking that needed transformation. As a strategy, TOT was deliberately chosen because of its multiplier effect in spreading the message wider and sooner. This strategy was highly successful, and it was documented and celebrated in the tenth-year EHAIA Impact Assessment.[59] Citing a 2008 "Workshop on Transformative Masculinities"[60] organized by the Association of Lesotho Theologians, for example, the EHAIA impact assessors reported that this workshop "included the state correctional services, policemen and taxi drivers." It "triggered spinoff training activities" that demonstrated the multiplier and ripple effect of the training of trainers strategy. "As a result of this multiplier and ripple effect, the EHAIA Impact Report asserts that over the period 2002–2009, there were 222 EHAIA Training events conducted in various places across the continent. These trainings and workshops involved over 12,000 participants."[61]

Secondly, Dube participated in and also spurred more assertive and contextual research and publication on theology and HIV/AIDS in Africa. For example, she urged changes in theological curricula in light of HIV/AIDS, and contributed to the project by publishing a template curriculum, which could be adopted and adapted throughout the continent as needed.[62] She also edited the volume *Africa Praying: A Handbook on HIV/AIDS Sensitive Sermon Guidelines and Liturgy.*[63] This has become a great resource for church leaders seeking to communicate effectively on HIV/AIDS to their respective contexts.

A third strategy Dube employed was to urge and model contextual biblical studies in the service of educating to transform the African mind in relation to HIV/AIDS. Both as a member of the Circle of Concerned African Women Theologians and as a seasoned scholar of the Bible, she pioneered in writing and editing books on reading the Bible in the context of HIV/AIDS. With Musimbi Kanyoro, she edited *Grant Me Justice: HIV/AIDS & Gendered Readings of the Bible.*[64] As a strategy, contextual biblical studies became a tool for introducing sensitive aspects of the crisis, particularly those related to sexual and gender violence as a major factor in the prevalence and spread of HIV/AIDS in Africa. A major success here has been the contextual reading of the story of Tamar, which within the context of EHAIA has grown to be a Pan-African project, suitably named the Tamar Campaign.[65]

A fourth strategy has mobilized church leaders and theologians and all of Dube's audiences through presentations in conferences and other fora, in which she challenges all to move from denial to engagement. Dube often does this through the use of metaphor and story. She explains the rationale and viability of storytelling as a preferred method in the quest for transformation of consciousness as a stepping-stone to social transformation by citing the work of the Circle of Concerned African Women.[66] She observes, "Storytelling is emerging as a central method of highlighting the situation of women in the struggle against HIV/AIDS."[67] According to Dube, this method has great potential in articulating a feminist and womanist theology of healing and liberation in an HIV/AIDS context. She concludes, "When we listen to each other's stories we create a space of breaking the silences, of understanding, of empathy, of being prophetic to one another and, hopefully, of giving justice a better deal."[68]

It is not surprising that she uses this storytelling method in a self-reflective essay discussing insights from her work in curriculum transformation in HIV/AIDS contexts.[69] Comparing responses to the crisis of HIV/AIDS to various responses that people might have to a (hypothetical) burning hut, she identifies a typology of responses to HIV/AIDS in Africa. She says some may be indifferent to the "burning hut" and continue with a "business as usual" attitude, while others may be in so much shock that they become overwhelmed, paralyzed, and helpless. Others might instinctively jump into action and try to put out the fire, though they may not have the skills or even equipment to deal with the fire. Others trained and fully equipped may approach the fire as professional firefighters.

She notes that HIV/AIDS has evoked a similar spectrum of responses, and she goes on to situate her own journey as an African scholar responding to the raging fire of HIV/AIDS in Africa. She reflects on how, as an academic, she moved from seeming indifference and inaction, possibly borne out of a sense of helplessness in the face of the magnitude and complexities of HIV/AIDS, to her role as an active "firefighter." Initially she fought the fire at the personal level through her own research and writing. Later, she became a "lead firefighter" as she was appointed as such by EHAIA. There, and elsewhere, she collaborated and benefited from being in company with other "firefighters," particularly colleagues and fellow sisters in the Circle of Concerned African Women Theologians.[70] In the meantime, as she puts it, she continued to inhabit a "burning hut"—that is, the university where she was teaching and where matters to do with HIV/AIDS were yet to be adequately recognized and addressed. She notes the challenge and opportunities for her as an African scholar concerned with the crisis of HIV/AIDS.

The moral of the story, she concludes, is that HIV/AIDS is a global and enduring fire. It demands that we all become active firefighters, and not bystanders or people who adopt a "business as usual" attitude. She reminds us of the ethical problematic of a "business as usual" attitude in the middle of a raging fire—in fact, multiple raging fires. It is imperative to become "firefighters," in other words, to engage in transformative research and teaching. In her view, HIV/AIDS and other "fires" call for a commitment to "producing and disseminating knowledge for utilisation by students, communities and the world at large."[71] In being such a committed scholar determined to research and teaching to transform, through the EHAIA platform among others, Dube has been an exemplary trailblazer in Africa and beyond.

Conclusion: Celebrating the "Already" and Reckoning with the "Not Yet"

As I draw to the conclusion of this chapter and search for language to describe the road map ahead while providing a rearview-mirror look at the journey so far, I am struck by the title of a recent panel at Santa Clara University convened by the Ignatian Center for Jesuit Education. Suitably entitled "Already but Not Yet," the panel was to assess both the achievements and the gaps in the implementation of SCU's vision of diversity, inclusion, and call of justice in Jesuit Catholic higher education.

Invoking the notion of "already but not yet" becomes a suitable way of concluding this chapter, while at the same time encouraging similar assessment of the "already but not yet" in the implementation of teaching to transform in global contexts. We will definitely find reasons to celebrate the achievements already in place as exemplified in the two case studies discussed in this chapter. In both cases, there is *already* a palpable awareness and commitment to the very idea of teaching to transform. At Santa Clara, the emphasis on education as a means toward helping students to become "citizens of competence, compassion and conscience" is an *already* to be celebrated and emulated. Similarly, the deliberate adoption of education as a (shared) practice of freedom and the deliberate involvement of people living with HIV/AIDS in the work of transformation is an *already* that bell hooks and Freire would surely celebrate.

At the same time, it is clear in both cases that the journey of transformation is not completed. The panel on the "Already but Not Yet" in matters of diversity and inclusiveness at Santa Clara revealed that whereas bold steps have already been made in making Santa Clara inclusive and sensitive to the reality of diversity, there are specific areas where more is needed to be done.[72] In the meantime, in a bid to show evidence of achievement of goals and to discern enduring challenges and emerging issues, EHAIA conducted a detailed impact assessment of its strategies and activities in the past ten years. In this self-assessment, EHAIA confirmed that whereas so far there is a lot to be celebrated, there is much as yet to be addressed to bring transformation and healing in the context of HIV/AIDS. This "not yet" character of the project of transformation arises out of the fact that we have multiple and entrenched contexts that need transformation. We have multiple fires: some are perennially "simmering" under the surface, and some are brand new ones for which we may be the least prepared. The multiple and enduring fires demand a correspondingly enduring vigilance and commitment as "firefighters" in the sense discussed by Dube. Moreover, these "already" and "not yet" situations call for a willingness to evaluate critically the impact of what we do. The examples of SCU and EHAIA in this regard are commendable practices worthy of emulating and scaling up.

In short, recognizing the "already but not yet" of the project of transformation is reminiscent of Freire's view that both the world and humans in it are in the process of becoming. It is reminiscent of the African worldview that all are in the process of ongoing formation and transformation. What we will become as a transformed community of scholars engaged in the process of teaching/educating to transform is itself a "not yet" to be discovered, evaluated, shared, and celebrated.

✦ 9 ✦

Hablando Se Entiende la Gente
Tower of Babble or Gift of Tongues?

LOIDA I. MARTELL-OTERO

I am a bicoastal Puerto Rican. I was born in New York City but eventually moved to the island. I was not unfamiliar with being called a "spic" in New York and being told to "go back where I came from." Yet, it was quite disconcerting then to be called a "gringa" in Puerto Rico and be told to "go back where I came from." Thus I, and others like me, learned early on to maneuver and survive between these two linguistic worlds and the various cultural minefields that were implicit within them. We spoke fluently, crossing the linguistic and cultural borders between our hyphenated existences that so perplexed others.[1] We shrugged. We were born into these multiple worlds and learned to breathe in and between them. After many years in Puerto Rico, I admit that I assimilated to the island mindset and eventually lost my "gringa accent," speaking Spanish like a native. I thought I had finally arrived home.

My vocational call to ministry not only led me away from my veterinary practice; it also took me from the island to a Massachusetts seminary to begin my theological training. Once again, I found myself treading cultural and linguistic minefields. It was shocking, and yet in a curious way unsurprising, for me to hear a classmate interrupt a conversation I was holding in Spanish with other Latin@ students and stridently declare, "This is America. We speak English here!" In that one racist and ignorant statement, my classmate summarized what I had experienced continuously over a lifetime: a xenophobia, a resistance to difference, a fear of being in the presence of that which one does not understand, and an ignorance of the global reality of the linguistic, cultural, social, religious, and political differences that surround us not only in the wider world but in our local neighborhoods. Perhaps he was angry that we could so blithely cross multiple worlds in ways that he could not fathom. Whatever the cause of his caustic remark, what my colleague failed to understand was that this is not *America* but the United States, located within the *Americas*, where English is actually only one among multiple languages. It is a nation where indigenous dialects, Spanish, different dialects of Chinese, Korean and other Asian languages, French, Greek, Russian, and so many other languages are spoken.[2] He failed to perceive the many worlds in which he lived that comprise our present diverse and global reality.

That incident points to the ongoing need of theological education: we must educate our students so that they can deal effectively with an increasingly diverse and global world. We are called to give them the tools to speak in "difference," to speak "multilingually," to enable them to traverse and transgress borders with ease. To fail to do so is to conceive of theological education as an entrenched framework of homogenic purity and sameness that uses increasingly irrelevant pedagogical paradigms to perpetuate the belief that Eurocentric power and privilege is "*el ombligo del mundo*" (the navel of existence). Such paradigms ultimately serve no one and achieve nothing creative or life-giving. To speak "difference," which may seem nothing more than political correctness and babble-speak, is a paradigm shift that invites all participants—students, staff, and faculty—to cease being diversity "tourists" at the borders.[3] That is to say, we cannot be effective ministers, scholars, or a people called of God if we only pay lip service to diversity by including the occasional reading from James Cone or Gustavo Gutiérrez. Rather, the very nature of our vocational calling requires us to wrestle with the difficult questions, ambiguities, conflicts, weariness, and, yes, even joy that living in the liminal spaces of the border entails.

In this chapter, I address what it means to educate for difference, what it means to speak "multilingually." In our current social climate, difference is encapsulated in the global realities we face, both locally and abroad. Since part of my concern is that theological education must help our students become aware of global issues and how they impact our everyday surroundings (*en lo cotidiano*), I begin with a brief discussion on "globalization." Globalization is a term that has a somewhat ambiguous meaning: different scholars use it in different ways. Therefore, I define how I am using it in this discussion. In light of the issues of globalization, I then discuss my understanding of education, and in particular what it means to be *una persona educada* (an educated person): one who is hospitable and welcoming to the stranger and to the neighbor, one who creates sacred spaces of communal living. A *persona educada* is *sensible* (sensitive, attentive) to the cries of the suffering in an increasingly globalized world.

Finally, I discuss a method I created for the introductory "Systematic Theology and Ethics" course taught at my institution. In Puerto Rico, we have a saying: "*hablando se entiende la gente*" (speaking, people understand [each other]). The spirit of this saying is partly behind the Latino/a theological practice of *teología en conjunto*, a collaborative and dialogical approach to theology.[4] Based on this notion of dialogue and collaborative spirit, I created a pedagogical tool that I call "roundtable dialogue groups." Such a method creates a safe (and sometimes sacred) space where students learn the value of difference as a normative way of being and relating. In so doing, it raises their consciousness (*conscientiçao*) and leads them to seek praxeological responses to situations of injustice, both at a local and at a global level. It is meant to be not *the* method but a complementary pedagogical approach that when added to others prepares students to engage a global reality in a diverse world. One of the most satisfying consequences of this method is that it helps students become *personas educadas*. It teaches them to appreciate and respect those who are different, primes them to be open to speak "in other tongues," as well as realize that difference is a fundamental aspect of community formation.

Globalization: Now We See It Even When We Don't

It is claimed that we live in an increasingly globalized reality. Generally, "globalization" refers to "an emerging 'neo-liberal' democratic world order cemented by a new, dynamic, transnational, market capitalism" that raises sociopolitical, religious, and even environmental consequences.[5] It is a system that is "associated with . . . extension of forms of production, rapid mobility of capital, information and goods, denationalization of culture, interpenetration of local communities by global media networks, and dispersal of socioeconomic power."[6] These processes are not innocent. They follow the old trade routes of colonization and empire, exacerbating the ills of labor exploitation, land displacement, and resource diminishment in overt and covert ways. Corporate gains and productivity are the goals of globalization, and these take precedence over human well-being and dignity or creation care. One of the consequences of global corporate policies has been the increased migrant movement of populations—displaced due to the loss of their lands and the tectonic shifts of their local economies. Scholars have described this aspect of globalization in various ways: "deterritorialization," "denationalization," or simply as the perception that "the world has shrunk." We have gone to the wider world—are more aware of it—and, in many ways, the world has also come to us.

This latter reality, "that the world has come to us," is apparent in many neighborhoods. As a bicoastal Puerto Rican, part of my years were spent in the northeastern United States, where inevitably I encountered so-called "little Italys" or "Chinatowns": places where one experienced some sense of the tastes and sounds of the peoples of northern Italy or certain regions of China. Yet this phenomenon of "the world coming to us" has subtly changed that dynamic. Currently, I encounter enclaves of immigrant neighborhoods in various locations of the United States, Puerto Rico, and Canada. The anti-immigrant fervor impacting Europe and increasing xenophobic violence in the United States give witness to the presence of the global world permeating the wider world. To use theological language: there seems to be an (anti)perichoretic "interpenetration" of global communities into local communities.[7] This interpenetration of the global into the local is what I refer to as the "glocal." "Glocal" is a term first used by Roland Robertson, who adapted it from its Japanese meaning to refer to "a global outlook adapted to local conditions."[8] Other scholars have since used the word in a number of ways.[9]

While globalization and glocality are, on the one hand, pressing issues in our seemingly shrinking world—and I do contest this view, since it seems to me that the allocation and distribution of space has itself political and economic intentionality, and while for the poor it is indeed shrinking, for those benefiting from global markets it is, in fact, expanding—it is curious that, on the other hand, it has led to a disembodied disconnection from the very issues it causes. We do not seem to fully comprehend that the "Walmartization" of our neighborhoods has anything to do with sweatshops in Vietnam, that the use of ethanol as fuel might affect farmers in Mexico, or that the sale of flat screen television sets is in any way related to the rapes, murders, or disappearances of women along the border towns of the southwest.

Theological education seems to be working on an older paradigm, or at least on an idealized paradigm of a homogenized world, when the global—particularly the poor, brown, and broken—stayed on their respective side of the border and did not invade the lily-white towers of intellectual purity. Seminaries still look to prepare missionaries to cross oceans "to help the poor" who are "over there" in a replica of imperial paternalism. Very few seminaries encourage their students to learn languages other than the requisite biblical ones of Hebrew and Greek. I have yet to find a missional training program that prepares leadership to work with people not across oceans but across the street where global communities now reside. The world is "global," and yet, in many of our seminaries, it seems that we teach and act as if that world has nothing to do with us "here."

Globalization thrives on absence and hiddenness. While seemingly making the world smaller and more accessible, it hides from us its most pernicious effects, including the presence of the "absent ones" of history. This absence is most visible in our seminaries—not only because there is a dearth of diversity and lack of "speaking of tongues," but also because we have ill-prepared our students to live in a global world. We provide educational credentialing, but too many of our students graduate *mal educados*—with a lack of a holistic spirit of hospitality toward, or concern for, the cultural, religious, and linguistic "other." In failing to prepare our communities for difference, we have fostered conditions that have allowed those with "eyes to not see, and ears to not hear." In so doing, we inadvertently become complicit with the sin of globalization and contribute to the suffering of those consumed by capitalism's *habitus* of consumption. We are *gente mal educada*, tourists of the border.

Persona Educada: A Holistic Spirituality of Hospitality

Education has been defined in various ways. Elliot W. Eisner defines it as "an art guided by educational values, personal needs, and by a variety of beliefs or generalizations that the teacher holds to be true."[10] While such conceptualizations of education try to consider its creative dimension (i.e., education as "an art"), Parker Palmer is closer to the truth when he chastises the general trend in education to emphasize post-Enlightenment Cartesian pedagogical values: "Education portrays the self as *knower*, the world as *known*, and mediates the *relation* of the two, giving the knowing self supremacy over the known world."[11] Such a pedagogical approach produces a "well-educated people who have been schooled in a way of knowing that treats the world as an object to be dissected and manipulated, a way of knowing that gives us power over the world."[12] Of course, Palmer does not point out that the "us" in the "power over" refers to a very select group of people. In a hierarchalized system of privilege and empire, the "known" are often the poor, the brown, the colonized indigenous women and children, the marginalized, and the exploited.

Indeed, an educational system so conceived ultimately serves only to ensure that power structures of the privileged stay in place. Gloria Ladson-Billings has found that, by and large, most "schools, society, and the structure and production of knowledge are designed to create individuals who internalize the dominant worldview and knowledge production. . . . The hegemony of the dominant paradigm makes it more than just another way to view the world—it claims to be the only legitimate way to view the world."[13] It is no wonder that Michel Elias Andraos and others find that there is a tendency toward a "colonial differential" in theological education: the views and theologies of the dominant and westernized culture are privileged and accorded "universal" acceptance and respect, while non-Western perspectives and those espoused by faculty of color are judged to be only of passing perspectival interest.[14]

Education envisioned in this way cannot adequately prepare students for a global world. On the contrary, it often produces students who at worst reinscribe attitudes of intolerance, colonizing and patriarchal arrogance, and racist blindness, and at best are ineffective at ministering to a changing, diverse, and increasingly multilingual world. While Palmer considers such students "well-educated" because they are better "credentialed," in Puerto Rico, we would consider such persons *mal educadas* (poorly educated) because there *educada* is understood not simply as the amount of formal schooling one receives but more importantly as how one treats the neighbor and the stranger. A person who greets the other with respect, treats people with dignity, is hospitable (especially to the stranger and the guest), and makes people feel welcome in his or her home is a *persona educada*. There is an understanding that such a person is wise; the community defers to such a person.[15]

Gente (people) *mal educada* bring shame upon the home and upon the community. If you are *mal educado*, it means that you were not raised right; your parents did not teach you manners. The worst thing in the world is a person with a formal education who is nonetheless *mal educado*. Such a person is considered to be worse than foolish. Our educational system too often prepares *personas mal educadas*, people with titles who believe their worldview to be "the only legitimate" one and who make the "other" feel unwelcome and small.

Perhaps we need to change our educational paradigm. Elsewhere I have suggested that theological education develop a "spirituality of pedagogy."[16] Such an approach to education is not only critical but also holistic. Such a pedagogy construes education in terms of a journey. Elizabeth Conde-Frazier notes that education means to "lead out," or "to bring forth."[17] It is a journey that should lead us to borderlands and subsequently to create spaces that allow difference and mutuality to flourish.[18] Laura I. Rendón echoes a similar understanding of education in her notion of *sentipensante* (literally, "feelingthinking") pedagogy. She observes that indigenous languages have no word for "education" but rather consider learning to be a process of "coming-to-know." Thus she affirms that education is "a journey, a process, or quest for knowledge or understanding."[19] It must, she insists, lead to life.

Such a conceptualization of education insists on two aspects: that its purpose is to create a space of hospitality that nurtures community amid its celebration of difference, and that it must be holistic. A holistic view of education prizes relationality as intrinsic to rationality. Roberto S. Goizueta has challenged the Cartesian view of rationality as a purely objective and intellectual endeavor, arguing that it is always an intersubjective undertaking.[20] We do not simply know "facts" about someone, but we must always know the person. John D. Zizioulas, in his elaboration of Trinitarian theology, defines "personhood" by this capacity for relationality.[21] We know communally. A holistic education should therefore include an environment that fosters a healthy relationality among the various constituencies of the educational community. It is part of the journey.[22] It cannot simply be about knowing facts and figures, but must also be about knowing each other and ourselves as whole persons: our emotional, physical, and spiritual selves. While articulating an understanding of education in this way might sound foreign (after all, I am speaking in a "foreign tongue!"), I do believe that the concept is not far from what educators mean by "multiple intelligences"—that in seeking to approach learning through the senses, the visual, the kinesthetic, and so forth, we are implicitly acknowledging the whole person. I am simply expanding that notion and joining others in insisting that learning is a deeply communal enterprise.

Pedagogy, then, must intentionally create "sacred spaces" that allow for the flourishing of community and personhood. What do I mean by "sacred space"? Elsewhere, I have defined sacred space as the intersection between divine *kairos* and space, and created time and space.[23] Simply put, it is a worldview that posits that to be attentive to the *where* is to be attentive to the relations of those located there, and that taking time to forge relations is a holy enterprise. To emphasize sacred space is to pay attention to the people and relations within creation that comprise our community, to pay attention to that which is life-giving. Community leads to life, just as the indigenous understanding of "coming-to-know" is about life. For American Indians, community is not simply the hermeneutical framework for learning: it is the very goal of coming-to-know.[24]

Unfortunately, our current educational systems are not structured to allow for the formation of sacred spaces that nurture the flourishing of life, community, and full personhood. At present, we live under the tyranny of overwork and overscheduling because, as Catherine Keller has argued, time has been monetized.[25] We exploit people to do more with less and less time in order to make a greater profit margin. This is the reality of a globalized (and I would add, a colonized) world. Such a worldview is counterproductive to learning, to humanization, and to the formation of community. It leads to the formation of *gente mal educada*. A spirituality of pedagogy resists such models of exploitation and seeks instead to create spaces that allow for the formation of community. It acknowledges the priority of place over and above time and schedules, because "place" is where relations among people are nurtured. It allows for everyone in the classroom to interact and to learn about each other, as well as to learn from each other. An important aspect of such an approach is to create the means for dialogue. In Spanish we say, *hablando se entiende la gente* (speaking, people understand [each other]).

Hablando Se Entiende la Gente

Dialogue is a crucial pedagogical and epistemological tool. It is a process, an engagement, a pooling of voices, and an encounter of life narratives. It is, for example, the coming together of two strangers at a well: he a rabbi from the village; she an oppressed Samaritan woman; at the end of the day, both transformed and wiser by their exchange. In a collaboratively written article, Arch Chee Keen Wong describes dialogue as a "subject-to-subject encounter" that allows people to share their stories and visions. Thus, according to Wong, "telling and listening" are essential to the process of dialogue.[26] In the same article, Emma Emgård defines dialogue as a "flow of meaning." Differentiating between discussion and dialogue, she notes that the former often leads to arguments but does not necessarily provide understanding or cross-cultural learning.[27] Dialogue teaches, enlightens, and transforms. It is like a river of living water! As such, it is a messy enterprise. In Puerto Rico, we are often known for speaking over each other in social situations; in some cultures, this would be considered rude. For us, it is a sign of good conversation, in which one is engaged and truly listening. There is, indeed, a flow. Palmer believes that in some way, such a dialogical flow leads us to trúths.[28]

It does not surprise me that dialogue is so essential to our understanding as a people. Theologically and biblically, dialogue lies at the core of our existence. Genesis records the beginning of human history as a word; God spoke and it came to be. The Hebrew notion of *dabar* connotes the belief that speaking is creative and transformational. Indeed, in the First Testament, *ruach* (Spirit) and *dabar* (Word) are often closely associated. Words are not simply passive. They *do*. Thus, for Franz-J Leenhardt, the very existence of the world is a "speech act":

> The world is therefore the result of a speech act, it is a language of divinity . . . the world is a word [speaking], the instrument of a dialogue. It has meaning. It says something about the one who ordered it. Human beings are called to respond. Whether astonishment or anguish, through the voice of conscience or through the silence of infinite spaces, the world troubles and questions human beings. If humans know how to listen to the word addressed to them, this disquiet generates personality, responsibility, freedom.[29]

If God speaks and if the world is the result of a speech act, then we are called not only to respond but also to continue this dialogue. Leenhardt seems to share this conclusion when he insists that God speaks "to the silent of the world . . . human beings were governed, created and directed by a God who continuously speaks."[30] The world is a dialogue. The whole world is needed to engage in it.

The Incarnation is the embodiment of that dialogue. It is the *dabar*, the Word, *el Verbo* (the doing and speaking of God with all of creation) made flesh—that is to say, the divine intimately entangled in the affairs of the creation. God has crossed borders to listen as well as to speak, to know as well as to be known. In the process, *vínculos*—intimate communal ties—are forged. The Incarnation is an affirmation that true dialogue does not take place when one stays ensconced in one's own places of comfort, but requires that one cross borders, to venture "outside the gate"—as Orlando E. Costas so eloquently insisted—and remain there, as Gary Riebe-Estrella calls us to do, to engage with difference, to be willing to wrestle with conflict, and to truly learn the cultural, social, and historical language of the other.[31]

Dialogue is a flow, but it can be a turbulent one. This is evident in the embodied dialogical event of Pentecost. A true blowing of the Spirit (*ruach*) took place to create a multilingual, multicultural, intentionally diverse encounter. People were disturbed when barriers were eliminated that allowed them talk to one another. There is no place for "tourists of diversity" in this spirit of dialogue. This is not a spirit of debate, nor is it a spirit of vacuous oral posturing. To dialogue in the midst of difference, in a spirit of respect that listens and shares, is to engage in deep conversation and to critically engage with others. It is through such a process that true community can be forged. One must go into dialogue unafraid. True dialogue leads to *conscientiçao* (conscientization). Paulo Freire first coined this term to define a "process by which a person acquires and develops a critical consciousness, not only of the social reality that conditions their lives, but also of the capacity to transform that reality."[32] Thus, dialogue is praxeological. It is creative. It can be liberative. Fernando Cascante-Gómez has found that it can lead people to transform "unequal and unjust realities of the world in which they live."[33]

Roundtable Groups: Exercise in Collaborative Dialogue amid Diversity

In order to engage my students in this critical dialogical approach in an introductory course in "Systematic Theology and Ethics," I adapted a technique I had developed in my youth ministry in Puerto Rico. I had created something called *la ronda pastoral* (pastoral round), organizing my young adult Sunday school group into a literal circle of "pastoral agents," in which they would counsel each other on pressing issues they faced. It was very successful, and upon the group's request, we continued these rounds on a monthly basis. When I began teaching at my current institution, I developed similar "roundtable dialogue groups." I believed this system could provide a solution for two dilemmas I faced. On the one hand, I wanted to underscore to my students that theology is discourse—a dialogue that entails a diversity of voices. I did not want to privilege white, male, European voices or treat voices of color or those of white women as marginalized "others." On the other hand, given time and cost, I could not possibly assign all the books required to achieve this dialogical end. My experience with *la ronda pastoral* led me to think I could adapt it for the course as a tool to solve both dilemmas. As one group noted,

> Time constraints . . . [did] not permit limitless hours of reading. So the group structure provided an avenue to discover, vicariously, what other theologians have stated on particular topics. (Group 2, 2006)

Adapting a technique I learned from a former professor, S. Mark Heim, Samuel Abbot Professor of Christian Theology at Andover Newton Theological School, I assigned what I called "dialogue partners" to each student. The model works as follows. There are six dialogue partners, each representing a particular contextual perspective (see Table 1).[34]

TABLE 1

Group Represented	*Dialogue Partner*
African American	James Cone, *A Black Theology of Liberation*
Latin American	Gustavo Gutiérrez, *A Theology of Liberation*
Native American	Clara Sue Kidwell, Homer Noley, and George E. "Tink" Tinker, *A Native American Theology*
Feminist	Rosemary R. Ruether, *Sexism and God-Talk*
Asian American	C. S. Song, *The Believing Heart*
Womanist	Delores S. Williams, *Sisters in the Wilderness*[35]

Initially, I was responsible for assigning a partner to each student. In response to students' feedback, I changed tactics and eventually allowed them to form their own groups of six and then, within groups, to negotiate who would read which partner. This did not always result in as great a diversity within groups as when I assigned them, but it did allow students to take responsibility for their learning, and this meant they were more open for the challenges they encountered in the roundtable process.[36] In addition to their dialogue partners, I assigned students a class textbook that contains chapters written by a variety of authors, and other readings that provide a variety of perspectives on a given topic at any one time.

Thus each roundtable group is comprised of six students reading different dialogue partners, such that all six are represented per group. The groups meet approximately every two weeks to share with each other what their dialogue partners have or have not written about theological topics discussed in class. In this way, everyone in the circle is informed about the books they are not personally reading. Given the tendency of some students toward loquaciousness and of others toward tardiness in the completion of assigned readings—thus affecting group dynamics—I request that each student write a summative three key points on an index card. These cards are collected at the beginning of class to ensure that students indeed have completed their assigned readings, and then returned before the roundtable meetings. I also assign a leader from within each group who is tasked with monitoring the time, to ensure that everyone has a turn to speak. To avoid ill will toward the person thus assigned, I further request that the group supervise the leader to ensure that she/he not overstep her/his time limit. This request inserts good humor into the process and underscores the sense of mutual collaboration.

At the end of the semester, each group submits an evaluation report based on guided questions that analyze its process critically and theologically. Since this is a group grade, and I realize that on occasion there may be someone who has not done the work, has been consistently late or absent from the roundtable meetings, has been recalcitrant in reporting, or has shirked duties in the writing of the report, I further require that each member of the group evaluate each other. The individual evaluations allow me to adjust the grade to be fair to those who have worked responsibly, as well as to allow students to acknowledge those who have shown outstanding leadership or initiative among them. It also gives them ownership in the grading process. The individual evaluations must be signed and are submitted on the day the group evaluation report is due.

An analysis of these reports from the inception of the class process through December of 2013 has provided me with some critical insights about the learning that the students achieved around issues of diversity and, interestingly, around the larger issues of global concerns.

Creation of Safe Spaces and the Formation of Communities

The reports reveal that oftentimes students found the roundtable groups to be spaces where mutual dialogue, critique, exploration, and struggle (*lucha*) could take place safely.[37]

> The intimacy of the group setting allowed for more risk taking in seeking an understanding. It enabled members to address topics and ask questions that may not have been entertained in the larger lecture setting. (Group 2, 2006)

> [Sensitivity and vulnerability with a sense of humility] allowed for a safe atmosphere of theological exploration, where we were able to "try on" different theological perspectives, to engage with "marginal" theologies, without the pressure of having to be an "expert" on a particular doctrinal statement . . . [or] denying our own admitted "greenness" about the subject matter. (Group 1, 2007)

> Our interaction with our dialogue partners and with each other provided a safe forum in which to wrestle with the various theologies that both challenged and inspired us. (Group 3, 2008)

It was a place of true dialogue and not debate or argument.

> ["Y"] noted the importance of being aware of differing opinions was not to convince someone where they are wrong, but to "make room for everyone at the table." (Group 3, 2008)

This eventually led to a fostering of communal ties that at times transcended the class assignments. When difficulties arose, they discovered a support group that showed grace, concern, and friendship. It was the journey together that allowed them to bond in this way. Interestingly, the most common complaint was that I did not allow them sufficient time together. That is to say, the constructive nature of the process and the formation of community were such that they desired to be together more often and for longer periods of time.[38]

> As a group, we welcomed the gift of these interactions, recognizing that is a rare thing to be part of a community in which each voice is valued and wanted and heard without requiring conformity or complete agreement. (Group 1, 2008)

> These conversations led each person into deeper understanding of our own selves. In the creation of these relationships, through moments of laughter, intellectual discussion and emotional vulnerability, we created community. (Group 4, 2008)

> It was truly beautiful to see new partners develop from this class assignment. (Group 1, 2011)

> If this course and our round table discussions have taught us anything, it is that community matters. (Group 1, 2013)

> Last semester, we spent the majority of our time together working to create an environment that encouraged and valued open and honest dialogue between our group members. Our decision to stay together as a group speaks not only to the sense of community established during that time, but also indicates our desire to strengthen these connections. The

> familiarity and camaraderie developed last semester allowed us to once again come together and wrestle with new dialogue partners and theological topics in a safe and encouraging space. (Group 3, 2013)

Appreciation for Diversity on the Road to Damascus

One of the most important results of the roundtable experience is its ability to make students not simply aware of diversity but aware of how essential being "multilingual" is—that is to say, being culturally attuned to the multiplicity of voices of a larger world. They discover the ability and the foundational importance of listening and giving space to those voices, and that welcoming others "to the table" is essential to a true meaning of community. Allowing them as a group to grapple directly with difference and to speak to difference increases their sensitivity to being more open to difference. It was a more effective tool than if they had solely read about dialogue in a book, or if I simply lectured on the importance of "diversity."

> Examining doctrine in this context encouraged us to stretch beyond the traditional and our familiar. Our proverbial theological bones were altered as we continued our discussions. As a group we learned to listen more, read more and ask more questions. Learning theology from many perspectives and in a group setting is an excellent way to become more self-reflective and increasingly conscious of other traditions and worldviews. We appreciated the opportunity to learn from one another and our dialogue partners. (Group 1, 2006)

> We have all grown with these discussions. Generally speaking, we have all learned to listen in a new way. We have been exposed to a "mixed bag" of theologies and have realized that our ability to listen to other opinions is crucial for doing theology. Our discussions have taught us the value of listening to the "underside" or the "other"—those who are not afforded a theological voice or who have been repressed for centuries. . . . We noticed that through this discourse we acknowledged that different does not mean "bad" or "wrong." (Group 2, 2009)

> Listening to contributions of group members concerning the theology of their dialogue partners challenged us to become more open-minded about how we respond to voices different from our own. We all gained new insights from the discussions concerning the theological themes of our dialogue partners. As a group, we had to look beyond our Eurocentric points of view and engage in theological positions of authors from different countries, ethnicities, cultures and languages. . . . We were able to walk alongside our authors and hear their personal stories. (Group 2, 2010)

> We quickly appreciated [that] the scope of our theological endeavors concerned not only our ideology, but virtually that of the entire globe. . . . Everyone in our group came from a tradition and context significantly different from that of her or his dialogue partner. Being entrusted to represent such different viewpoints increased our appreciation and respect for our assigned theologians and the ethnic, linguistic and cultural lenses through which they see. It also increased our questions and stretched our theological perspectives. (Group 3, 2011)

> Much value in the roundtable discussions came from the sheer number of different voices present during each discussion. . . . It was particularly beneficial that the majority of our group were reading books from perspectives completely foreign to our own. . . . The diversity of perspectives taught us new ways of thinking about theology as a product of culture and context. (Group 1, 2012)

The students invariably described the experience as being a difficult task, one that involved disagreement as well as wrestling with difference. Yet they also described it as being deeply satisfying, an "eye-opening" experience. That is to say, it involved a *metanoia* of sorts, as students who were heretofore either unaware of or resistant to "speaking in other cultural, religious, or faith tradition tongues" engaged in these different perspectives. They discovered that difference was *not threatening* and, more important, that it was actually necessary for the formation and well-being of community. Indeed, they often linked the *imago Dei* to a sense of diversity-as-community. To be other than community, and to be a community that was other than diverse, seemed somehow to fall short of the vision of God for creation. In other instances, the students drew on imagery of the eschatological or eucharistic banquet as a way of affirming the need to include the marginalized and voiceless "at the table."

> Our dialogue partners helped us dismantle many . . . presuppositions. (Group 1, 2006)

> For [M], the lone Caucasian in the group, recognizing the variegated starting points of the dialogue partners shed light on a reality that he had taken for granted—that in our North American context, scholarship in the fields of history, social sciences, theology, [etc.] have largely been dominated by, and voiced the concerns/worldview of, the racial, social, and political [dominant culture]. . . . His greatest lesson was in learning the necessity of humility in order to truly *listen* and engage with the voices of the "other." (Group 1, 2007)

> One of our white male group members indicated that his participation in the group discussions exposed him to hidden sin. . . . The group allowed him to sit and hear the voices of people who were oppressed in the name of the God he loved. His unconscious desire to make everything instantly okay has been changed. He now wants to be a part of healing those wounds in whatever manner he is able to. (Group 3, 2008)

> Our discussions allowed us to hear others, especially our dialogue partners, in new ways. One group member shared how his conservative theological background was shaken by the diversity of theological perspectives we discussed, especially the womanist and feminist perspectives. Instead of interpreting these voices as threats to his embedded theology, he "heard" them as good and necessary voices that would "balance out [his] own theology." Other group members heard their dialogue partners calling them to go beyond the classical voices of Western Christianity in search of new answers and explanation. Listening to the voices of those who have been oppressed and overlooked was both refreshing and challenging. At times, the voices of our dialogue partners were very unsettling as they shared their anger over suffering and injustice. We were challenged in these times to be quiet and simply listen. This experience was important for our group because we realized how easily we assign greater value to certain voices simply because they are championed by the status quo and conveniently ignore the voices of those who speak on behalf of the marginalized. (Group 1, 2012)

Part of that "conversion" was realizing that their educational journeys had been skewed to privilege a Eurocentric interpretation of the world. They now realized that the world was a larger place.

> Through our sharing we gained a better understanding of some of the various theological positions held within Christianity, beliefs which differ from our positions. . . . We realized that the European theological tradition is not superior to other theologies. (Group 1, 2006)

> Our North American mindsets and cultural understandings of Christianity in general, and theological issues specifically, were broadened when we were exposed to the writings and theology of Christian theologians from around the world. . . . [There is] ample benefit to the practice of coming to understand the diversity of thought present in our world, even within our Christian community. (Group 2, 2006)

> The group celebrated the realization that the Western theological perspective is not the only paradigm for understanding Christian mission through the exploration of various contextual and contemporary voices. Group members reported "hearing" formerly hushed or neglected voices . . . as well as countless stories of oppression. (Group 1, 2010)

It also made them sensitive to the "absent" voices, and it created commitments to make present the invisible, the marginalized, and the oppressed.

> Many times, those not included in the dialogue of Western theology have grown comfortable in accepting their "non-voice" at the table, and even perhaps, not realizing that they have a voice. . . . Now, we can be more aggressive in having other voices heard and we can actually bring those voices to the table. . . . Other perspectives give us yet another context and make us realize the need for other voices. (Group 3, 2010)

Formation of Sa cred Spaces of Self-Learning

The greatest satisfaction in developing this pedagogical tool is that it has created a sacred space for students to engage in a learning process that is theirs for the making. While I provide literature and questions to guide the process, I intentionally create spaces that are theirs to shape. I largely refrain from interacting with the groups. I am present only to answer questions that might be initiated from a group. I gauge the full extent to which they wrestled with the readings, and the degree to which they helped each other in that struggle, only when I read the final reports. It is extremely gratifying for me to read findings or insights that are not part of the lesson plan. One of these is how groups grow to value the process of group learning, even when they initially express skepticism based on past experiences.

> The "roundtable discussions" we shared together were rewarding, challenging, and in some cases cognitively and spiritually transforming. . . . In retrospect, most group members expressed some initial skepticism and hesitancy towards working in groups in general. Others acknowledged the fear of potential conflict due to a number of strong personalities in the group. However, despite our initial misgivings or ambivalence, what began as [what] one group member described as "a bad idea" grew to be an enjoyable and constructive process. (Group 1, 2007)

> Many of us were skeptical about working in groups due to past experiences or assumptions about the group dynamic; this roundtable discussion group put those doubts to rest for us. We feel that we could continue to meet as a group if that option is available to us. It was a safe place and a place for growth. (Group 2, 2009)

Part of what contributes to a positive experience is the dialogical aspect: oftentimes, clarity and understanding come because their wrestling was done not alone but communally.

> Each member gently pushed other members into a better understanding of a particular theological issue that was placed into the context of their Dialogue partner. There were several times where a good conversation ensued from another person asking a deep question about what was mentioned. . . . It allowed for further examination of each of our dialogue partners and brought about a greater clarity of the group's understanding of each position. (Group 1, 2011)

Some students admitted that had they been assigned the reading as a solo project, they would not have completed it or appreciated it. The fact that they had to explain their dialogue partners to others pushed them to learn to listen and respect the voices of "others."

The roundtable group experience was a journey that entailed a critical dialogical process. Over the years, most groups have reported that the dialogical process has helped them develop their critical thinking skills and helped them in their process of "self-awareness." It became a journey in which they "came-to-know." They learn about diversity in the process of engaging diverse voices; they live out community in the process of learning communally.

> The community that was formed through this process really serves as a microcosm of what we (hopefully) learned this semester. We live in an individualistic society, and as one member of our group pointed out, there is not a lot of emphasis placed on small group interaction in our seminary journey. Yet if the God whom we [*sic*], as individual beings-in-community, is truly the Triune, relational, self-giving God, a God who values unity in diversity, that has created us as men and women in God's very image and likeness, then would it not be a sad irony if we walked away from a semester of "systematically" studying the Christian faith, as individual islands of intellect? Isn't it more appropriate that as children of God, representing different races, ethnicities, and backgrounds, we grew together in the process of listening together to the distinct voices of others? (Group 1, 2007)

> We learned about community by "doing" community. (Group 1, 2008)

> Just as God is community and unity in diversity, Christians should strive to live in community and in unity celebrate our diversity. Our experience as a group this semester did just that. . . . The struggle to listen is worth it. The struggle to give ideas that we strongly disagree with equal time and space with our own ideas made us sharper theologians and more strongly committed to the faith that brought us to the table in the first place. (Group 1, 2013)

It is my belief that in the "coming-to-know" journey they experienced being *personas educadas*, who are conscientized about the suffering of the world and understand that they cannot be tourists if they are truly to engage difference in the world.

Conclusion

Education is the creation of sacred spaces that allow true dialogue to take place. It is the formation of *personas educadas* who learn the value of multilingual, multicultural dialogue. Such persons not only cultivate a *habitus* of critical dialogue that flourishes in diffierence but seek to expand their knowledge of the world in which we are embedded and of which we are a part. *Personas educadas* are keenly aware that through dialogue we learn about God, ourselves, the stranger, and the world. We are awakened to the injustice of the world as we occupy spaces and go to places beyond our borders of comfort, and we experience what it means to be a stranger in a strange land. It is in dialogue that we also learn to hear and respect the silences of the voiceless and the absent of the world. This comes about because, as we are exposed to more and more diverse voices, we become aware of the voices *not present*, the ones *not speaking*.

Education is also a journey, a process of "coming-to-know." As such, no one class, teacher, experience, or educational institution can possibly teach all that one needs to learn. With each learning, we are shown new paths, new peoples, and new experiences. As one group articulated it, learning makes one increasingly aware "of the enormity" of what one does not know and still needs to learn, particularly in light of an increasingly globalized reality.[39] The motto of my institution is to "share the whole gospel with the whole world through whole persons." In the face of the challenges of globalization and glocalization, the "whole world" demands whole people, *personas educadas*. The "enormity" of such a task requires an institutional approach. In this chapter, I sought to demonstrate that the roundtable groups can be used as a pedagogical tool to provide students with a taste, perhaps it is even better to say a "foretaste," of what diversity and difference are like when experienced communally. Yet I am ever mindful that this is a small step of a long journey where others share of their wisdom and experiences. I am grateful for colleagues and their holistic pedagogies, and in particular for courses that expose our students to the larger world of Africa, Latin America, the Middle East, and beyond.

To be "multilingual" is to understand that the world will never conform to our comfort zones. True vocation is to go where we are sent. The prophet said, "Here I am. Send me," and not "Bring them to me."[40] Theological education is called to shift paradigms: to teach how to be community by preparing *personas educadas* and creating spaces that nurture communities of difference.

> More than anything, the idea of wrestling with material so different from your own perspective has become less of a fear and more of a growth process. . . . Our ways of thinking and talking have been stretched and maybe in some way even transformed. (Group 2, 2007)

> We have come to understand that there can be no true liberation until the voices of all the oppressed of the world can be heard. (Group 2, 2012)

Only then can we begin to experience the Spirit-filled joy of a true Pentecost, even as we prepare people called to be seekers of justice, and an embodiment of the love of the triune God—that is to say, a people who seek to live out the reality of the Reign of God in the world.

✦ 10 ✦

The Geopolitical and the Glocal

Situating Global Theological Voices in Theological Education

ELEAZAR S. FERNANDEZ

In this chapter I will present global geopolitics as an entry point in the discourse about transnational theological education. I will articulate the constructive geopolitical nature of regional or nation-state boundaries as well as the hybrid, porous, fluid, shifting, and multiple identities and belongings of various agents and entities. To sharpen the constructed and complex dynamics of our globalized world, I will employ the term "glocal." This term, which is the interweaving of the global and the local, offers a lens in understanding the nature and dynamics of the global. Following an account of the glocal, this chapter articulates the crucial characteristics of a transnational theological education and pedagogy. What insights can we derive from the notion of the glocal that may help us articulate the architecture of a transnational curriculum and pedagogy? What are the basic presuppositions that must undergird this transnational pedagogy and curriculum? What are the interacting dynamics that we must be attentive to?

Constructing Boundaries, Identity, and Belonging

Why are we often insistent and hard when putting up boundaries, both physically and discursively? Why are we insistent in delineating what/who belongs here, what/who belongs there, or what/who belongs to the East and what/who belongs to the West? Are we afraid of hybridity? Of contamination? Are we worried of blurring identity and belonging? Or, is there a complete ignorance of the constructed and geopolitical nature of boundaries that we make?

Essentialist, territorial-based thinking served an important purpose in the era of the formation of nation-states and their struggles for national independence. While geographical territory is a given reality that makes nation-states possible, it is not only geography that defines the life of a nation-state. Much of what defines the quality of life and people's interaction within a nation-state is a construct—a geopolitical construct. To be sure, there are geographical places called Asia, the Middle East, Africa, Latin America, and so on (discourse exists in relation to geographic place; nothing exists out of thin air), but these geographical designations are geopolitical constructs. They are constructs in relation to Europe, to the United States of America, and to what Michael Hardt and Antonio Negri call "Empire," a network of power relations that transcends nation-states even if it is enforced and propagated by more powerful nation-states, especially the United States.[1]

We may understand better the constructed nature of boundaries if we take the example of Tan Dun in relation to Johann Sebastian Bach. I do not need to belabor over an account of Bach, but I will focus on Tan and what his works suggest. Tan became widely known for his score for the movie *Crouching Tiger, Hidden Dragon*, and he came to prominence when he won the Academy Award in 2003. To be sure, Bach and Tan have distinctive geographic provenance, birthed and shaped by certain localities. Bach is a child of Germany (West) as Tan is of China (East). But what is Germany or China, Europe or Asia? There was not even a nation-state called Germany when Bach was born. Where is the demarcation line that separates the East from the West? Who is making the line and for what purpose? Boundaries are constructs that people make, and, in many instances, they change. Bach belongs to the West as Tan belongs to the East (where is the reference point?) as they both belong to the earth and to humanity.[2]

Similar to Bach, Tan employs counterpoints. But what is distinctive about Tan's creative compositions is that he goes a step further in using counterpoints to bridge or blend traditional divides/binaries between East and West. In doing so, he produces magnificent musical scores that are pleasant to the ears of his folks in Hunan, China, and to the ears of his Western listeners. Tan's works demonstrate the artificial nature of boundaries and encourage others to exercise freedom to transgress constructed boundaries for the sake of producing magnificent works.

The greater freedom claimed by later generations of Asian North American theologians to use pieces from various places and cultural traditions to compose new theological overtures reflects not only a greater embrace of the constructed, dynamic, shifting, and fluid character of realities but also a new understanding of our global context—particularly our global connectivity. In the spirit of Tan Dun, they have exercised greater freedom in fusing horizons to compose new theological overtures. This is not simply because no one can own a horizon but because the well-being of one locality or group is connected to another. With a fluid and unstable construal of borders and an expansive sense of belonging, they have become more daring in transgressing constructed boundaries of various sorts, whether those of geography, race/ethnicity, nation-state, or fields of discipline. They have become more daring in fusing horizons for the sake of that which promotes life.

The Glocal as Hermeneutic Lens

With a constructed and geopolitical notion of borders, we are now in a better position to understand the character of our globalized world. We live in a globalized world. This has become a cliché that people accept without much scrutiny of what it really means. Often, it is taken simply to mean that the local is impacted by global realities. It comes with this question: What are the impacts of globalization in the local neighborhood? This question needs to be asked, but this line of inquiry is one-dimensional and one-directional. In this articulation, the flow between the global and the local follows the linear, one-way traffic approach. We must not just reverse the question but ask the question that helps us see the multiple interactions. A term that would help us understand the multidimensional and multidirectional character of our globalized world is "glocal" and its extension, "glocalization." What "glocalization" does, says Charles Van Engen, is help us see the "interrelationship between the local and the global in their multifaceted, multidirectional, interactive dynamic influence one upon the other."[3]

I have said elsewhere that in a globalized world, the global is lived locally and the local is lived globally.[4] The global is not simply "out there" but also "in here," wherever our location is. The global has no reality *apart from* the local, even as the reality of the global is more than the sum of the locals. The local constitutes the global even as the global is not equivalent to the sum of all the parts. The slogan "think globally and act locally" is not as simple as it sounds. Through the local we see the global, not outside the local. In fact, awareness that one is seeing through the local is constitutive of seeing the global. Global thinking is located thinking; it is not nowhere-thinking. After all, nowhere-thinking is somewhere-thinking that has forgotten it is thinking from, in, and through somewhere. To articulate the slogan differently, "thinking globally demands seeing locally." But we must also underscore the converse. If we want to see the local, we have to see it globally. The reality of the local would come to full light only when seen globally. Only in seeing globally is the local taken seriously. Seeing globally is seeing through the local but using a wider frame that is able to analyze the various threads in their systemic interconnections. Apart from seeing the systemic or structural interconnections of the locals, we have not really taken the local seriously. In short, the global is not a separate reality from the local but a way of seeing the interconnections of the local.

The Geopolitical and the Glocal in Theological Education

The geopolitical and the glocal offer insights on how we may pursue theological education. They suggest the basic premises and the thrust and scope as well as the context, the identity of the main actors (teachers and students), the content or the curriculum, and the pedagogy of theological education. The geopolitical, as I indicated earlier, suggests the constructed and political character of boundaries and interaction of nation-state and non–nation-state players. These boundaries and interactions are creations of the power-knowledge nexus, constructs that often appear or are made to appear rigid because they serve some interests in the power-knowledge nexus. If the geopolitical underscores the political and constructed nature of boundaries, the glocal, on the other hand, helps us see the glocalized character of reality. The understanding that reality is glocal has important bearings on how we do theological education, especially if we are intentional in building a transnational curriculum and pedagogy. It has bearings on the content of the curriculum, the pedagogy, and how we mentor students. I will spell this out in the next few pages.

The geopolitical and the glocal suggest, as well, how we might see and consider the context of theological education. Context is not simply a reality out there but a reality we engage through our interpretation. How do the notions of the geopolitical and the glocal inform how we see our context? What do they suggest about the contextualization of theological education? How might we perform theological education in the interweaving of the local and the global?

What do the geopolitical and the glocal have to say about identity, particularly the identity of the teachers and the students? Identity needs to be factored into thinking about theological education in general and about curriculum and pedagogy in particular. How shall we think about identity in a globalized/glocalized world? Who are the teachers and the students? What context do they come from, and what experiences do they bring? Are we preparing students to do ministry in their globalized context, and in what ways?

How about the content of theological education in a globalized world? What do the geopolitical and the glocal suggest about the scope and thrust of theological education and the content of the curriculum? What architectural design shall we pursue so that our theological dwelling place meets the desires of all and nourishes all and opens a place for future inhabitants? What degree programs must we offer, and what competencies must we expect from our students? On what bases are we defining competencies?

Finally, how do the geopolitical and the glocal inform us about pedagogy? How do multiple and shifting identities and belonging inform how we teach? How does the teacher navigate or negotiate with his or her own shifting and multiple identities in the classroom in relation to students? What pedagogical principles, strategies, and tools might he or she use to let multiple worlds saturate his or her classroom?

Our Globalized World: The Context of Theological Education

Our globalized world has become the context in which we must do theological education. In spite of the many positions and disagreements regarding what globalization is, there is one point of agreement among various interpreters: heightened connections and interweaving of our lives. John Tomlinson speaks of globalization as "complex connectivity," which he describes as "the rapidly developing and ever-densening network of interconnections and interdependencies that characterize modern social life."[5] Anthony Giddens speaks of a similar point by articulating globalization as "the intensification of worldwide social relations which link distant localities in such a way that local happenings are shaped by events occurring many miles away and vice versa."[6] In line with the heightening reality of our connectivity or interrelatedness is the heightening awareness of our interconnections or the increasing recognition that our lives are intertwined, and that we have shared vulnerabilities and hopes even if we have suffered unevenly. The question "Who is my neighbor?" is becoming more complex and difficult to answer.

With or without globalization, we have, of course, always been connected. Globalization has only heightened these connections and made us more acutely aware of them. With connections heightened, so are the consequences of our actions on others, even those who were once geographically far. With our abilities to reach and connect heightened, so are our abilities to affect the lives of others, for good or for ill. The mobility of people goes along with the mobility of pathogens and the spread of diseases. Fast and efficient technology has made investing in the global market much easier, but there is also a downside. What happens in the global market affects all. The economic recession in the United States is affecting not only the United States but other countries as well. Many victims of downsizing in the Global North know painfully well the connection of downsizing, overseas outsourcing, and poorly compensating the workers employed in the Global South. The Third World is present not only in the Global South but also in the Global North.

Given the opportunity, a great number of the world's poor have found their way into the heartland of the Global North, such as the United States. Many of them are refugees from civil wars and from wars that the United States has been involved in, directly or indirectly. They carry with them their suitcases full of dreams and subversive desires—a dream of a new and better tomorrow: a tomorrow of radical hospitality. This has changed significantly the ethnic and religious demographics of the Global North. Ethnic diversity is fast becoming the reality in many areas. We can observe a similar phenomenon in relation to religious diversity. Encounters of people of various faiths are becoming common, along with the challenges that they entail. It should be noted that many of the newcomers are Christians. The much-touted Christian vitality in the Global South has come to the Global North through those living in diaspora. The idea of the post-Christian West may not be accurate (or not yet accurate) because of this phenomenon.

We need to be clear on what we mean by context for theological education. This context is our glocalized and highly diverse world. We need to move beyond the narrow notion of context, which is often equated to a small and limited geographical boundary. We still need to be attentive to the specificity of our localities, but our context is glocal. In short, our context embraces the interweaving of the many locals that shape our lives.

Identity: Who Are the Teachers? Who Are the Students?

If we speak of geopolitical space as a complex, broad, transnational, porous, hybrid, fluid, unstable, and contested space, we must do the same when we speak of the identity and subjectivity of teachers and students. The homogenous identity does not exist. Teachers and students are humans assuming multiple identities, subjectivities, and belongings. Moreover, there are multiple subjectivities at the individual level. An individual may be Chinese by ethnicity, born in Malaysia, adopted by white Canadians, and an immigrant to the United States. We may add other categories: gender, sexuality, class, and religious affiliation. If this person is gay or lesbian, he or she may seek affinity with white gays and lesbians but may also encounter racism within that group. On the other hand, while she or he may feel at home ethnically with Asian North Americans, she or he may experience marginalization in the Asian North American communities because of her or his sexual identity.

Another example of multiple, fluid, and shifting identity came to me in one of the immersion trips I led with my students to Palestine-Israel. One day our group went to the Golan Heights (a territory occupied by Israel since 1967 that belongs to Syria). Its terrain, resources (e.g., water source), green vegetation, and so forth make one understand that it is strategic in a comprehensive sense, not only militarily. Our group stopped by a cherry farm, and I had the chance to ask a few questions to a farmer by the name of Jamil. I asked him if he was in the area during the war with Israel and if he was Syrian. He confirmed that he is Syrian by birth and nationality and also carries an Israeli ID. Afterward he spoke about his love for his land, which explains why he did not leave the place even during the war that led to the occupation. As a person living in a land (his own land) now under Israeli occupation, he said that he is loyal to whoever is the ruling power (now the State of Israel). He abides by the rules of the occupier in order to survive. But, at the end of the conversation, he expressed his longing for the return of the territory to Syria.

With heightened transnational connection brought about by the compression of time and space and the extension of reach, we must articulate an anthropology that takes a serious account of glocalized identity. There is a need to speak of identity not only in terms of multiplicity but also in terms of translocality. Translocal is not simply an adjective we attach to a person: it is an aspect that is constitutive of one's identity; it is an evolving form of identity. The translocal is a self that is porous to the interweaving of the many localities in one's own self. This person is locally rooted and globally winged. A translocal is one who experiences the interweaving, the tension, and the possibilities of both one world and many worlds.

Complexifying the multiplicity, fluidity, and instability of identity is what Fumitaka Matsuoka calls "amphibolous" life.[7] He speaks of himself as one living with an amphibolous faith, not completely at home in one religion such as Christianity. A person or community with an amphibolous faith embodies more than one epistemological and cosmological orientation. Most often the Eurocentric-Christian worldview expects or forces the individual to make an either/or decision, but the diverse orientations do not submit for easy compromise. Thus the person or community experiences tensions with the wider society and tension within itself. There have been tensions within white churches that see Hmong members, for example, practicing their indigenous and Buddhist religious practices even when they have become baptized Christians. They expect Hmong members to stick to a single Christian, if not Eurocentric, worldview.

The multiple identities of the teacher must be considered as an important factor in the discourse about curriculum and pedagogy. These multiple identities shift, and, consequently, power differentials shift. The teacher carries or embodies his or her multiple and shifting identities in the classroom. This is particularly obvious with teachers identified as "marked" bodies in terms of ethnicity, color, gender, and sexuality. As a professor/person of color in a white society and in a predominantly white theological institution with two decades of experience in teaching, I surely have witnessed how race/ethnicity (and other forms of "marked" identities) has played out in the classroom, in research and publication, in administration, and in policy making. The "marked" teacher encounters racism in multiple forms from various groups, including racism from students in her or his classroom. Though often subtle, it comes in the stereotyped expectations of students and faculty colleagues. If a racial/ethnic teacher, particularly new to the United States, introduces a little bit more of his or her country of origin's culture in the classroom, she or he may get the comment that she is "into her ethnic stuff" and not really teaching the core substance of the course. If the racially/ethnically "marked" person does not include her or his ethnic identity/culture, she or he may get the comment that her or his teaching or writing is generic, just like what one can expect from a white teacher and scholar. To add to the complexity, if the racial/ethnic person is identified as a liberationist theologian, she or he might be under observation to monitor whether she or he is teaching the "real stuff."

The identity of the teacher is a text; it is not a neutral text. It is read and interpreted by various agents in the teaching and learning process. This "marked body text" either impedes or facilitates learning. The teacher who is identified as a "marked" body must be fully aware of the constructed and political nature of his or her teaching presence and must continue to find ways to decenter the educational normativity of certain bodies. She or he must point to her or his "marked" body as "implicit" curriculum and expose in the explicit curriculum its vestiges of assumptions about "marked bodies" as "racial-ethnic texts."

Likewise, we need to be attentive to the multiple, shifting, and translocal identities of our students and the nature of the communities they come from. Strangely, even as the ethnic demographic landscape in the United States has become more diverse, religious congregations from which most seminary students are coming have remained relatively homogenous. How shall we do theological education for a multiracial, religiously diverse, and glocalized world? With the greater possibility that students may be serving pastoral settings that are different from their ethnic-racial background, how shall we do theological education for that ministry? With white students mostly shaped by their more homogenous congregations, how shall we prepare them for a different world? And how shall we prepare racial-ethnic minority students whose identity has been contested and precarious?

Curriculum Content

Transnational theological curriculum and pedagogy that take account of our globalized world must reframe the context, which is glocal; promote a way of thinking/reasoning that transgresses Eurocentric and binaristic assumptions; be multilingual—understood in a deeper sense to mean various ways of apprehending the world through language—and transcultural; and be interfaith-engaged, hermeneutically dialogical, and interdisciplinary and integrative.

A transnational pedagogy must embrace a glocalized framework. When we see reality as glocal, we gain the ability to connect our seemingly local context and concerns with the wider world. Only in seeing the local through the global (interconnections of the locals) can we truly honor the local. Conversely, only in being attentive to our local specificities can we celebrate the global. Attentiveness to the local when seen through the lens of the global is our way to avoid narrowing and making exclusive our particularities. To be particular is not the same as to be exclusive and narrow. Particularity is a necessary mode for something to become universal.

Kwame Anthony Appiah offers a way of interpreting the local/particular in relation to the global in his concept of "rooted cosmopolitanism."[8] Rootedness or connection to the particular is not antithetical to cosmopolitan vision. In fact, recognition of our rootedness in specific geographies and cultures and nexuses of relations is a critical point for a credible account of cosmopolitanism. We can say that we are all citizens of the earth, but that does not take seriously into account our specific locations, much less address the power differentials between inhabitants of the Global South and the Global North. Once rootedness is accepted, the critical point is whether our rootedness is self-enclosed or porous to the presence and claims of other human beings in their particularities.

To be true to its name, a transnational curriculum and pedagogy must continue the educational project of transgressing Eurocentric and binaristic assumptions. It must transgress Western sociopolitical imaginary, such as what Edward Said calls Orientalism.[9] Transgression of Eurocentric assumptions must happen not only in the materials assigned but also in ways of learning and ways of evaluating student performance. It must continue to examine and problematize alternative views, exposing the multiple angles in which they may reinscribe Euro-hegemonic assumptions. Binaristic thinking—such as the notion of East and West, which puts the West as the reference point and relegates the East to the lower status—needs to be exposed and transgressed. The work of Tan Dun that I cited earlier, transgressing and bridging binaries to produce magnificent pieces, is an inspiration for theological education.

Transnational curriculum and pedagogy must seek to promote multiple linguistic ways of "apprehending" the world. People inhabit different worlds; they see the world through their worldviews. An excellent theological education must expose teachers and students to the various worlds in which people dwell. A sort of "mindwalk" to the worlds of various groups and cultures will help teachers and students to be more respectful of the worlds of others and help them understand the limits and idiosyncrasies of their own world.

Obviously, we need to broaden our theological education to include the voices and concerns of the Global South and the new diaspora communities in our midst. We need to study world Christianity and the global ecumenical movement vis-à-vis the trend toward being absorbed with domestic, local church affairs, especially when church survival has become the primary concern of many. We need to study church history from a non-Eurocentric perspective. Broadening the perspective of theological education is not, however, as simple as adding electives. Many liberal seminaries already have a list of course offerings that deal with the Global South, and many students have taken them. More crucial is how we see these courses in relation to the overall curriculum and our approach in studying them. Unfortunately, these courses are often treated like "exotic fruits" to supplement the traditional, main Euro-American dishes.

Changing our framework is a step in the direction of moving beyond the exotization of the so-called foreign courses. Unless we see the connection between the global and the local, we will always have students who say, "Studying about Global South or Third World theologies is informative, but that is not relevant to my context in North America." But I say that it is irrelevant only for someone who has not seen the connections or the interweaving of the global and the local, or the connections between our comforts and the sufferings of people in the Global South. Hence, it is crucial that whatever subject we teach, it should be framed in the context of the interweaving of the global and the local.

The interweaving of the global and the local must move in accord with the approach of integrating the various academic disciplines in the context of people's day-to-day lives. In accord with moving beyond offering "exotic fruits," we should not be satisfied with requiring students to take courses on major religions. What is crucial is our method or approach. The dominant approach remains captive to the secularist and essentialist hegemony. We study religions—often learning the basic teachings and comparing them with other religions—as if they were isolated from sociopolitical and economic conditions. I suggest that we study religions as part of the whole web of sociopolitical interactions. This means changing our approach and focus from simply concentrating on the core teachings of religions to considering how religions are embodied in flesh-and-blood people in the context of social interaction at the local and global level.

Transnational theological education must be interdisciplinary and integrative. Global complexity, geographic/geopolitical deterritorialization and reterritorialization, border crossings, threshold dwelling, transnationality, fluidity, and hybridity must bear on how we construct fields of disciplines and the curriculum. The academic community has abundant institutional forms of insistent individualism, such as disciplinary fields, which have become specialty silos. These specialty fields, says John Cobb Jr., "constitute self-contained communities of research whose selection of topics is little affected by any needs but their own."[10] The "hands-off" agreement among specialty fields breeds a kind of indifference to common concerns that everyone must address.[11] Disciplinary silos have been obstacles for transformative work; they have been disempowering for individuals and communities. We need to recognize the need for interdisciplinary work that, in the prevalence of sacralized disciplinary silos, requires the unholy act of transgression. We need to promote discourses that transgress disciplinary boundaries: boundaries that make academic disciplines captive to hegemonic interests; boundaries that are less useful in the life and practice of communities; and boundaries or disciplinary silos that make scholars prisoners of their academic disciplines.

When disciplinary silos are transgressed, we will be in a better position to integrate the various courses. When adding another course in what is construed as an already overloaded curriculum would not be readily welcome, even though it remains an option, the notion of the glocal provides a way for addressing the matter of transnational pedagogy. When reality is understood as glocal—that is, the constant interweaving of the global and the local—the global is rescued from being remote and far, and it is brought to the immediate context and into the heart of the local. When the current notion of the global peripheralizes global-oriented courses as electives or, in the case of global justice immersion courses, as experiences accessible only to those who have the means to travel, the adoption of the glocal perspective brings global or transnational concerns to the center and saturates every aspect of the educational enterprise. "The rest of the world" is no longer identified with courses that deal with the global, but all courses can be vehicles of understanding the transnational character of our daily lives, because there is no local entity that is not at the same time global or affected by the global.

On Transnational Pedagogy

Transnational pedagogy starts with the fundamental assumption of our glocalized reality and the teacher's understanding of his or her glocalized identity. It is out of this fundamental assumption that the teacher crafts her or his course, the syllabus, the objectives and learning outcomes, learning activities, readings, and evaluation.

How does a glocalized understanding of identity and belonging affect/inform pedagogy? How does one teach as a racially-ethnically "marked body" in ways that honor one's identity as well as take the students' life experiences and multiple identities seriously and promote cultural-ethnic diversity? How shall we teach to prepare our students to do ministry in a glocalized and culturally and racially diverse context? Do we have a broad repertoire of teaching methods that are culturally sensitive and respectful of ethnic differences and are able to address various learning styles? How do we assess effective teaching in a multicultural, multiethnic, and multireligious classroom? What approaches, exercises, and evaluative or assessment tools are we going to use? What kind of teaching-learning environment are we creating? What is the classroom culture, and what are the classroom norms?

Doing transnational pedagogy calls for the creation of a learning environment in which students understand deeply the glocalized reality of our world and develop glocalized identities. Learning activities must be conducted in ways that deepen and broaden their self-understandings as individuals connected to the wider community. Moreover, learning activities must be geared toward enlarging one's heart, with the capacity to transcend national and ethnic interests.

In light of its commitment to enlarging the students' hearts and imaginations, transnational pedagogy is by nature transgressive: it is teaching to transgress. This pedagogy seeks ways to transgress constructed boundaries that limit one's world, shrink one's heart, and narrow one's social imagination. Or, in another way of putting it, transnational pedagogy is disruptive because it must disrupt various forms of hegemony. It must develop pedagogical principles and strategies for disruptive teaching.

Moreover, transnational pedagogy cultivates and practices hermeneutic companionship with others, especially giving an ear and voice to strangers. In dialoguing with strangers and letting strangers remain subjects, strangers or the "others" are more able to represent, following Raúl Betancourt, "the exteriority that widens the frontiers of our horizon of understanding." In allowing this to happen, "we discover a new world": we are "born again."[12]

Conclusion: Moving Ahead

While it is true that technology and communications have compressed our time and space, and the global village has become a reality, we are also experiencing global fragmentation and global conflict. Our increasing connections and their challenges demand that we pursue the goal of developing and promoting transnational pedagogy. We need to intensify our efforts in pursuit of theological education that breaks walls of separation and fences of division. I hope this attempt to articulate transnational pedagogy will contribute to the betterment of our globalized world. So we, along with others, must dare to pursue, to articulate, and to practice transnational curriculum and pedagogy.

Notes

Chapter 1: Kwok Pui-lan

1 Joerg Rieger and Kwok Pui-lan, *Occupy Religion: Theology of the Multitude* (Lanham, Md.: Rowman & Littlefield, 2012), 5–6.

2 John Tomlinson speaks of globalization as "complex connectivity" in his *Globalization and Culture* (Chicago: University of Chicago Press, 1999), 2.

3 Anthony Giddens, *The Consequences of Modernity* (Stanford, Calif.: Stanford University Press, 1990), 64.

4 Roland Robertson, "Glocalization: Time-Space and Homogeneity-Heterogeneity," in *Global Modernities*, ed. Mike Featherstone, Scott Lash, and Roland Robertson (London: Sage, 1995), 25–44.

5 Harold A. Netland, "Introduction: Globalization and Theology Today," in *Globalizing Theology: Belief and Practice in an Era of World Christianity*, ed. Craig Ott and Harold A. Netland (Grand Rapids: Baker Academic, 2006), 25–27.

6 Gustavo Gutiérrez, *A Theology of Liberation: History, Politics, and Salvation*, trans. Caridad Inda and John Eagleson (Maryknoll, N.Y.: Orbis, 1973).

7 Sergio Torres and John Eagleson, eds., *Theology in the Americas* (Maryknoll, N.Y.: Orbis, 1976).

8 Robert J. Schreiter, *Constructing Local Theologies* (Maryknoll, N.Y.: Orbis, 1985), 5.

9 Stephen B. Bevans, *An Introduction to Theology in Global Perspective* (Maryknoll, N.Y.: Orbis, 2009), 4.

10 Andrew Walls, *The Significance of African Christianity* (Edinburgh: St. Colm's Education Center and College, 1989), 3; quoted in Tite Tiénou, "Christian Theology in an Era of World Christianity," in Ott and Netland, *Globalizing Theology*, 40.

11 Philip Jenkins, "The Next Christianity," *Atlantic*, October 1, 2002, http://www.theatlantic.com/magazine/archive/2002/10/the-next-christianity/302591/.

12 Lamin Sanneh, "Missionary Enterprise," in *Encyclopedia of Africa: South of the Sahara*, ed. John Middleton (New York: Scribner's, 1997), 296.

13 Lamin Sanneh, *Whose Religion Is Christianity? The Gospel beyond the West* (Grand Rapids: Eerdmans, 2003), 22.

14 Walter Hollenweger, "Intercultural Theology: Some Remarks on the Term," in *Towards an Intercultural Theology: Essays in Honour of J. A. B. Jongeneel*, ed. Martha Fredris, Meindert Dijkstra, and Anton Hontepen (Zoetermeer, Netherlands: Uitgeverij Meinema, 2003), 94; quoted in Tiénou, "Christian Theology," in Ott and Netland, *Globalizing Theology*, 42.

15 Soong-Chan Rah, *The Next Evangelicalism: Freeing the Church from Western Cultural Captivity* (Downers Grove, Ill.: InterVarsity, 2009).

16 The syllabi can be found on the Wabash Center Web site, http://www.wabashcenter.wabash.edu/resources/result-browse.aspx?advkey1=Theology&advkey2=&advconj=and&type=syllab.

17 William A. Dyrness, ed., *Emerging Voices in Global Christian Theology* (Grand Rapids: Zondervan, 1994), 13.

18 Veli-Matti Kärkkäinen, *An Introduction to Ecclesiology: Ecumenical, Historical, and Global Perspectives* (Downers Grove, Ill.: InterVarsity, 2002); *Christology: A Global Introduction* (Grand Rapids: Baker Academic, 2003); *The Doctrine of God: A Global Introduction* (Grand Rapids: Baker Academic, 2004); *The Trinity: Global Perspectives* (Louisville, Ky.: Westminster John Knox, 2007).

19 Hans Schwarz, *Theology in a Global Context: The Last Two Hundred Years* (Grand Rapids: Eerdmans, 2005).

20 Namsoon Kang, "Re-constructing *Asian* Feminist Theology: Toward a *Glocal* Feminist Theology in an Era of Neo-empire(s)," in *Christian Theology in Asia*, ed. Sebastian C. H. Kim (Cambridge: Cambridge University Press, 2008), 210–11.

21 See the discussion in Dipesh Chakrabarty, *Provincializing Europe: Postcolonial Thought and Historical Difference* (Princeton: Princeton University Press, 2000).

22 Tiénou, "Christian Theology," in Ott and Netland, *Globalizing Theology*, 38.

23 Andrew Walls, "Globalization and the Study of Christian History," in Ott and Netland, *Globalizing Theology*, 74.

24 For a detailed discussion of the stele, see P. Y. Saeki, *The Nestorian Monument in China* (London: Society for the Promotion of Christian Knowledge, 1916).

25 Kwok Pui-lan, "2011 Presidential Address: Empire and the Study of Religion," *Journal of the American Academy of Religion* 80, no. 2 (2012): 285–303.

26 Simon Shui-Man Kwan, *Postcolonial Resistance and Asian Theology* (London: Routledge, 2014).

27 See Lai Pan-chiu's chapter in this volume.

28 Robert J. Schreiter, *The New Catholicity: Theology between the Global and the Local* (Maryknoll, N.Y.: Orbis, 1997).

29 Schreiter, *New Catholicity*, 132–33.

30 Schreiter, *New Catholicity*, 16–20.

31 Orlando O. Espín, *Idol and Grace: On Traditioning and Subversive Hope* (Maryknoll, N.Y.: Orbis, 2014), 17.

32 Espín, *Idol and Grace*, 10–13.

33 Mary McClintock Fulkerson and Sheila Briggs, "Introduction," in *The Oxford Handbook of Feminist Theology*, ed. Mary McClintock Fulkerson and Sheila Briggs (Oxford: Oxford University Press, 2012), 7–9.

34 Musa W. Dube, "Feminist Theologies of a World Scripture(s) in the Globalization Era," in Fulkerson and Briggs, *Oxford Handbook of Feminist Theology*, 387.

35 Ellen T. Armour, "Beyond the God/Man Duo: Globalization, Feminist Theology, and Religious Subjectivity," in Fulkerson and Briggs, *Oxford Handbook of Feminist Theology*, 373; and Sharon D. Welch, "Beyond Theology of Religions: The Epistemological and Ethical Challenges of Inter-religious Engagement," in Fulkerson and Briggs, *Oxford Handbook of Feminist Theology*, 353–70.

36 Gayatri Chakravorty Spivak, *Other Asias* (Malden, Mass.: Blackwell, 2008), 1.

37 The Association of Theological Schools in the United States and Canada published the issue "Globalizing Theological Education in North America" in spring of 1986, and other issues on globalization and theological education in autumn of 1986 and spring and autumn of 1993.

38 Edward W. Said, *Orientalism* (New York: Vintage, 1979).

39 Corey D. B. Walker, "Theology and Democratic Futures," *Political Theology* 10, no. 2 (2009): 200.

40 Dube, "Feminist Theologies," in Fulkerson and Briggs, *Oxford Handbook of Feminist Theology*, 394.

41 Gayatri Chakravorty Spivak was the first critic to use the term "transnational literacy" extensively; see the discussion in Jessica Schagerl, "Transnational Literacy," http://globalautonomy.uwaterloo.ca/global1/servlet/Glossarypdf?id=CO.0065.

42 Gutiérrez, *Theology of Liberation*.

43 Rauna Kuokkanen, *Reshaping the University: Responsibilities, Indigenous Epistemes, and the Logic of the Gift* (Vancouver: University of British Columbia Press, 2007), 1.

44 William A. Dyrness, "Why Don't We Hear Much from the Global Church?" *Teaching Theology in a Global and Transnational World* (blog), November 28, 2011, http://teachingtheology.blogspot.com/2011/11/why-dont-we-hear-much-from-global.html.

45 Althea Spencer Miller, "Feminist Pedagogies: Implications of a Liberative Praxis," in *Feminist New Testament Studies: Global and Future Perspectives*, ed. Kathleen O'Brien Wicker, Althea Spencer Miller, and Musa W. Dube (New York: Palgrave Macmillan, 2005), 34.

46 Spencer Miller, "Feminist Pedagogies," in Wicker, Miller, and Dube, *Feminist New Testament Studies*, 35.

47 A helpful resource is Eleazar S. Fernandez, ed., *Teaching for a Culturally Diverse and Racially Just World* (Eugene, Ore.: Cascade Books, 2014).

48 The digital natives are those who were born into the culture of the Internet and digital media. Others are digital immigrants who have to learn the culture and catch up with the digital age. For the culture of the digital natives, see John Palfrey and Urs Gasser, *Born Digital: Understanding the First Generation of Digital Natives* (New York: Basic Books, 2010).

Chapter 2: William A. Dyrness

1 I would like to express appreciation to Professor Joseph Prabhu for extended conversations that gave rise to some of the arguments in this paper.

2 See Lamin Sanneh, *Translating the Message: The Missionary Impact on Culture*, rev. ed. (Maryknoll, N.Y.: Orbis, 2009).

3 Andrew Walls, "The Rise of Global Theologies," in *Global Theology in Evangelical Perspective: Exploring the Contextual Nature of Theology and Mission*, ed. Jeffrey P. Greenman and Gene L. Green (Downers Grove, Ill.: InterVarsity, 2012), 23.

4 W. H. C. Frend, *The Rise of Christianity* (Minneapolis: Fortress, 1984), 144–45.

5 James H. Charlesworth, *The Old Testament Pseudepigrapha* (New York: Doubleday, 1985), 725. Quotes from these hymns are from this source.

6 Andrew Walls comments on this hymn, "I cannot think of anything in second-century Greek theology that puts trinitarian relationships so clearly." See Walls, "Rise of Global Theologies," in Greenman and Green, *Global Theology*, 28.

7 Mercy Amba Oduyoye, *Hearing and Knowing* (Nairobi: Acton, 2000), 25. She notes, "The theological implications of this for women and for the church are tremendous."

8 Oduyoye, *Hearing and Knowing,* 20.

9 In a letter to Bishop Alexander of Alexandria (312–328), in Frend, *Rise of Christianity*, 494.

10 Henry Chadwick, *East and West: The Making of a Rift in the Church; From Apostolic Times until the Council of Florence* (Oxford: Oxford University Press, 2003), 27. It was in the context of this challenge, Chadwick notes, that Augustine wrote "On the Trinity," insisting that the Son participates in the Spirit's proceeding from the Father (thus the "filioque" clause in the creed).

11 Oduyoye, *Hearing and Knowing*, 23. Great as Augustine and Cyprian were, she says, "their theology did not reflect the spirituality of the Berbers."

12 A good overview of Nestorius and his influence is found in Samuel Hugh Moffett, *A History of Christianity in Asia* (San Francisco: HarperSanFrancisco, 1992).

13 Quoted in Moffett, *History of Christianity in Asia*, 176.

14 Walls, "Rise of Global Theologies," in Greenman and Green, *Global Theology*, 32. Moffett notes that Islam treated both Jews and Christians with generosity, in *History of Christianity in Asia*, 325.

15 Moffett, *History of Christianity in Asia*, 200.

16 Malcolm Lambert, *Medieval Heresy: Popular Movements from Bogomil to Hus* (New York: Holmes & Meier, 1977), 8.

17 For a description of this period and its religious tolerance, see María Rosa Menocal, *The Ornament of the World: How Muslims, Jews, and Christians Created a Culture of Tolerance in Medieval Spain* (Boston: Little, Brown, 2002); and Sidney H. Griffith, *The Church in the Shadow of the Mosque: Christians and Muslims in the World of Islam* (Princeton: Princeton University Press, 2008).

18 See R. I. Moore, *The Origins of European Dissent* (New York: St. Martins, 1977), 4.

19 R. I. Moore, *The Formation of a Persecuting Society: Power and Deviance in Western Europe: 950–1250* (Oxford: Basil Blackwell, 1987), 69.

20 Moore, *Persecuting Society*, 4. Quote that follows is from p. 5. Moore's focus is on the Western Church; he acknowledges that persecution continued in the Eastern Church.

21 This is the way David J. Collins explains matters in his review of *The War on Heresy*, in "Collateral Damage," *America*, November 12, 2012, 25.

22 Moore, *Origins of European Dissent,* 44. In addition to the two cited, see his *The War on Heresy* (Cambridge, Mass.: Belknap Press of Harvard University, 2012). One might similarly argue that this dynamic lay behind the rise of Islam as well.

23 Malcolm Lambert argues, e.g., that the Waldensians were drawn into heresy by the inadequacies of the church authorities, in *Medieval Heresy,* 67.

24 Collins, "Collateral Damage," 26.

25 The review by David J. Collins gives some idea of the debate it has inspired.

26 Enrique Dussel, *The History of the Church in Latin America: An Interpretation* (San Antonio: Latin American Cultural Center, 1974), 15.

27 Willie James Jennings, *The Christian Imagination: Theology and the Origins of Race* (New Haven: Yale University Press, 2010), 81–82. For what follows, see p. 79.

28 On this, see the excellent study by Cristián Parker, *Popular Religion and Modernization in Latin America: A Different Logic* (Maryknoll, N.Y.: Orbis, 1996).

29 See Robert D. Woodberry, "The Missionary Roots of Liberal Democracy," *American Political Science Review* 106, no. 2 (2012): 244–74.

30 I owe this point to conversation with my colleague Oscar Garcia-Johnson. On this, see Enrique Dussel, "World-System and 'Trans-modernity,'" *Nepantla: Views from the South* 3, no. 2 (2002): 221–44.

31 Herman Bavinck, "Theology and Religious Studies in Nineteenth-Century Netherlands," in Herman Bavinck, *Essays on Religion, Science, and Society*, ed. John Bolt (Grand Rapids: Baker Academic, 2008), 284.

32 Francis X. Clooney, "Comparative Theology," in *The Oxford Handbook of Systematic Theology*, ed. John Webster, Kathryn Tanner, and Iain Torrance (New York: Oxford University Press, 2007), 654. For an appreciative evaluation of this movement, see Reid B. Locklin and Hugh Nicholson, "The Return of Comparative Theology," *Journal of the American Academy of Religion* 78, no. 2 (2010): 477–514. I have tried to do something similar in religious aesthetics; see William A. Dyrness, *Senses of Devotion: Interfaith Aesthetics in Buddhist and Muslim Communities* (Eugene, Ore.: Cascade, 2013).

33 A. N. Williams, "Assimilation and Otherness: The Theological Significance of *Négritude*," *International Journal of Systematic Theology* 11, no. 3 (2009): 250.

34 Quoted in Williams, "Assimilation and Otherness," 250–51.

35 Williams, "Assimilation and Otherness," 265.

Chapter 3: Veli-Matti Kärkkäinen

1 "Religious Plurality and Christian Self-Understanding," ¶2, ¶3, World Council of Churches Ninth Assembly (Porto Alegre, Brazil, 2006, February 14–23), http://www.oikoumene.org/en/resources/documents/assembly/porto-alegre-2006/3-preparatory-and-background-documents/religious-plurality-and-christian-self-understanding.html. The latest revision of the document (at the

moment of this writing, yet unpublished) will be presented at the Tenth General Assembly in Korea in November 2013 and subsequently published.

2 Paul Tillich, *The Future of Religions*, ed. Jerald C. Brauer (New York: Harper & Row, 1966), 91.

3 My own long-term project, *A Constructive Christian Theology for the Pluralistic World* (Grand Rapids: Eerdmans, 2013–2017), seeks to correct that lacuna. *Christ and Reconciliation*, the first of five volumes, was published in 2013, and volume two appeared in the beginning of 2014.

4 Francis X. Clooney, *Comparative Theology: Deep Learning across Religious Borders* (Oxford: Wiley-Blackwell, 2010), 9.

5 The Roman Catholic Jacques Dupuis preferred to name it "theology of religious pluralism." See his monumental work, *Toward a Christian Theology of Religious Pluralism* (Maryknoll, N.Y.: Orbis, 1997).

6 Veli-Matti Kärkkäinen, *An Introduction to the Theology of Religions: Biblical, Historical and Contemporary Perspectives* (Downers Grove, Ill.: InterVarsity, 2003), 20.

7 For discussion of Muslim theology of religions in dialogue with Christian traditions, see the work of my former doctoral student Lewis E. Winkler, *Contemporary Muslim and Christian Responses to Religious Plurality: Wolfhart Pannenberg in Dialogue with Abdulaziz Sachedina* (Eugene, Ore.: Pickwick, 2011).

8 For a penetrating critique of theology of religions, see James L. Fredericks, *Faith among Faiths: Christian Theology and Non-Christian Religions* (New York: Paulist, 1999); and Richard Schebera, "Comparative Theology: A New Method of Interreligious Dialogue," *Dialogue and Alliance* 17, no. 1 (2003): 7–18.

9 David Tracy, "Comparative Theology," in *The Encyclopedia of Religion*, ed. Mircea Eliade and Charles J. Adam (New York: Macmillan, 1987), 14:446.

10 This section as a whole depends heavily on my *Christ and Reconciliation*, 21–29; I also glean from the following recent writings of mine: "Theologies of Religions," *Evangelical Interfaith Dialogue* 1, no. 2 (2010): 3–7, http://cms.fuller.edu/EIFD/issues/Spring_2010/Theologies_of_Religions.aspx; "Dialogue, Witness, and Tolerance: The Many Dimensions of Interfaith Encounters," *Theology, News & Notes* 57, no. 2 (2010): 29–33, http://cms.fuller.edu/TNN/Issues/Fall_2010/Dialogue,_Witness,_and_Tolerance/; "Theologies of Religions," in *Witnessing to Christ in a Pluralistic World: Christian Mission among Other Faiths*, ed. Lalsangkima Pachuau and Knud Jørgensen (London: Regnum Books, 2011), 110–18.

11 Clooney, *Comparative Theology*, 10. "Comparative theology must not be confused with comparative religion, since faith is a necessary and explicit factor in the former and not in the latter, where its influence might even be ruled out. But the fields need not be separated entirely, since comparative theology still has to measure up to expected disciplinary standards regarding the religions being compared" (12).

12 Clooney, *Comparative Theology*, 8.

13 This is the fallacy of Ninian Smart and Steven Konstantine, *Christian Systematic Theology in a World Context* (Minneapolis: Fortress, 1991), whose work seeks to develop a Christian-based, more-or-less generic account of some key doctrinal

themes. For a discussion and critique, see Veli-Matti Kärkkäinen, *The Trinity: Global Perspectives* (Louisville, Ky.: Westminster John Knox, 2007), chap. 16.

14 For fine insights, see Clooney, *Comparative Theology*, 10–11.

15 Francis X. Clooney, *Theology after Vedānta: An Experiment in Comparative Theology* (Albany: State University of New York Press, 1993), 7.

16 Francis X. Clooney, "Comparative Theology: A Review of Recent Books (1989–1995)," *Theological Studies* 56, no. 3 (1995): 521–22.

17 See Jürgen Moltmann, *Experiences in Theology: Ways and Forms of Christian Theology*, trans. Margaret Kohl (Minneapolis: Fortress, 2000), 43.

18 Clooney, *Comparative Theology*, 78.

19 A liturgical ritual tradition in Hinduism.

20 Clooney, *Comparative Theology*, 78.

21 For an up-to-date and highly useful mapping out and analysis of the most important contributions to comparative theology, see Clooney, *Comparative Theology*, chap. 3.

22 Keith Ward, *Religion and Community* (Oxford: Clarendon, 2000), 339.

23 See further Keith Ward, *Religion and Revelation: A Theology of Revelation in the World's Religions* (Oxford: Clarendon, 1994), 1–2. The remaining two volumes are *Religion and Creation* (Oxford: Clarendon, 1996) and *Religion and Human Nature* (Oxford: Clarendon, 1998).

24 Moltmann, *Experiences in Theology*, 19–20.

25 Moltmann, *Experiences in Theology*, 18.

26 Moltmann, *Experiences in Theology*, 18–19.

27 Clooney, *Comparative Theology*, 7.

28 Timothy C. Tennent, *Theology in the Context of World Christianity: How the Global Church Is Influencing the Way We Think about and Discuss Theology* (Grand Rapids: Zondervan, 2007), 55.

29 All important Hindu scriptures can be found on the Sacred Texts Web site at http://www.sacred-texts.com/index.htm. Some (mainly Mahayana) Buddhist texts can likewise be found there, and a major part of the necessary portions of the Tipitaka (Theravada) is available on the Web site Access to Insight: Readings in Theravāda Buddhism (www.accesstoinsight.com). The Qur'an (with several modern versions) can be easily found, e.g., at ALTAFSIR.COM (http://altafsir.com), and much of Hadith is available in the Hadith Collection at http://www.hadithcollection.com/.

30 See "Ecumenical Theological Education," World Council of Churches, accessed July 30, 2013, http://www.oikoumene.org/en/what-we-do/ecumenical-theological-education.

31 Dietrich Werner, David Esterline, Namsoon Kang, and Joshva Raja, eds., *Handbook of Theological Education in World Christianity: Theological Perspectives, Ecumenical Trends, Regional Surveys* (London: Regnum Books International, 2010). For the work done around the *Handbook* in the Edinburgh 2010 Centennial Process, see "Theological Education and Formation," Edinburgh 2010, accessed July 30, 2013, http://www.edinburgh2010.org/en/study-themes/main-study-themes/theological-education-and-formation.html.

32 "Teaching Christianity in Dialogue with Other Faith Traditions," World Council of Churches, October 23, 2000, http://www.oikoumene.org/en/resources/documents/wcc-programmes/interreligious-dialogue-and-cooperation/christian-identity-in-pluralistic-societies/teaching-christianity-in-dialogue-with-other-faith-traditions.

33 "Magna Charta on Ecumenical Theological Education in the 21st Century—ETE Reference Document," World Council of Churches, June 3, 2008, http://www.oikoumene.org/en/resources/documents/wcc-programmes/education-and-ecumenical-formation/ete/wcc-programme-on-ecumenical-theological-education/magna-charta-on-ecumenical-theological-education-in-the-21st-century-ete-reference-document.

34 "Global Digital Library on Theology and Ecumenism," GlobalEthics.net, accessed July 30, 2013, http://www.globethics.net/web/gtl.

35 Stephen R. Graham, "Christian Hospitality and Pastoral Practices in a Multifaith Society: An ATS Project, 2010–2012," *Theological Education* 47, no. 1 (2012): 1–10.

36 "Current Initiatives," Association of Theological Schools, http://www.ats.edu/resources/current-initiatives.

37 Gregory Mobley, "Taking Interfaith Off the Hill: Revelation in the Abrahamic Traditions" (Andover Newton Theological School special project, Association of Theological Schools, 2012), http://www.ats.edu/uploads/resources/publications-presentations/chapp-reports/andover-newton-theological-school.pdf.

38 David A. Roozen, "Curriculum Development Project: Educating Parish Clergy for a Multifaith World" (document produced by Hartford Seminary for a project administered by the Association of Theological Schools, 2012), http://www.ats.edu/uploads/resources/publications-presentations/chapp-reports/hartford-theological-seminary.pdf.

39 Mary Hess, on behalf of the Luther CHAPP team, "The Pastoral Practice of Christian Hospitality as Presence in Muslim-Christian Engagement: Contextualizing the Classroom" (document produced by Luther Seminary for a project administered by the Association of Theological Schools, 2012), http://www.ats.edu/uploads/resources/publications-presentations/chapp-reports/luther-seminary.pdf.

40 Sang-Ehil Han, "Christian Hospitality and Neighborliness: A Wesleyan-Pentecostal Ministry Paradigm for the Multi-faith Context" (document produced by Pentecostal Theological Seminary for a project administered by the Association of Theological Schools, 2012), http://www.ats.edu/uploads/resources/publications-presentations/chapp-reports/pentecostal-theological-seminary.pdf.

41 "Research: Multifaith Education in Seminaries," AuburnSeminary.org, 2009, http://www.auburnseminary.org/seminarystudy/.

42 Justus Baird, "Case for Multifaith Education," AuburnSeminary.org, http://www.auburnseminary.org/thecase, excerpted from Baird, "Multifaith Continuing Education: Leading Faithfully in a Religiously Diverse World," in *A*

Lifelong Call to Learn: Continuing Education for Religious Leaders, ed. Robert E. Reber and D. Bruce Roberts (Herndon, Va.: Alban Institute, 2010).

43 Jürgen Moltmann, *The Trinity and the Kingdom of God: The Doctrine of God*, trans. Margaret Kohl (San Francisco: Harper & Row 1981), xii–xiii (emphasis in original).

Chapter 4: Cecilia González-Andrieu

1 In the U.S. context, see, for instance, Philip G. Altbach, Patricia J. Gumport, and Robert O. Berdahl, eds., *American Higher Education in the Twenty-First Century: Social, Political, and Economic Challenges* (Baltimore, Md.: Johns Hopkins University Press, 2011). UCLA's Civil Rights Project continues to produce key research in how civil rights and educational access are linked at http://civilrightsproject.ucla.edu/; Excelencia in Education produces research particularly targeting access to higher education for Latino populations in the United States at http://www.edexcelencia.org/; and see also Jennie E. Brand and Yu Xie, "Who Benefits Most from College? Evidence for Negative Selection in Heterogeneous Economic Returns to Higher Education," *American Sociological Review* 75, no. 2 (2010): 273–302.

2 *Documento Conclusivo, V Conferencia General del Episcopado Latinoamericano y del Caribe*, Aparecida, May 13–17, 2007, 2nd ed., 64. Hereafter, Aparecida. My translation.

3 Aparecida, 65.

4 Aparecida, 65.

5 Aparecida, 329.

6 Aparecida, 330.

7 The Association of Jesuit Colleges and Universities (AJCU) says in "Jesuit Higher Education: An Overview," "Since its beginnings in 1548 when the first Jesuit institution opened its doors in Messina, Sicily, Jesuit higher education remains committed to expansive and critical thinking, to service, leadership and to care for the whole person" (http://www.ajcunet.edu/about?Page=DTN-20120530014006).

8 Donal Dorr writes, "An option for the poor is a commitment by individual Christians and the Christian community at every level to engage actively in a struggle to overcome social injustices which mar our world. To be genuine it must come from real experience of solidarity with the victims of our society." See Dorr, *Option for the Poor: A Hundred Years of Catholic Social Teaching* (Maryknoll, N.Y.: Orbis, 1992), 3.

9 Justo L. González, *Mañana: Christian Theology from a Hispanic Perspective* (Nashville: Abingdon, 2010), 85.

10 Beth McMurtrie, "Worldly Challenges for Theology Schools," *Chronicle of Higher Education* 49, no. 23 (2003): A29.

11 Donald Senior and Timothy Weber write, "The changing status of religion in contemporary culture has left many denominations and congregations in a state of crisis, torn by theological and moral disputes, pressured by pluralism and relativism, and compromised by a consumer approach to life. As a result,

many religious institutions downsize and drift, unsure of their own identity and direction." See Senior and Weber, "What Is the Character of Curriculum, Formation, and Cultivation of Ministerial Leadership in the Good Theological School?" *Theological Education* 30, no. 2 (1994): 29.

12 Walter Brueggemann, *The Prophetic Imagination* (Philadelphia: Fortress, 1987), 20.

13 Brueggemann, *Prophetic Imagination*, 21.

14 "Undocumented Students, Unfulfilled Dreams," UCLA Center for Labor Research and Education, http://ccaucla-laborcenter.electricembers.net/wp-content/uploads/downloads/2014/04/Undocumented-Students.pdf.

15 After the DREAM act was defeated in 2010, the student group at Loyola Marymount University constituted of undocumented youth and their allies renamed themselves "Resilience."

16 "Undocumented Students, Unfulfilled Dreams," 3.

17 Richard Fry, "Hispanic Youth Dropping Out of U.S. Schools: Measuring the Challenge," Pew Hispanic Center, June 12, 2003, iii, http://www.pewhispanic.org/files/reports/19.pdf.

18 In my writing, I never use the term "American" to refer to the land or people of the United States. For me such usage points to the hubris of calling oneself or one's country as if it were the only one in the entire hemisphere, thus the only "America." My own father-in-law, Yvon Andrieu, a French émigré and World War II veteran, routinely referred to his new home, Venezuela, and to all of the "New World" as "L'America." Clearly, to a non-American like him, the hemisphere represented a kind of cohesive whole that from this side of the Atlantic we seldom see.

19 I am grateful to my colleague Herbert Medina, a mathematician and leading advocate for educational justice, for his attentive reading of my draft of this text.

20 Prior to the pope's oft-quoted interview on the plane traveling back from Brazil on July 28, 2013, he gave a long and candid one-on-one exclusive interview in Spanish and Portuguese to the Latin American television network Red Globo. The entire interview is available on the Vatican's new Spanish language Web site "La Comunicación al Servicio de una Autentica Cultura del Encuentro" ("Communication at the Service of an Authentic Culture of Encounter"). See "Entrevista completa que Papa Francisco concedió a la Red Globo en Brasil," Pontificio Consejo para las Comunicaciones Sociales video, 43:23, July 30, 2013, http://www.pccs.va/index.php/es/news2/attualita/item/1597-entrevista-completa-que-papa-francisco-concedio-a-la-red-globo-en-brasil. Pope Francis said, "Today the diverse confessions cannot go to sleep peacefully while there is one child who dies of hunger, or one child without an education" (my translation).

21 See Ada María Isasi-Díaz, *En la Lucha, In the Struggle: Elaborating a Mujerista Theology* (Minneapolis: Fortress, 1993), esp. 166–85.

22 Stephen B. Bevans, *Models of Contextual Theology* (Maryknoll, N.Y.: Orbis, 1992), 2.

23 González, *Mañana*, 22.

24 David Tracy writes, "To become educated is to be freed to enter the conversation of all the living and the dead; to enter that conversation independently and critically, to be sure, but nonetheless to enter." See Tracy, "On Theological Education: A Reflection," in *Theological Literacy for the Twenty-First Century*, ed. Rodney L. Petersen (Grand Rapids: Eerdmans, 2002), 13.

25 Bevans, *Models of Contextual Theology*, 5.

26 Tracy, "On Theological Education," in Peterson, *Theological Literacy*, 15.

27 Alex García-Rivera, *A Wounded Innocence: Sketches for a Theology of Art* (Collegeville, Minn.: Liturgical, 2003), 33.

28 A United Nations' report for UNESCO states bluntly, "In disaster and conflict-ridden countries, 18 million children are estimated not to attend school. Only 2 per cent of aid to education goes to countries in conflict." "The Education for All Agenda," United Nations Economic and Social Council, 2011,

29 Ricardo D. Stanton-Salazar, "A Social Capital Framework for the Study of Institutional Agents and Their Role in the Empowerment of Low-Status Students and Youth," *Youth & Society* 43, no. 3 (2011): 1075.

30 Roberto S. Goizueta writes, "To say that God's love is universal is not to say that God's love is neutral; indeed, it is to say the very opposite. Only if God is identified preferentially with the poor, then, is God's love truly universal." See Goizueta, *Caminemos con Jesús: Toward a Hispanic/Latino Theology of Accompaniment* (Maryknoll, N.Y.: Orbis, 1995), 77.

31 I asked "Ignacio" if he would give me permission to quote this text. He was happy to share it and stressed that he was motivated by the hope that readers would know what it was like to be an undocumented student.

32 Application essay from student (name changed), spring 2012.

33 "Frequently Asked Questions: Application Process," Harvard Divinity School, http://www.hds.harvard.edu/admissions-aid/frequently-asked-questions.

34 Desmond Tutu writes this in the foreword for Ross Kinsler, *Diversified Theological Education: Equipping All God's People* (Pasadena, Calif.: William Carey International University, 2008), 5–6.

35 Claudia Buchmann, Dennis J. Condron, and Vincent J. Roscigno, "Shadow Education, American Style: Test Preparation, the SAT and College Enrollment," *Social Forces* 89, no. 2 (2010): 435–61.

36 See Kaplan Test Prep, http://www.kaptest.com/index.jhtml.

37 I thank my colleague N. Frances Hioki of the Nanzan Institute for Religion and Culture for her help with the research into Japan's shadow education system. She adds, "So let's say you are weak in math and English and register for the two subjects, it's $900 for one term. And let's say you take these classes for a year—it will be $3600 . . . most high school students start taking these classes as soon as they enter high school (which is age 16–18). Meaning, $3600 x 3 years = $10,800." Personal communication, October 19, 2013.

38 "Admissions," Kaplan Test Prep, http://www.kaptest.com/gre/enroll?zip=&tab=admissions (emphasis in original).

39 Peter Scott, "Society Is Becoming Less Equal, Less Just . . . and Higher Education Seems to Be Following Suit," *Guardian*, September 2, 2013, http://www.theguardian.com/education/2013/sep/02/oxford-cambridge-elite-brands.

40 Anand Giridharadas, "Escaping the Heat in Art's Fortress," *New York Times*, August 22, 2013, http://www.nytimes.com/2013/08/23/arts/design/escaping-the-heat-in-arts-fortress.html?_r=0.

41 The Web site says, "These general admission prices are suggested contribution amounts." Visit: Hours and Admission, Brooklyn Museum, https://www.brooklynmuseum.org/visit/.

42 Kinsler, *Diversified Theological Education*, 8–10.

43 As an example, a Web service called Cappex offers a "What are my chances?" online calculator that plots a student's "chances" of being accepted to a particular institution based on GPA and scores on standardized tests. This could be profoundly discouraging to students from low-status backgrounds and preempt any attempts at gaining admission.

44 González, *Mañana*, 79.

45 Buchmann, Condron, and Roscigno, "Shadow Education," 436.

46 Pius XI, *Quadresimo Anno*, 1931, section 79.

47 Higher education theorist Peter Scott summarizes the problem in England, saying that the "ultimate objective" appears to be "to reserve 'proper' higher education, the full university experience, for an elite—ostensibly of the talented but inevitably also the privileged—and to provide everyone else with higher education lite." Scott, "Society Is Becoming Less Equal, Less Just."

48 John L. Allen Jr., "Global Priest Shortages, Faith and Reason in the U.K. and a Loss in Ohio," *National Catholic Reporter*, December 9, 2011, http://ncronline.org/blogs/all-things-catholic/global-priest-shortages-faith-and-reason-uk-and-loss-ohio.

49 Allen, "Global Priest Shortages."

50 Allen, "Global Priest Shortages."

51 Allen, "Global Priest Shortages."

52 Committee on the Laity of the United States Conference of Catholic Bishops, *Co-workers in the Vineyard of the Lord: A Resource for Guiding the Development of Lay Ecclesial Ministry* (Washington, D.C.: United States Conference of Catholic Bishops, 2005), 34 (emphasis added).

53 Committee on the Laity of the USCCB, *Co-workers in the Vineyard*, 34n70.

54 In a particularly ironic image from the now-closed National Pastoral Life Center, the cover of *Ministries, A Parish Guide* (2005), subtitled "The Changing Face of Parish Pastoral Ministers," features a group of persons all of whom are Euro-Americans and overwhelmingly middle aged or older.

55 Office of Media Relations of U.S. Conference of Catholic Bishops, "Hispanics in the United States and the Catholic Church" (Washington, D.C.: 2013), http://www.usccb.org/about/leadership/holy-see/benedict-xvi/upload/Papal-Transition-2013-Hispanics.pdf.

56 Stephen Graham, "Some Reflections on ATS and Racial/Ethnic Faculty," Association of Theological Schools, March 14, 2013. This report was presented during a meeting of racial/ethnic faculty. Earlier ATS devoted an

issue of *Theological Education* to questions surrounding race and ethnicity, vol 45, no.1 (2009), at http://www.ats.edu/uploads/resources/publications-presentations/theological-education/2009-theological-education-v45-n1.pdf. The 2013 report by Graham further segmented the race and ethnicity questions to include faith traditions. Roman Catholics make up only 16 percent of the 6 percent of students of color in ATS schools. On rates of ordination for Hispanic priests, see J. D. Long-Garcia, "Hispanics in the Pews, Not on the Altar," *U.S. Catholic*, September 2011, http://www.uscatholic.org/church/2011/07/hispanics-pews-not-altar.

57 For much more about this, see Antonia Darder's *Culture and Power in the Classroom: Educational Foundations for the Schooling of Bicultural Students* (Boulder, Colo.: Paradigm, 2012).

58 Gustavo Gutiérrez, *La densidad del presente* (Salamanca: Ediciones Sígueme, 2003), 70. In the original Gutiérrez capitalizes *Iglesia*.

59 Matt 22:36-40; Matt 19:18-19; Lev 19:18; and Rom 13:9.

60 As Ada María Isasi-Díaz stresses in her groundbreaking articulation of what she terms *Mujerista* theology, "When the professional theologian is not herself part of the community—that is, when she has no vested interest in the liberation of those involved because her liberation is not connected to the liberation of others in the group—the dialogue becomes dishonest, the group being researched is objectified, and theology itself becomes a tool of oppression." See Isasi-Díaz, *En la Lucha*, 71.

61 Isasi-Díaz, *En la Lucha*, 41.

62 Stanton-Salazar, "Social Capital Framework," 1093.

Chapter 5: Miguel A. De La Torre

1 Jacques Lacan, *Écrits: A Selection*, trans. Alan Sheridan (New York: Norton, 1977), 1–7.

2 Miguel A. De La Torre, *Latina/o Social Ethics: Moving Beyond Eurocentric Moral Thinking* (Waco, Tex.: Baylor University Press, 2010), x.

3 Michel Foucault, *Discipline and Punish: The Birth of the Prison*, trans. Alan Sheridan (New York: Vintage, 1995), 202–3.

4 Frantz Fanon, *The Wretched of the Earth* (New York: Grove, 1965), 249.

5 Edward W. Said, *Culture and Imperialism* (New York: Vintage, 1994), 14, 96, 228–30.

6 Michel Foucault, *The History of Sexuality*, trans. Robert Hurley, vol. 1, *An Introduction* (New York: Vintage, 1978), 93–101; idem, *The Foucault Reader*, ed. Paul Rabinow (New York: Pantheon, 1984), 60–61.

7 Latin American liberationist thinkers have taught us to reflect on autobiographical elements to avoid creating lifeless theoretical concepts. The methodological inclusion of one's story powerfully connects theory with reality, producing a "feet-on-the-ground-theology," as per Clodovis Boff, *Feet-on-the-Ground-Theology: A Brazilian Journey*, trans. Phillip Berryman (Maryknoll, N.Y.: Orbis, 1987). Of course, the danger of including one's story is falling into the fallacy of an exaggerated individualism, as in a conversion testimony. While it is not my

intention to write my memoirs, I find it important to situate myself within the dilemma of uncovering the extent of the colonization process upon this particular Hispanic mind. I recognize the risk that some within the dominant culture will dismiss such an exploration as unscholarly.

8 The term "empire" can no longer be narrowly defined as the physical possession of foreign lands that must pay tribute. Empire is understood today as a globalized economy that provides economic benefits to multinational corporations whose influences are secured through the military might of one superpower.

9 Pierre Bourdieu, *Outline of a Theory of Practice*, trans. Richard Nice (Cambridge: Cambridge University Press, 1977), 96.

10 Miguel A. De La Torre, "The Value of a Peso," in *My Neighbor's Faith: Stories of Interreligious Encounter, Growth, and Transformation*, ed. Jennifer Howe Peace, Or N. Rose, and Gregory Mobley (Maryknoll, N.Y.: Orbis, 2012), 261–63.

11 See the scholarly report composed by the organization with which I work: *A Culture of Cruelty: Abuse and Impunity in Short-Term U.S. Border Patrol Custody*, No More Deaths, 2011, http://forms.nomoredeaths.org/abuse-documentation/a-culture-of-cruelty/.

12 Miguel A. De La Torre, *Trails of Hope and Terror: Testimonies on Immigration* (Maryknoll, N.Y.: Orbis, 2010), 175–81.

13 See the Catholic Church documents *Gaudium et Spes* and *Octogesima Adveniens*.

14 Miguel A. De La Torre, *Doing Christian Ethics from the Margins* (Maryknoll, N.Y.: Orbis, 2004), 58–69.

15 Although citizens may leave this section of the identification card blank, they are prohibited to profess any adherence to indigenous or atheist beliefs.

16 Paulo Freire, *Pedagogy of the Oppressed* (New York: Continuum, 1994), 25–30.

17 I am indebted to one of my mentors, John Raines, who would constantly remind me of this fact during my doctoral studies.

Chapter 6: Lai Pan-chiu

* The research work for this chapter is funded by a research grant gratefully received from the Research Grants Council of Hong Kong (project no. 14405214).

1 For my understanding of the task of Chinese Christian theology in the contemporary global context, see Lai Pan-chiu, "Inheriting the Chinese and Christian Traditions in Global Context: A Confucian-Protestant Perspective," *Religion & Theology* 10, no.1 (2003): 1–23; and idem, "Theological Translation and Transmission between China and the West," *Asia Journal of Theology* 20, no. 2 (2006): 285–304.

2 The seven ancient Chinese texts include a Jesus-Messiah Sutra (*Xuting mishihe jing*), a Treatise on Monotheism (*Yi shen lun*), a Sutra on the Origin of Origins (*Xuan yuan zhi ben jing*), a book on spirituality named Sutra on Mysterious Rest and Joy (*Zhi xuan an le jing*), a Baptismal Hymn in Adoration of the Trinity (*Sanwei meng du zan*), a Hymn in Adoration of the Transfiguration of Our Lord (*Da sheng tong zhen gui fa zan*), and a prayer dedicated to the living and the dead titled Honor Sutra (*Zun jing*). See further P. Y. Saeki, *The Nestorian Monument*

in China (London: Society for the Promotion of Christian Knowledge, 1916); idem, *The Nestorian Documents and Relics in China* (Tokyo: Academy of Oriental Culture, Tokyo Institute, 1937).

3 Some of the misunderstandings or misidentifications of *Jingjiao* are rectified in Chu Sin Jan, *An shen yu li ming: Dongfang jiaohui zai Hua xuanjiao shi* [*Being Human: The Church of the East Mission in China (635–1368)*] (Taipei: Taiwan Baptist Theological Seminary, 2009).

4 Lai Pin-chao (Lai Pan-chiu), "Jidu lun de zhengbian yu kaerxidun da gong huiyi: Shenxue yu zhengzhi" [Christological Controversy and the Chalcedon Ecumenical Council: Theology and Politics], in *Zhexuejia de Yadian, Jidutu de Luoma* [*Philosophers' Athens, Christians' Rome*], ed. Mei Qianli (Thierry Meynard) and Zhang Xianyong (Beijing: China Social Sciences, 2012), 31–52.

5 For the inadequacy of the term "Nestorian" for the Church of the East, see Christoph Baumer, *The Church of the East: An Illustrated History of Assyrian Christianity* (London: I. B. Tauris, 2006), 7–8.

6 Philip Jenkins, *The Lost History of Christianity: The Thousand-Year Golden Age of the Church in the Middle East, Africa, and Asia—and How It Died* (New York: HarperOne, 2008).

7 Some of the publications by or related to "cultural Christians" and Sino-Christian Theology were translated into English. See Yang Huilin and Daniel H. N. Yeung, eds., *Sino-Christian Studies in China* (Newcastle: Cambridge Scholar, 2006); Lai Pan-chiu and Jason Lam, eds., *Sino-Christian Theology: A Theological Qua Cultural Movement in Contemporary China* (Frankfurt am Main: Peter Lang, 2010).

8 One of the best-known examples is probably Yang Tingyun; see N. Standaert, *Yang Tingyun, Confucian and Christian in Late Ming China: His Life and Thought* (Leiden: E. J. Brill, 1988).

9 Similar attempts can be found in Nicolas Standaert, *The Fascinating God: A Challenge to Modern Chinese Theology Presented by a Text on the Name of God Written by a 17th Century Chinese Student of Theology* (Rome: Pontifical Gregorian University, 1995). However, this exploration is made against the background of contemporary Chinese context rather than in a global context.

10 The concept of *da-fu-mu* can be found in the Confucian classics. Under the influence of some Neo-Confucians of the Sung dynasty—especially Zhang Zai (1020–1077), who recognized the male cosmic force/principle (*qian*) as the father (*fu*) of humankind and the female cosmic force/principle (*kun*) as the mother (*mu*) of humankind in his "Western Inscription" (*xi ming*)—some Neo-Confucians of the Ming dynasty employed the expression *da-fu-mu* to refer to the Heaven and the Earth. This expression was then adopted by Matteo Ricci and also some Chinese Catholics (e.g., Yang Tingyun) to refer to the Christian God (*Deus*). For the historical development of this concept, see further Ji Jianxun, "*Ming mo Tianzhu jiao Deus zhi 'Dafumu' shuofa kaoquan*" [*Da-fu-mu (the Parents): Another Name of God in Chinese*], *Dao Feng* [*Logos & Pneuma*] 37 (2012): 103–40.

11 Ricci articulated his criticisms of the idea of "ten thousand things of one body" in the fourth chapter of his *Tianzhu shiyi*; see Matteo Ricci, *The True Meaning of*

the Lord of Heaven, trans. with introduction and notes by Douglas Lancashire and Peter Hu Kuo-chen, a Chinese-English edition edited by Edward J. Malatesta (Taipei: Ricci Institute, 1985), 174–237. For his use of the concept of *da-fu-mu*, see the second chapter, 130–31.

12 See Li Tiangang, ed., *Ming mo Tianzhu jiao san zhushi wenjian zhu: Xu Guangqi, Li Zhizao, Yang Tingyun lun jiao wenji* [*Catholic Documents of Xu Guangqi, Li Zhizao, Yang Tingyun: An Exposition of Three Great Late Ming Thinkers in China*] (Hong Kong: Logos & Pneuma, 2007), 238–40, 247.

13 Li Tiangang, *Ming mo Tianzhu jiao san zhushi wenjian zhu*, 324–27.

14 See Lai Pinchao (Lai Pan-chiu) and Wang Tao, "Zai si Shengduomasi de shengtai lunli" [Reconsidering St. Thomas's Ecological Ethics], *Zhexue yu wenhua* [*Universitas: Monthly Review of Philosophy and Culture*] 37, no. 11 (2010): 155–73; and idem, "Cong Jidu zongjiao rujia, ji yanhua lun kanli ta zhuyi" [Altruism in Christian, Confucian and Evolutionary Perspectives], *Hanyu Jidu jiao xueshu lun ping* [*Sino-Christian Studies: An International Journal of Bible, Theology and Philosophy*] 15 (2013): 183–214.

15 Han Lin, *"Duo Shu" jiao zhu* ["The Book of the Bell" *with Annotation and Commentary*], with introduction, annotation, and commentary by Sun Shangyang, Xiao Qinghe, et al. (Beijing: Huaxia chu ban she, 2008).

16 Sun Shangyang, "Shangdi yu Zhongguo huangdi de xiangyu" [The Encounter between God and the Emperor of China], in Han Lin, *"Duo Shu" jiao zhu*, 4–7.

17 Sun Shangyang, "Shangdi yu Zhongguo huangdi de xiangyu," in Han Lin, *"Duo Shu" jiao zhu*, 12–17.

18 Sun Shangyang, "Shangdi yu Zhongguo huangdi de xiangyu," in Han Lin, *"Duo Shu" jiao zhu*, 17–22.

19 Lai Pan-chiu, "Christian Ecological Theology in Dialogue with Confucianism," *Ching Feng* 41, no. 3–4 (1998): 309–44; Lai Pan-chiu, "God of Life and Ecological Theology: A Chinese Christian Perspective," *Ecumenical Review* 65, no. 1 (2013): 67–82.

20 Lai Pan-chiu, "Beyond Anthropocentrism and Ecocentrism: Eco-theology and Confucian-Christian Dialogue," *Ching Feng* (N.S.) 2, no. 1–2 (2001): 35–55.

21 This approach to ecological theology is further elaborated in Lai Pinchao (Lai Pan-chiu) and Lin Hongxing, *Ru-Ye duihua yu shengtai guanhuai* [*Christian-Confucian Dialogue and Ecological Concern*] (Beijing: Religious Culture, 2006); and it was reviewed favorably in Sun Xiangchen, "A New Approach to Ecological Theology in the Frame of Confucian-Christian Dialogue: On *Confucian-Christian Dialogue and Ecological Concern*," *Ching Feng* (N.S.) 10, no. 1–2 (2010–2011): 179–88.

22 The aforementioned article "Christian Ecological Theology in Dialogue with Confucianism" published in 1998 was translated into German and published in Monika Gänssbauer, ed., *Christsein in China* (Hamburg: Evangelisches Missionwerk in Deutschland, 2000), 54–81; it was also reprinted with modifications in Katrin Fiedler and Freddy Dutz, eds., *Ökologische Perspektiven in China* (Hamburg: Evangelisches Missionwerk in Deutschland, 2011), 41–61.

23 Some of their studies are published in Li Chichang (Archie C. C. Lee) et al., eds., *Wenben shijian yu shenfen bian shi: Zhongguo Jidu tu zhishifenzi de zhongwen*

zhu shu, 1583–1949 [*Textual Practice and Identity Making: A Study of Chinese Christian Writings, 1583–1949*] (Shanghai: Shanghai Guji chubanshe, 2005).

24 See Lai Pinchao (Lai Pan-chiu), ed., "Bijiao shenxue" [Comparative Theology], *Dao Feng* [*Logos & Pneuma*] 25 (2006): 17–164.

25 See Lai Panchao (Lai Pan-chiu), "Bijiao shenxue yu Hanyu shenxue" [Comparative Theology and Sino-Christian Theology], *Dao Feng* [*Logos & Pneuma*] 25 (2006): 147–64.

26 Lai Pincho (Lai Pan-chiu), *Dasheng Jidu jiao shenxue: Hanyu shenxue de sixiang shiyan* [*Mahayana Christian Theology: Thought-Experiments of Sino-Theology*] (Hong Kong: Logos & Pneuma, 2011).

27 Some chapters of it had been published in English before. See Lai Pan-chiu, "Buddhist-Christian Complementarity in the Perspective of Quantum Physics," *Studies in Interreligious Dialogue* 12, no. 2 (2002): 148–64; "A Mahayana Reading of Chalcedon Christology: A Chinese Response to John Keenan," *Buddhist-Christian Studies* 24 (2004): 209–28; "Doctrine of the Trinity, Christology and Hua-yen Buddhism," *Ching Feng* (N.S.) 5, no. 2 (2004): 203–25; "The Kingdom of God and the Pure Land: A Dialogical Study of Eschatology and Praxis," *Ching Feng* (N.S.) 7, no. 1–2 (2006): 183–210; and "Barth's Doctrines of Sin and Humanity in Buddhist Perspective," *Studies in Interreligious Dialogue* 16, no.1 (2006): 41–58.

28 Lai Pinchao, *Dasheng Jidu jiao shenxue*, 7–8.

29 For the Chinese Buddhist method of doctrinal classification, see Mun Chanju, *The History of Doctrinal Classification in Chinese Buddhism: A Study of the Panjiao Systems* (Lanham, Md.: University Press of America, 2006).

30 Lai Pinchao, *Dasheng Jidu jiao shenxue*, 55–64.

31 For Zhang's Mahayana Christian theology, see Lai Pan-chiu and So Yuen-tai, "Mahayana Interpretation of Christianity: A Case Study of Zhang Chunyi (1871–1955)," *Buddhist-Christian Studies* 27 (2007): 67–87; and Su Yuantai (So Yuen-tai), *Zhang Chunyi de fo hua Jidu jiao shenxue* [*Zhang Chun-yi's Buddhist-Christian Theology*] (Hong Kong: Logos & Pneuma, 2007).

32 See Lai Pan-chiu and So Yuen-tai, "Zhang Chun-yi's Buddhist-Christian Pneumatology," *Ching Feng* (N.S.) 4, no.1 (2003): 51–77.

33 For the debate in the English-speaking world, see Thomas Cattoi, "What Has Chalcedon to Do with Lhasa? John Keenan's and Lai Pan-chiu's Reflections on Classical Christology and the Possible Shape of a Tibetan Theology of Incarnation," *Buddhist-Christian Studies* 28 (2008): 13–25; and John Keenan, "The Prospects for a Mahāyāna Theology of Emptiness: A Continuing Debate," *Buddhist-Christian Studies* 30 (2010): 3–27. For the debate in the Chinese-speaking world, see Zhang Xuefu, "Jiakedun xingjing de quanshi yu Jidu de zuixing: Ping Deng Shaoguang yu Lai Pinchao zhi jian you guan 'ye-fo' duihua de taolun" [The Interpretation of Chalcedon Creed and the Sinful Nature of Christ: A Review on the Recent Christianity-Buddhism Dialogues], *Shandao qikan* [*Hill Road*] 8, no.1 (2005): 107–24.

34 Lai Pinchao (Lai Pan-chiu), "Dasheng Jidu jiao shenxue: Jing fu pinglun zhe" [Mahayana Christian Theology: A Rejoinder], *Shandao qikan* [*Hill Road*] 16, no. 1 (2013): 207–8.

35 See Lai Pinchao, "Zhongjiao duoyuan shiye xia de zongjiao zhexue" [Philosophy of Religion in the Perspective of Religious Plurality], *Dao Feng* [*Logos & Pneuma*] 37 (2012): 21–44.

36 Lai Pinchao, "Zhongjiao duoyuan shiye xia de zongjiao zhexue," 37.

37 E.g., Wesley J. Wildman, *Religious Philosophy as Multidisciplinary Comparative Inquiry: Envisioning a Future for the Philosophy of Religion* (Albany: State University of New York Press, 2010).

38 Lai Pinchao (Lai Pan-chiu), "Xiumo de *Ziran zongjiao duihua lu* di shi zhi shiyi zhang: Yi ke kua wenhua de shijiao" [Reading David Hume's *Dialogues Concerning Natural Religions*, Chapters 10 and 11: A Cross-Cultural Perspective], *Zhexue men* [*Beida Journal of Philosophy*] 14 (2006): 97–123; "Chong du Shenganshelun dui Shangdi cunzai de benti lun lunzheng: Yi ke kua wenhua de shijiao" [Rereading St. Anselm's Ontological Argument for the Existence of God: A Cross-Cultural Perspective], *Fu Zhexue pinglun* [*Fudan Philosophical Review*] 2 (2005): 111–25.

39 See Archie Lee, "The Chinese Creation Myth of Nu Kua and the Biblical Narrative in Genesis 1–11," *Biblical Interpretation* 2, no. 3 (1994): 312–24.

40 E.g., Lin Yan, *Zai hanji chuangshi shenhua de liangguang xia chong du "Chuangshiji" 1–3 zhang* [*Re-reading Genesis 1–3 in the Light of Creation Myths from Ancient Chinese Texts*] (Lanzhou: Lanzhou University Press, 2008).

41 See Grace Hui Liang, "Interpreting the Lord's Prayer from a Confucian-Christian Perspective: Wu Leichuan's Practice and Contribution to Chinese Biblical Hermeneutics," in *Reading Christian Scriptures in China*, ed. Chloë Starr (London: T&T Clark, 2008), 118–33; and Tian Haihua, "Confucian Catholic Appropriation of the Decalogue: A Case Study in Cross-Textual Reading," in Starr, *Reading Christian Scriptures*, 163–80.

42 See Lai Pan-chiu, "Sino-Theology, Bible and the Christian Tradition," *Studies in World Christianity* 12, no. 3 (2006): 266–81.

43 E.g., Alexander Chow, *Theosis, Sino-Christian Theology and the Second Chinese Enlightenment: Heaven and Humanity in Unity* (New York: Palgrave Macmillan, 2013) examines the major types of Chinese Christian theology according to the typology offered in Justo L. González, *Christian Thought Revisited: Three Types of Theology* (Maryknoll, N.Y.: Orbis, 1999), and explores the significance of the Eastern Orthodox doctrine of theosis for contemporary Chinese Christian theology.

Chapter 7: Dwight N. Hopkins

1 This eight-year global network engaged in international youth-student exchanges and women's advocacy. It published one book: Dwight N. Hopkins (U.S.A.) and Marjorie Lewis (Jamaica), eds., *Another World Is Possible: Spiritualities and Religions of Global Darker Peoples*, Cross Cultural Theologies (London: Equinox, 2009). Because white Christians from the mainland United States of America participated in the colonizing of the sovereign nation Kingdom of Hawaii in January 1893, by international law a colonized nation is still a nation, akin to how Iraq was occupied and initially colonized by the United States in

2003 and then, subsequently, resumed its sovereign nation status. See, Ward Churchill and Sharon H. Venne, ed. *Islands in Captivity: The International Tribunal on the Rights of Indigenous Hawaiians* (Cambridge, Mass.: South End Press, 2004) and the documentary film "Act of War: The Overthrow of the Hawaiian Nation."

2 My pedagogical paradigm is partially informed by Anthony G. Reddie's *Nobodies to Somebodies: A Practical Theology for Education and Liberation* (London: Epworth, 2003); *Dramatizing Theologies* (Sheffield: Equinox, 2006); *Working Against the Grain: Black Theology in the 21st Century* (Sheffield: Equinox, 2008); "Teaching for Racial Justice: A Participative Approach," *Teaching Theology and Religion* 13, no. 2 (2010): 95–109; *Black Theology* (London: SCM Press, 2012); and by bell hooks, *Teaching to Transgress: Education as the Practice of Freedom* (New York: Routledge, 1994); Noel L. Erskine, *Black Theology and Pedagogy* (New York: Palgrave Macmillan, 2008); and Paulo Freire's *Pedagogy of the Oppressed*, 30th anniv. ed. (New York: Continuum, 2000).

3 Some possible helpful texts on presuppositions to theological anthropology are Bo-Myung Seo, *A Critique of Western Theological Anthropology: Understanding Human Beings in a Third World Context* (Lampeter, UK: Edwin Mellen, 2005); Andrew Sung Park, *The Wounded Heart of God: The Asian Concept of Han and the Christian Doctrine of Sin* (Nashville: Abingdon, 1993); Eleazar S. Fernandez, *Reimagining the Human: Theological Anthropology in Response to Systemic Evil* (St. Louis: Chalice, 2004); George E. Tinker, *Spirit and Resistance: Political Theology and American Indian Liberation* (Minneapolis: Fortress, 2004); Mercy Amba Oduyoye, *Hearing and Knowing: Theological Reflections on Christianity in Africa* (Maryknoll, N.Y.: Orbis, 1986); Nyambural J. Njoroge, *An African Christian Feminist Ethic of Resistance and Transformation* (Legon, Ghana: Legon Theological Studies, 2000); Karen Baker-Fletcher, *Sisters of Dust, Sisters of Spirit: Womanist Wordings on God and Creation* (Minneapolis: Fortress, 2008); Phillis Isabella Sheppard, *Self, Culture, and Others in Womanist Practical Theology* (New York: Palgrave Macmillan, 2011); Riggins R. Earl Jr., *Dark Symbols, Obscure Signs: God, Self, and Community in the Slave Mind* (Knoxville: University of Tennessee Press, 2003); John W. De Gruchy, *Being Human: Confessions of a Christian Humanist* (London: SCM Press, 2006); Spencer Wells, *The Journey of Man: A Genetic Odyssey* (Princeton, N.J.: Princeton University Press, 2002); and Archie Smith Jr., *The Relational Self: Ethics & Therapy from a Black Church Perspective* (Nashville: Abingdon, 1982).

4 I have an expanded inquiry and definition of "culture" in my *Being Human: Race, Culture and Religion* (Minneapolis: Fortress, 2005). Additional texts with further insights: Africa Information Service, ed., *Return to the Source: Selected Speeches of Amilcar Cabral* (New York: Monthly Review, 1973); Amilcar Cabral, *Unity and Struggle: Speeches and Writings* (New York: Monthly Review, 1979); David Morley and Kuan-Hsing Chen, eds., *Stuart Hall: Critical Dialogues in Cultural Studies* (New York: Routledge, 1996); Delwin Brown, Sheila Greeve Davaney, and Kathryn Tanner, eds., *Converging on Culture: Theologians in Dialogue with Cultural Analysis and Criticism* (Oxford: Oxford University Press, 2001); and Dwight

N. Hopkins and Sheila Greeve Davaney, eds., *Changing Conversations: Religious Reflection & Cultural Analysis* (New York: Routledge, 1996).

5 At least one East Asian student shared this insight and then produced his family's millennial documentation. African students have represented similar memory through orality.

6 See Philip Jenkins, *The Next Christendom: The Coming of Global Christianity*, rev. ed. (Oxford: Oxford University Press, 2007); Adrian Hastings, ed., *A World History of Christianity* (Grand Rapids: Eerdmans, 1999); Lamin Sanneh, *Disciples of All Nations: Pillars of World Christianity* (Oxford: Oxford University Press, 2008); idem, *Translating the Message: The Missionary Impact of Culture* (Maryknoll, N.Y.: Orbis, 1990); Laurenti Magesa, *Anatomy of Inculturation: Transforming the Church in Africa* (Maryknoll, N.Y.: Orbis, 2004); Jose Miguez Bonino, ed., *Faces of Jesus: Latin American Christologies* (Maryknkoll, N.Y.: Orbis, 1984); and Kwok Pui-lan, *Postcolonial Imagination and Feminist Theology* (Louisville, Ky.: Westminster John Knox, 2005).

7 Friedrich Engels, *Origins of the Family, Private Property and the State* (New York: Penguin Classics, 2010); David Parkin and Linda Stone, eds., *Kinship and Family: An Anthropological Reader* (Hoboken, N.J.: Wiley-Blackwell, 2004); Allen Johnson and Timothy Earle, *The Evolution of Human Societies: From Foraging Group to Agrarian State*, 2nd ed. (Stanford, Calif.: Stanford University Press, 2000); David Carrasco, *Religions of Mesoamerica: Cosmovision and Ceremonial Centers* (Prospect Heights, Ill.: Waveland, 1998); Michael Loewe and Edward L. Shaughnessy, *The Cambridge History of Ancient China: From the Origins of Civilization to 221 BC* (Cambridge: Cambridge University Press, 1999); and Basil Davidson, *African Civilization Revisited: From Antiquity to Modern Times* (Trenton, N.J.: Africa World Press, 2001).

8 In his *Dialogue with the Other: The Inter-religious Dialogue* (Louvain: Peeters, 1990,), xi, David Tracy writes, "Indeed, I believe we are fast approaching the day when it will not be possible to attempt a Christian systematic theology except in serious conversation with the other great ways."

9 David Tracy writes, "Conversation is questioning itself. It is a willingness to follow the question wherever it may go." See Tracy, *Plurality and Ambiguity: Hermeneutics, Religion, Hope* (San Francisco: Harper & Row, 1987), 18. Ukachukwu Chris Manus reminds us that all conversations and interpretations are particular. See his *Intercultural Hermeneutics in Africa: Methods and Approaches* (Nairob: Acton, 2003). Patricia Hill Collins further claims that voice in conversation is political. See her *Fighting Words: Black Women and the Search for Justice* (Minneapolis: University of Minnesota Press, 1998).

10 For instances of questioning traditions, see Michel Foucault, *Lectures on the Will to Know (Lectures at the College de France 1970–1971 and Oedipal Knowledge)* (New York: Palgrave Macmillan, 2013); Michel Foucault, *The Archaeology of Knowledge* (New York: Vintage, 1982); and James H. Cone, *Black Theology and Black Power* (Maryknoll, N.Y.: Orbis, 1997). Also see my "Postmodernism, Black Theology of Liberation, and the U.S.A.: Michel Foucault and James H. Cone," in *Liberation Theologies, Postmodernity, and the Americas*, ed. David Batstone, Eduardo

Mendieta, Lois Ann Lorentzen, and Dwight N. Hopkins (London: Routledge, 1997), 205–19.

11 See Eduardo Mendieta, "Imperial Somatics and Genealogies of Religion: How We Never Became Secular," in *Postcolonial Philosophy of Religion*, ed. Purushottama Bilimoria and Andrew B. Irvine (Dordrecht, Netherlands: Springer, 2009), 235–50.

12 See Lydia Johnson and Joan Alleliua Filemoni-Tofaeono, eds., *Weavings: Women Doing Theology in Oceania* (Suva, Fiji: Weavers, South Pacific Association of Theological Schools, 2003).

13 See Mary N. Getui, Tinyiko Maluleke, and Justin Ukpong, eds., *Interpreting the New Testament* (Nairobi, Kenya: Acton, 2001).

14 Western European creation of new knowledge is emblematic of how one episteme gave way to another; that is to say, the prism of thought of feudalism dialectically sprouted into new bodies of knowledge under capitalism. See Marimba Ani Yurugu, *An African-Centered Critique of European Cultural Thought and Behavior* (Trenton, N.J.: Africa World Press, 1994); and Ian F. McNeely and Lisa Wolverton, *Reinventing Knowledge: From Alexandria to the Internet* (New York: Norton, 2009). To entertain one's curiosity about the formation of knowledge, in a contrasting approach, see Christian Jennings and Toyin Falola, eds., *Africanizing Knowledge: African Studies across the Disciplines* (Piscataway, N.J.: Transactions, 2002); and Colina Mason and Felicity Rawlings-Sanaei, eds., *Academic Migration, Discipline Knowledge and Pedagogical Practice: Voices from the Asia-Pacific* (Berlin: Springer, 2013).

15 See the work of my University of Chicago Divinity School colleague: Willemien Otten, "Middeleeuwen tot en met Reformatie. (Ont)spanning tussen geloof en rede," in *Perspectief op leren. Verkenningen naar onderwijs en leren vanuit de christelijke traditie*, ed. A. de Mynck and B. Kalkman (Gouda: Driestar Educatief, 2005), 57–69. Other helpful texts: Joseph H. Lynch, *The Medieval Church: A Brief History* (London: Longman, 1992); and Catherine M. Chin, "The Grammarian's Spoils: *De Doctrina Christiana* and the Contexts of Literary Education," in *Augustine and the Disciplines: From Cassiciacum to Confessions*, ed. Karla Pollmann and Mark Vessey (Oxford: Oxford University Press, 2005), 167–83.

16 Dwight N. Hopkins, *Down, Up & Over: Slave Religion and Black Theology* (Minneapolis: Fortress, 1999).

17 Liberation theologies from Asia to Africa write on these notions of Jesus, wealth, and social connections. For Latin America's form of liberation theology and these ideas, see Ignacio Ellacuria and Jon Sobrino, eds., *Mysterium Liberationis: Fundamental Concepts of Liberation Theology* (Maryknoll, N.Y.: Orbis, 1993); especially refer to Gustavo Gutiérrez' chapter "Transcendence and Historical Liberation: Option for the Poor." Also check out J. B. Banawiratma and J. Miller, *Contextual Social Theology: An Indonesia Model* (Quezon, Philippines: East Asian Pastoral Institute) (a book of the *East Asian Pastoral Review* 36 [1999], nos. 1 and 2). And see my *Heart and Head: Black Theology; Past, Present and Future* (New York: Palgrave, 2002), especially "The Preferential Option for the Poor and the Oppressed" and "A New Commonwealth" chapters. From South Africa, review Itumeleng J. Mosala, *Biblical Hermeneutics and Black Theology in*

South Africa (Grand Rapids: Eerdmans, 1989). And from Cameroon, Jean-Marc Ela writes *My Faith as an African* (Maryknoll, N.Y.: Orbis, 1989).

18 In my talks on being human in South Korea and Cuba, I introduced the African American religious song "This Little Light of Mine." To my amazement and delight, both audiences immediately joined in the English lyrics and sang with much gusto, though they added their own flavor that would have been fascinating to black Americans but was somewhat culturally particularized by the South Korean and Cuban realities. Similarly, the African American freedom song "We Shall Overcome" has been sung all over the world by people bearing the brunt of asymmetrical power relations. And, furthermore, perhaps one of the most global classics is Bob Marley's reggae music.

19 The United Kingdom and U.S. universities remain influential on the world stage. Harvard University's endowment is about $33 billion.

20 See Jia Xue Rui, *A Comparative Study of Chinese and American Communication Styles* (Harbin, China: Harbin Institute of Technology Press, 2008).

21 Cf. Matt 28:16-20 and Mark 6:7-13 on what people think Jesus said about going to foreign neighbors.

22 A comic strip character who first appeared in 1931 in the *Detroit Mirror*, Tracy was a smart futuristic detective. Actually, Samsung has, indeed, produced the first commercial wrist watch (the Samsung Galaxy Gear) that is basically the beginnings of a smart phone.

Chapter 8: Teresia Hinga

1 This refers to Peter Singer's book *One World: The Ethics of Globalization* (New Haven: Yale University Press, 2002).

2 Thomas L. Friedman refers to globalization as "a flattening of the world." He cites several breakthroughs, particularly in computer and information technology, that have accelerated globalization and a "flattening of the world." See Friedman, *The World Is Flat: A Short History of the Twenty-First Century* (New York: Farrar, Straus & Giroux, 2005).

3 Consider, e.g., the debates about genetically modified organisms and the ethically ambiguous implications of breakthroughs in biotechnology.

4 Consider, e.g., the recent crisis in the United States as the nation contemplates ethical and practical quandaries resulting from the sudden influx of child immigrants from Central America.

5 Martha C. Nussbaum, *Cultivating Humanity: A Classical Defense of Reform in Liberal Education* (Cambridge, Mass.: Harvard University Press, 1997); and Paulo Freire, *Pedagogy of the Oppressed* (New York: Continuum, 1995).

6 R. Sambuli Mosha, *The Heartbeat of Indigenous Africa: A Study of the Chagga Educational System* (New York: Garland, 2000).

7 bell hooks, *Teaching to Transgress* (New York: Routledge, 1994).

8 Nussbaum, *Cultivating Humanity*, 9.

9 Nussbaum, *Cultivating Humanity*, 10.

10 Nussbaum, *Cultivating Humanity*, 10.

11 Nussbaum, *Cultivating Humanity*, 10.

12 Nussbaum, *Cultivating Humanity*, 10.
13 Nussbaum, *Cultivating Humanity*, 10–11.
14 Nussbaum, *Cultivating Humanity*, 11.
15 Freire, *Pedagogy of the Oppressed*, 54.
16 Freire, *Pedagogy of the Oppressed*, 54.
17 Freire, *Pedagogy of the Oppressed*, 54.
18 Freire, *Pedagogy of the Oppressed*, 72.
19 Freire, *Pedagogy of the Oppressed*, 73.
20 Freire, *Pedagogy of the Oppressed*, 83 (emphasis in original).
21 Freire, *Pedagogy of the Oppressed*, 83.
22 Freire, *Pedagogy of the Oppressed*, 84 (emphasis added).
23 Freire, *Pedagogy of the Oppressed*, 84.
24 *Ipvunda* is the Chagga name for the indigenous education system. The term is a metaphor from the world of pottery; it means molding (as one molds clay), particularly the inner moral core of the student. *Ipvunda* has a two-sided goal: education for living (i.e., preparing one with survival skills as well as an education for life—that is, nurturing someone's inner core so that one gradually acquires positive human dispositions or virtues such as reverence, self-control, courage, communality, and diligence). For details, see Mosha, *Heartbeat of Indigenous Africa*, 16–18.
25 This definition of the individual in context of community is well summed up by John Mbiti, who says that Africans say, "We are therefore I am," as compared to the Western view, attributed to Descartes, "I think therefore I am."
26 Mosha, *Heartbeat of Indigenous Africa*, 87–88.
27 Mosha, *Heartbeat of Indigenous Africa*, 88.
28 Mosha, *Heartbeat of Indigenous Africa*, 146.
29 Mosha, *Heartbeat of Indigenous Africa*, 15.
30 Mosha, *Heartbeat of Indigenous Africa*, 14–15.
31 hooks, *Teaching to Transgress*, 21.
32 hooks, *Teaching to Transgress*, 22.
33 See hooks, "Paulo Freire," chap. 4 in *Teaching to Transgress*, where she presents a playful imaginary dialogue on Freire's work (45–58).
34 hooks, *Teaching to Transgress*, 52.
35 hooks, *Teaching to Transgress*, 54.
36 A recent report, e.g., claims that 27 million people, most of them women and girl children, live in bondage as slaves. Slavery, the ultimate subversion of one's humanity, seems to have escalated and to thrive under globalization. For details, see "Human Trafficking," Polaris Project, http://www.polarisproject.org/human-trafficking/overview.
37 Nussbaum, *Cultivating Humanity*, 115.
38 hooks, *Teaching to Transgress*, 35–44.
39 hooks, *Teaching to Transgress*, 36.
40 hooks, *Teaching to Transgress*, 44.

41 Peter-Hans Kolvenbach, "The Service of Faith and the Promotion of Justice in American Jesuit Higher Education" (unpublished manuscript, October 6, 2000).

42 "2014–15 Core Curriculum Guide, Santa Clara University," 1, http://www.scu.edu/provost/ugst/core/upload/Core-Guide-2013-2014.pdf.

43 Though these two courses are foundational in nurturing critical thinking, this is not the only place in the curriculum where such critical thinking is expected or nurtured. In fact, an overall goal of the whole educational experience is to nurture certain qualities or "habits of the mind and heart." Critical thinking is nurtured across the curriculum as one of the crucial qualities or habits of the mind that students ought to have not just in college but throughout life. Critical thinking is defined as "the ability to identify, reflect upon, evaluate, integrate, and apply different types of information and knowledge to form independent judgments." For details of SCU Core Curriculum goals and the intention to form critical thinking as a "habits of the mind and heart," see "Learning Goals and Objectives," Santa Clara University, http://www.scu.edu/provost/ugst/core/core-overview/learning-goals/.

44 "2014–15 Core Curriculum Guide," 10.

45 "2014–15 Core Curriculum Guide," 11.

46 "2014–15 Core Curriculum Guide," 11.

47 Nussbaum, *Cultivating Humanity*, 85.

48 "2014–15 Core Curriculum Guide," 13.

49 Kolvenbach, "Service of Faith."

50 Paul Farmer spells out how pathological power dynamics—including sexism, racism, and colonialism—have conspired in places like Haiti and post–Cold War Russia to create a context where AIDS and other diseases, particularly tuberculosis, thrive and bring death and massive suffering among the poor (or more accurately, the impoverished). See Farmer, *Pathologies of Power: Health, Human Rights, and the New War on the Poor* (Berkeley: University of California Press, 2005).

51 For a detailed discussion of how distortions in theological responses to the crisis of HIV/AIDS made the situation worse, particularly for women, see Teresia M. Hinga, "AIDS, Religion and Women in Africa: Theo-ethical Challenges and Imperatives," in *Women, Religion and HIV/AIDS in Africa: Responding to Ethical and Theological Challenges*, ed. Teresia M. Hinga et al. (Pietermaritzburg, South Africa: Cluster, 2008), 77–103.

52 This is one of the several projects under the World Council of Churches Health and Healing Desk. Other significant initiatives involve mental health as well as healing from violence and trauma.

53 See Susan Parry, *Beacons of Hope: HIV Competent Churches Framework for Action* (Geneva: World Council of Churches, 2008).

54 One very successful strategy is the deployment of people living with AIDS in various parts of Africa as staff members of EHAIA. They become part of the team in the transformational work in churches and neighborhoods and in the grassroots movements in their respective countries. Such people living with

AIDS are by this very strategy empowered, energized, and transformed from a mindset of that of a "victim" to a mindset of a transformative actor, with full agency that they can tap into on their own behalf and on the behalf of others.

55 For a detailed account of this strategy and how it was implemented in various parts of Africa, see Ezra Chitando, *Mainstreaming HIV and AIDS in the Theological Education* (Geneva: World Council of Churches, 2008).

56 Chitando, *Mainstreaming HIV and AIDS*, 91.

57 Chitando, *Mainstreaming HIV and AIDS*, 91.

58 Chitando, *Mainstreaming HIV and AIDS*, 92.

59 See "EHAIA Impact Assessment 2002–2009," World Council of Churches, last modified January 2, 2011, http://www.oikoumene.org/en/resources/documents/wcc-programmes/justice-diakonia-and-responsibility-for-creation/ehaia/ehaia-impact-assessment-2002-2009.

60 There is an awareness that hegemonic or dangerous masculinities have contributed to the escalation of the crisis in Africa. Therefore, the quest for "redemptive masculinities" is seen as a major strategy in the context of fighting HIV/AIDS. See Ezra Chitando and Sophie Chirongoma, eds., *Redemptive Masculinities: Men, HIV, and Religion* (Geneva: World Council of Churches, 2012).

61 According to the assessment report, this is an understatement of the number of people reached by these training of trainers workshops.

62 See *HIV & AIDS Curriculum for Theological Institutions in Africa* (MAP International, 2002), http://www.oikoumene.org/en/folder/documents-pdf/curriculum-for-theological-institutions-eng.pdf. It is commendable that EHAIA has made the publications under its umbrella freely accessible both online and as books.

63 Musa W. Dube, Isabel Apawo Phiri, et al., eds., *Africa Praying: A Handbook on HIV/AIDS Sensitive Sermon Guidelines and Liturgy* (Geneva: World Council of Churches, 2003). Many members of the Circle of Concerned African Women Theologians contributed to this volume.

64 As a member of the Circle of Concerned African Women Theologians, Dube coedited with Musimbi R. A. Kanyoro, *Grant Me Justice: HIV/AIDS and Gender Readings of the Bible* (Pietermaritzburg, South Africa: Cluster, 2004). This is one of the several volumes from the Circle's 2002 conference on the subject of HIV/AIDS and women in Africa.

65 The Tamar Campaign "seeks to acknowledge the existence of Gender-Based Violence in our society, with particular focus on sexual and domestic violence, and to challenge churches to address the problem." See "Tamar Campaign and Sexual Gender Based Violence," Fellowship of Christian Councils and Churches in the Great Lakes and Horn of Africa, http://www.fecclaha.org/index.php?option=com_k2&view=item&id=57:tamar-campaign-and-sexual-gender-based-violence&Itemid=202.

66 EHAIA has closed partnership with the Circle of Concerned African Women Theologians.

67 Musa W. Dube, "On Being Firefighters: Insights in Curriculum Transformation in HIV and AIDS Contexts," *Studia Historiae Ecclesiasticae* 35 (2009):

84, http://uir.unisa.ac.za/bitstream/handle/10500/4555/Dube-SHEXXXV-Supplement-Dec2009.pdf?sequence=1.

68 Musa W. Dube, ed., *HIV/AIDS and the Curriculum: Methods of Integrating HIV/AIDS in Theological Programmes* (Geneva: World Council of Churches, 2003), 109.

69 Dube, "On Being Firefighters," 82–89.

70 For details of Dube's appreciative yet analytical assessment of the Circle of Concerned African Women Theologians as "fellow firefighters against HIV/AIDS" who successfully partnered with EHAIA in fighting this particular fire, see Musa W. Dube, "In the Circles of Life: African Women Theologians' Engagement with HIV and AIDS," in *Compassionate Circles: African Women Theologians Facing HIV*, ed. Ezra Chitando and Nontando Hadebe (Geneva: World Council of Churches, 2009), 217.

71 Dube, "On Being Firefighters," 88.

72 One testimony came from a member of the lesbian, gay, bisexual, and transgender community at SCU. While she celebrated how SCU has offered this community, she pointed to a very practical "not yet" to be responded to—the provision of unisex restrooms in sufficient numbers to allow a more user-friendly campus for all. For many in the audience, this was the first time they had ever heard of the concept of unisex public restrooms, and they pushed to know what would be done in this regard to enhance inclusiveness for the diversely gendered in our midst.

Chapter 9: Loida I. Martell-Otero

1 This "translational ability" that involves the ability for "code switching" has been perceived for many years to be a sign of educational deficiency, in spite of studies that prove otherwise. See, e.g., Tyler Kimball Anderson and Almeida Jacqueline Toribio, "Attitudes towards Lexical Borrowing and Intra-sentential Code-Switching among Spanish-English Bilinguals," *Spanish in Context* 4, no. 2 (2007): 217–40.

2 Robert Bayley and Ruth King, "Languages Other than English Spoken in Canada and the United States," *American Speech* 88 (2003 Supplement): 164–65. The site www.ethnologue.com, which publishes *Ethnologue*, reports that the United States ranks about one-third of the most linguistically diverse countries of the world (accessed on November 14, 2013). In 2013 Camille Ryan reported that there were over 300 different languages spoken in the United States. See "Language Use in the United States: 2011," *American Community Survey Reports*, U.S. Department of Commerce/U.S. Census Bureau, accessed February 15, 2014, http://www.census.gov/prod/2013pubs/acs-22.pdf.

3 I am grateful to A. J. van den Blink's "Empathy amid Diversity: Problems and Possibilities" (*Journal of Pastoral Theology* 3, no. 1 [1993]: 5) for the wonderful phrase "tourist of diversity" for those who *theoretically* like the idea of diversity but do not want to face the conflicts it engenders or undertake the cost it entails to live out its reality.

4 For a greater discussion of *teología en conjunto*, see Loida I. Martell-Otero, "Introduction: *Abuelita* Theologies," in *Latina Evangélicas: A Theological Survey from the Margins*, by Loida I. Martell-Otero, Zaida Maldonado Pérez, and Elizabeth Cond-Frazier (Eugene, Ore.: Cascade, 2013), 6.

5 Carl Raschke, "Globalization and Theology," *Religion Compass* 5, no. 11 (2011): 638.

6 Gemma Tulud Cruz, "Between Identity and Security: Theological Implications of Migration in the Context of Globalization," *Theological Studies* 2 (2008): 357–58.

7 Unlike "perichoresis," which can be defined as "interdependent interpenetration" in theological language, globalization has none of the intimacy or fellowship (in Spanish, *vínculos*—ties that bind) that perichoresis implies. This is an antiperichoretic interlocation—an apartheid-like interpenetration!

8 Roland Robertson, "Glocalization: Time-Space and Homogeneity-Heterogeneity," in *Global Modernities: Theory, Culture and Society*, ed. Mike Featherstone, Scott Lash, and Roland Robertson (London: Sage, 1997), 28.

9 E.g., see F. Albert Tizon, *Transformation after Lausanne: Radical Evangelical Mission in Global-Local Perspective* (Oxford: Regnum, 2008), 203–30.

10 Elliot W. Eisner, *The Educational Imagination: On the Design and Evaluation of School Programs*, 3rd ed. (Upper Saddle River, N.J.: Prentice Hall, 2002), 154.

11 Parker Palmer, *To Know as We Are Known: Education as a Spiritual Journey*, 2nd ed. (New York: Harper Collins, 1993), 21 (emphasis added).

12 Palmer, *To Know as We Are Known*, 2.

13 Gloria Ladson-Billings, "Racialized Discourses and Ethnic Epistemologies," in *Handbook of Qualitative Research*, ed. Norman K. Denzin and Yvonna S. Lincoln, 2nd ed. (Thousand Oaks, Calif.: Sage, 2000), 258.

14 Michel Elias Andraos, "Engaging Diversity in Teaching Religion and Theology: An Intercultural, De-colonial Epistemic Perspective," *Teaching Theology and Religion* 15, no. 1 (2012): 7–8.

15 Indeed, Laura I. Rendón defines *persona educada* as a wise person in *Sentipensante (Sensing/Thinking) Pedagogy: Educating for Wholeness, Social Justice, and Liberation* (Sterling, Va.: Stylus, 2009), 88–91.

16 Loida I. Martell-Otero, "From Foreign Bodies in Teacher Space to Embodied Spirit in *Personas Educadas*: Or, How to Prevent 'Tourists of Diversity' in Education," in *Teaching for a Culturally Diverse and Racially Just World*, ed. Eleazar S. Fernandez (Eugene, Ore.: Cascade, 2014), 63–68.

17 Elizabeth Conde-Frazier, "From Hospitality to Shalom," in *A Many Colored Kingdom: Multicultural Dynamics for Spiritual Formation*, ed. Elizabeth Conde-Frazier, S. Steve Kang, and Gary A. Parrett (Grand Rapids: Baker Academic, 2004), 195.

18 Elizabeth Conde-Frazier, "Prejudice and Conversion," in Conde-Frazier, Kang, and Parrett, *Many Colored Kingdom*, 105.

19 Rendón, *Sentipensante*, 17.

20 Roberto S. Goizueta, "In Defense of Reason," *Journal of Hispanic/Latino Theology* 3, no. 3 (1996): 16–26.

21 John D. Zizioulas, *Lectures in Christian Dogmatics* (London: T&T Clark, 2008), 57.

22 I am grateful to Rendón for these insights. See *Sentipensante*, 15–17.

23 Loida I. Martell-Otero, "My GPS Does Not Work in Puerto Rico: An *Evangélica* Spirituality," *American Baptist Quarterly* 30, no. 3–4 (2011): 256–75. For more, see also Roger Friedland and Richard D. Hecht, "The Power of Place," in *Religion, Violence, Memory, and Place*, ed. Oren Baruch Stier and J. Shawn Landres (Bloomington: Indiana University Press, 2006), 18–36.

24 Jace Weaver, "From I-Hermeneutics to We-Hermeneutics: Native Americans and the Post-colonial," in *Native American Religious Identity: Unforgotten Gods*, ed. Jace Weaver (Maryknoll, N.Y.: Orbis, 1998), 22.

25 Catherine Keller, *Apocalypse Now and Then: A Feminist Guide to the End of the World* (Boston: Beacon, 1996), 118–19.

26 Arch Chee Keen Wong et al., "Learning through Shared Christian Praxis: Reflective Practice in the Classroom," *Teaching Theology and Religion* 12, no. 4 (2009): 307–8.

27 Emma Emgård, "Using Dialogue in Reflective Practice for Intercultural Studies," in "Learning through Shared Christian Praxis," by Arch Chee Keen Wong et al., *Teaching Theology and Religion* 12, no. 4 (2009): 317–18.

28 Palmer, *To Know as We Are Known*, 55.

29 Franz-J Leenhardt, "La signification de la notion de parole dans la pensée chrétienne," *Revue d'histoire et de philosophie religieuses* 35, no. 3 (1955): 267. I am grateful to Dr. Renata Furst, Professor of Scripture and Theology, Oblate School of Theology (San Antonio, Texas), who aided me in the translation of this passage.

30 Leenhardt, "La signification," 267.

31 Orlando E. Costas, *Christ outside the Gate: Mission beyond Christendom* (Maryknoll, N.Y.: Orbis, 1982), 188–94; Gary Riebe-Estrella, "Engaging Borders: Lifting Up Difference and Unmasking Division," *Theological Education* 45, no. 1 (2009): 21–24.

32 I find this definition by Daniel Schipani in his explanation of Paulo Freire to be quite succinct and helpful. See *El reino de Dios y el ministerio educativo de la Iglesia: Fundamentos y principios de educación Cristiana* (Miami: Editorial Caribe, 1983), 54.

33 Fernando A. Cascante-Gómez, "Advancing Racial/Ethnic Diversity in Theological Education: A Model for Reflection and Action," *Theological Education* 43, no. 2 (2008): 55.

34 These are meant to be not all-inclusive but rather an introduction to the many perspectives that could be discussed. Others are introduced through class discussions and in other assigned readings. However, we acknowledge the limits inherent in course programming.

35 The full bibliographic citation for all the books listed are as follows (in order of listing): James Cone, *A Black Theology of Liberation*, 2nd ed. (Maryknoll, N.Y.: Orbis, 1990); Gustavo Gutiérrez, *A Theology of Liberation: History, Politics and Salvation*, rev. ed., trans. Caridad Inda and John Eagleson (Maryknoll, N.Y.:

Orbis, 1988); Clara Sue Kidwell, Homer Noley, and George E. "Tink" Tinker, *A Native American Theology* (Maryknoll, N.Y.: Orbis, 2001); Rosemary Radford Ruether, *Sexism and God-Talk: Toward a Feminist Theology* (Boston: Beacon, 1993); C. S. Song, *The Believing Heart: An Invitation to Story Theology* (Minneapolis: Fortress, 1998); Delores S. Williams, *Sisters in the Wilderness: The Challenge of Womanist God-Talk* (Maryknoll, N.Y.: Orbis, 1993).

36 It should be noted that my institution does have an ethnically/racially diverse student population comprised of approximately 60 percent African Americans, and almost 50 percent women, and representing a variety of denominations.

37 Here *lucha* (struggle or wrestling) implies not only an intellectual endeavor but also a holistic exercise that includes spiritual, emotional, and interpersonal as well as personal struggle. The students' worldviews, assumptions, questions, theologies, and relationships at times undergo what feels like seismic shifts. Thus at times they refer to it as "wrestling." Group dynamics are such that they allow a safe space for this wrestling to take place.

38 I have increased their time together in response to this concern.

39 Group 2, 2011.

40 Isa 6:8 (NRSV).

Chapter 10: Eleazar S. Fernandez

1 Michael Hardt and Antonio Negri, *Empire* (Cambridge, Mass.: Harvard University Press, 2000).

2 See Eleazar S. Fernandez, "Orchestrating New Theological Overtures: Heterogeneity, Dissonance, and Fluidity vis-à-vis Imperial Monophony," in *New Overtures: Asian North American Theology in the 21st Century; Essays in Honor of Fumitaka Matsuoka*, ed. Eleazar S. Fernandez (Upland, Calif.: Sopher, 2012), 5–6.

3 Charles Van Engen, "The Glocal Church: Locality and Catholicity in a Globalizing World," in *Globalizing Theology: Belief and Practice in an Era of World Christianity*, ed. Craig Ott and Harold Netland (Grand Rapids: Baker Academic, 2006), 159.

4 Eleazar S. Fernandez, *Burning Center, Porous Borders: The Church in a Globalized World* (Eugene, Ore.: Wipf & Stock, 2011), 108–12.

5 John Tomlinson, *Globalization and Culture* (Chicago: University of Chicago Press, 1999), 2.

6 Anthony Giddens, *The Consequences of Modernity* (Stanford, Calif.: Stanford University Press, 1990), 64. Also see Harold Netland, "Globalization and Theology Today," in Ott and Netland, *Globalizing Theology*, particularly pages 18–23.

7 Fumitaka Matsuoka, "Asian North American Theology in the 21st Century: A Personal Reflection," in Fernandez, *New Overtures*, 46–48.

8 Kwame Anthony Appiah, *Cosmopolitanism: Ethics in a World of Strangers* (New York: Norton, 2007). Also William Schweiker, "Public Theology and the Cosmopolitan Conscience," in *Public Theology for a Global Society: Essays in Honor of Max L. Stackhouse*, ed. Deirdre King Hainsworth and Scott R. Paeth (Grand Rapids: Eerdmans, 2010), 134–35.

9 Edward W. Said, *Orientalism* (New York: Random House, 1978).

10 John B. Cobb Jr., "Theology against the Disciplines," in *Shifting Boundaries: Contextual Approaches to the Structure of Theological Education*, ed. Barbara G. Wheeler and Edward Farley (Louisville, Ky.: Westminster John Knox, 1991), 243.

11 Joseph Bessler, "Seminaries as Endangered Habitats in a Fragile Ecosystem: A New Ecology Model," in *Revitalizing Practice: Collaborative Models for Theological Faculties*, ed. Malcolm L. Warford (New York: Peter Lang, 2008), 9.

12 Raúl Fornet-Betancourt, "Hermeneutics and Politics of Strangers: A Philosophical Contribution on the Challenge of Convivencia in Multicultural Societies," in *A Promised Land, a Perilous Journey: Theological Perspectives on Migration*, ed. Daniel Groody and Gioacchino Campese (Notre Dame, Ind.: University of Notre Dame Press, 2008), 218.

List of Contributors

Miguel A. De La Torre is a scholar-activist and ordained minister. Since obtaining his doctoral degree in 1999, he has published over thirty books, five of which have won national awards. He presently serves as Professor of Social Ethics and Latino/a Studies at Iliff School of Theology in Denver, Colorado. He was the 2012 president of the Society of Christian Ethics. Additionally, he is the editor of the *Journal of Race, Ethnicity, and Religion* (www.raceandreligion.com), and the executive officer of the Society of Race, Ethnicity and Religion.

William A. Dyrness is Dean Emeritus and Professor of Theology and Culture at Fuller Theological Seminary. He is a founding member of the Brehm Center for Worship, Theology, and the Arts, and is director of its Visual Faith Institute. A former missionary and professor at New College Berkeley, Dyrness focuses on global issues in theology and, especially, the relation between theology and the visual arts. His most recent books include *Primer in Christian Worship*; *Poetic Theology: God and the Poetics of Everyday Life*; and *Senses of Devotion: Interfaith Aesthetics in Buddhist and Muslim Communities.*

Eleazar S. Fernandez was born in the Philippines and is Professor of Constructive Theology at United Theological Seminary of the Twin Cities, Minnesota. Some of his works include *Teaching for a Culturally Diverse and Racially Just World*; *Burning Center, Porous Borders: The Church in a Globalized World*; *New Overtures: Asian North American Theology*; *Reimagining the Human*; *Realizing the America of Our Hearts*; *A Dream Unfinished*; and *Toward a Theology of Struggle*. In

June 2013 he assumed his new post as President of Union Theological Seminary, Philippines.

Cecilia González-Andrieu is Cuban-American and grew up with the Mexican and Central American communities of Los Angeles, California. She is Associate Professor of Theological Studies at Loyola Marymount University. A Roman Catholic, she is the author of *Bridge to Wonder: Art as a Gospel of Beauty* and has contributed scholarship to the journals *Arts, Seen and Cithara*; *Journal of Hispanic/Latino Theology*; and *Princeton Lectures on Youth, Church, and Culture*, and to collaborative volumes on theater, Latino/a popular religion, and the visual arts.

Teresia Hinga was born in Kenya and earned her Ph.D. in Religious Studies/African Christianity from the University of Lancaster in England. Hinga's research focuses on religion and women's issues (particularly in Africa), African religious history, and expression in the global religious landscape, religion and public policy, and the ethics of globalization. She is a founding member of the Circle of Concerned African Women Theologians, a Pan-African association of women that studies the role and impact of religion and culture on African women's lives. She is also a member of the Black Catholic Symposium of the American Academy of Religion and a founding member of the Association for the Academic Study of Religion in Africa.

Dwight N. Hopkins is Professor of Theology at the University of Chicago Divinity School and Professor Extraordinarious, Department of Philosophy, Practical and Systematic Theology, University of South Africa (Pretoria, South Africa). He takes seriously the relation between theologies and cultures. He is the founding coordinator of a fourteen-country religious studies network. Hopkins is the author of *Being Human: Race, Culture and Religion* and *Shoes That Fit Our Feet: Sources for a Constructive Black Theology*. Some of his coedited works include *The Cambridge Companion to Black Theology*; *Global Voices for Gender Justice*; *Religions/Globalizations*; *Liberation Theologies, Postmodernity and the Americas*; and *Religious Reflection and Cultural Analysis*.

Veli-Matti Kärkkäinen is Professor of Systematic Theology at Fuller Theological Seminary in Pasadena, California, and Docent of

Ecumenics at the University of Helsinki. A native of Finland, he has also taught theology in Thailand and has participated widely in the ecumenical, theological, and interreligious work of the World Council of Churches. He is coeditor (with William A. Dyrness) of *The Global Dictionary of Theology*, and his most recent books are *Christ and Reconciliation* and *Trinity and Revelation*, the first two of the five volumes in the series Constructive Christian Theology for the Pluralistic World.

Kwok Pui-lan was born in Hong Kong and is the William F. Cole Professor of Christian Theology and Spirituality at the Episcopal Divinity School in Cambridge, Massachusetts. She is a past president of the American Academy of Religion. Her publications include *Globalization, Gender, and Peacebuilding*; *Postcolonial Imagination and Feminist Theology*; *Introducing Asian Feminist Theology*; and *Discovering the Bible in the Non-biblical World*. She is the editor of *Hope Abundant: Third World and Indigenous Women's Theology*, and *Women and Christianity* in four volumes.

Lai Pan-chiu was born in Hong Kong and is a professor in the Department of Cultural and Religious Studies, The Chinese University of Hong Kong. He delivered the Edward Cadbury Lectures at the University of Birmingham, England, in 2006. His recent publications include *Sino-Christian Theology: A Theological qua Cultural Movement in China* (coedited with Jason Lam); *Mahayana Christian Theology* (in Chinese); and *Sino-Christian Theology in the Public Square* (in Chinese). He is chief editor of *Ching Feng: A Journal on Christianity and Chinese Religion and Culture*.

Loida I. Martell-Otero is Professor of Constructive Theology at Palmer Theological Seminary/Eastern University in Pennsylvania. She is a licensed doctor in veterinary medicine as well as an ordained minister in the American Baptist Churches in the United States. She pastored in New York's urban centers for fifteen years after leaving a growing veterinary practice. She is coauthor of *Latina Evangélicas: A Theological Survey from the Margins* and coeditor of *Teología en Conjunto: A Collaborative Hispanic Protestant Theology*. She has published articles on soteriology, Christology, God, spirituality, vocation, and pedagogy. She is an avid amateur photographer.

Index